QUICK ESCAPES® SERIES

QUICK

ESCAPES®

DENVER

25 WEEKEND GETAWAYS
IN AND AROUND
THE MILE HIGH CITY

FOURTH EDITION

Sherry Spitsnaugle

The Globe Pequot Press

GUILFORD, CONN

D1444688

The prices and rates listed in this guidebook were confirmed at press time. We recommend, however, that you call establishments before traveling to obtain current information.

Interior design by Nancy Freeborn
Maps by M. A. Dubé
Photo Credits: pp. 1, 5, 54, 97, 118, 165: Dan Leeth; p. 136: courtesy of the National Mining Hall of Fame and Museum. All other photos by the author.

ISBN 0-7627-3022-6
ISSN 1540-4358

Manufactured in the United States of America
Fourth Edition/First Printing

To buy books in quantity for corporate use or incentives, call:
(800) 962–0973, ext. 4551, or e-mail premiums@GlobePequot.com.

CONTENTS

Acknowledgments vi

Introduction vii

NORTHERN ESCAPES 1

1. Boulder 2

2. Estes Park and Rocky Mountain National Park 11

3. Grand Lake 19

4. Central City and Black Hawk 27

5. Fort Collins 34

6. Saratoga, Wyoming 42

7. Steamboat Springs 50

DENVER AND POINTS EAST 61

1. Denver 62

2. Downtown Denver 71

3. Lower Downtown (LoDo) 80

4. Stratton 89

WESTERN ESCAPES 97

1. Winter Park and the Fraser Valley 98

2. Georgetown 107

3. Summit County 115

4. Vail and Beaver Creek 123

5. Leadville 133

6. Glenwood Springs 140

7. Aspen 148

8. Grand Junction and the Grand Valley 155

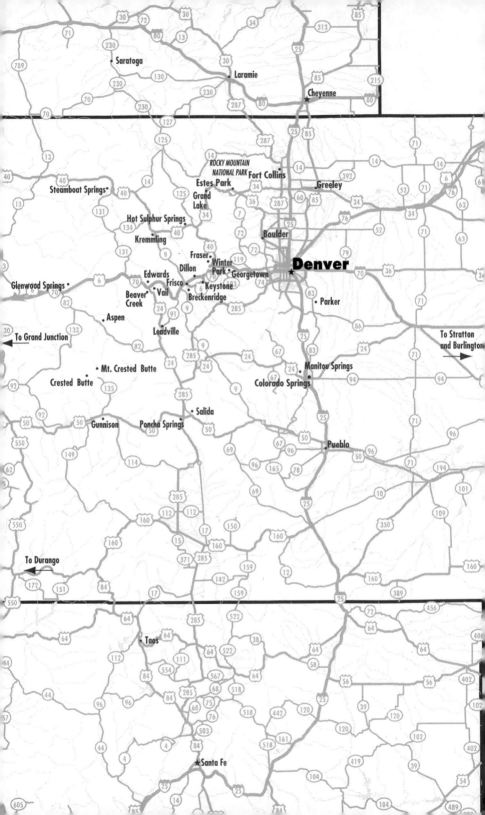

SOUTHERN ESCAPES 165

1. Colorado Springs 166
2. Salida and the Upper Arkansas Valley 177
3. Gunnison 184
4. Crested Butte and Mount Crested Butte 193
5. Durango 200
6. Taos and Santa Fe, New Mexico 209

Index 221

ACKNOWLEDGMENTS

Thank you, Doris and Gary Kennedy, for your guidance and friendship. I am forever in your debt.

INTRODUCTION

Colorado and its surrounding states are a traveler's nirvana. From statuesque mountains to wide-open prairies, opulent spas to rustic dude ranches, and rodeo to opera, it's all here. Described as "one big scenic drive," Colorado offers stunning landscape and compelling natural beauty. Take off in any direction and you'll discover peaks, grasslands, canyons, or deserts waiting to provide unlimited adventure.

It's difficult to describe the Centennial State without giving in to well-worn clichés and a list of superlatives. Sights can be portrayed, photographed, and visualized, but you'll want to experience the grandeur of the area firsthand.

Traveling spontaneously can work well when luck is on your side, but for the most part a little advance planning will help make a successful trip. Whether you're a local, a tourist, or a new resident, this book will escort you to places you've heard about, such as Aspen, Vail, and Colorado Springs. Other towns, such as Saratoga, Wyoming, may be new to you. The ritzy resorts and cosmopolitan cities provide an exceptional variety of activities, but the small towns reveal a special charm and homespun hospitality.

The majority of the trips are no more than three hours' driving distance from Denver, and several are a four-hour drive. Two chapters—Durango and Taos/Sante Fe, New Mexico—may push the envelope for a *quick* escape, but the beauty of both locations is well worth the seven- to eight-hour drive.

Each chapter details an itinerary for a different city and area. You'll want to set your own pace and may not be able to see all the sights on one trip, but that provides a good reason to plan a return visit. At the end of the chapter, **There's More** points you in the right direction for additional sights and activities. **Special Events** lists festivals and annual happenings, and **Other Recommended Restaurants and Lodgings** gives ideas for dining and accommodations in addition to those named in the itinerary. **For More Information** provides names, addresses, Web sites, and phone numbers of the tourist office of the area you're visiting.

Travel information can change at any time, and it's best to call ahead for confirmation.

This guidebook will steer you to well-known tourist sites and obscure finds. You'll travel on scenic byways and visit castles, hot springs, and dinosaur remains. Often the best way to see the countryside is to hike it, bike it, or raft it. As for skiing, trying to name the best downhill ski area is asking for a debate. Aspen takes the prize for glitz while Steamboat Springs revels in its reputation for bottomless powder.

The undisputed fact remains that sometimes you crave to escape the routine for a few days. So put the office on autopilot and hit the road. After all, isn't that what weekends are all about?

NORTHERN
ESCAPES

Boulder

Mecca for Bicyclists and Tea Lovers

1 Night

Politically and environmentally correct, hip, progressive, diverse, offbeat, alternative, and most of all outdoorsy, Boulder is where Birkenstocks, bicycles, and good vibes rule.

Spend some time strolling the wonderfully eclectic outdoor Pearl Street Mall and you're likely to see a grunge-clad performer crooning a 1970s tune or a guy dressed in a Dr. Seuss costume strolling the mall.

Geographically, the striking red sandstone slabs that form the backdrop of Boulder, along with the pine-covered foothills that surround this town, make for a positively stunning setting.

- [ ] Outdoor walking mall
- [ ] University of Colorado
- [ ] Western art gallery
- [ ] Boulder Dushanbe Teahouse
- [ ] Historic park
- [ ] Summer Shakespeare festival

With nearly 100 miles of hiking trails practically right in their backyard, it's no wonder that Boulderites are smitten by the great outdoors. Biking is big business in Boulder, and it's safe to say that the majority of residents own at least one bicycle.

Home to the **University of Colorado,** Boulder has that academic and youthful spirit unique to college towns.

Mo Siegel, founder of Celestial Seasonings, the nation's largest herb-tea manufacturer, is known as the local youth-turned-millionaire. Located outside Boulder on Sleepytime Drive, Celestial Seasonings offers tours of its facility.

Whether people-watching on the mall or hiking the trails of historic Chautauqua Park, you'll no doubt absorb the good karma of this wonderfully with-it city.

Day 1 / Morning

Connect with U.S. Highway 36 (also known as the Boulder Turnpike) off I–25 north for the 30-mile drive to Boulder.

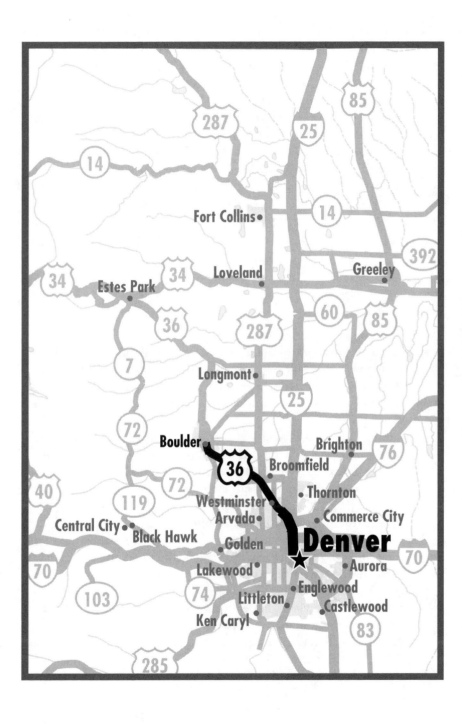

BREAKFAST: You'll get an instant flavor of the city at **Dot's Diner** (2716 Twenty-eighth Street; 303–449–1323). Here you'll find not only tofu, soy, and *huevos rancheros* but also "diner" food such as biscuits with ham and eggs covered with gravy. Open weekdays from 7:00 A.M. to 2:00 P.M. and weekends from 8:00 A.M. to 2:00 P.M.

Head to the lively **Pearl Street Mall** (on Pearl Street from Eleventh to Fifteenth Streets), which is the soul and true essence of Boulder. This outdoor, pedestrian-only walkway is lined with galleries, boutiques, sculptures, and flowers. Wooden benches and outdoor cafes provide the perfect opportunity to observe the characters and array of shoppers, strollers, and other people-watchers. January or July, noon or midnight, the mall entertains.

LUNCH: The outdoor cafes on Pearl Street Mall are packed on warm days. Snag a table on a patio, linger through a leisurely meal, and savor the mood.

Afternoon

Chautauqua Park (Ninth Street and Baseline Road; 303–442–3282) is a great place to explore year-round. Stop at the Park Ranger Cottage (first cottage to the right as you enter the park) and pick up a map of the trails. The Park Ranger Cottage is open from 8:30 A.M. to 4:00 P.M. Monday through Friday. For additional information call the Ranger Station at (303) 441–3408.

During summer the twenty-six-acre park hosts programs that feature dance, music, theater, and film. **Chautauqua Dining Hall** (303-440-3776) has a sprawling porch and good views. The historic restaurant is open year-round. If you want to spend the night in the cottages located at the park, call (303) 442–3282 for information.

Take a tour of **Celestial Seasonings** (4600 Sleepytime Drive; 303–581–1202) and discover how spices and herbs are squeezed into tea bags. Don't miss the exotic teapots from around the world, at the beginning of your tour. Be prepared to wear a hairnet for sanitary reasons; you'll look and feel a bit silly, but so does everyone else. Take a deep breath in the aromatic "Mint Room," where your eyes will water and your senses clear. The Tea Shop and Emporium is a good place to buy teas at a discount.

Celestial Cafe serves breakfast, lunch, and tea. Try one of more than forty choices as you enjoy the view of the Continental Divide and the Rocky Mountain Front Range from the patio. The cafe is open Monday

Chautauqua Dining Hall, Chautauqua Park.

through Friday for breakfast from 7:00 to 10:00 A.M. and for lunch from 11:00 A.M. to 2:00 P.M. Weekend hours vary; it's best to call ahead.

To get to Celestial Seasonings, take the Longmont Diagonal (Colorado 119) heading northeast. Turn east on Jay Road, go 1 mile to Spine Road, and turn north. Continue 0.5 mile to Sleepytime Drive and turn left into Celestial Seasonings. Tour times are Monday through Saturday from 10:00 A.M. through 3:00 P.M. on the hour and Sunday from 11:00 A.M. through 3:00 P.M. on the hour. Children under five years are not permitted on the factory portion of the tour.

DINNER: A legend for more than twenty-five years, **Flagstaff House** (1138 Flagstaff Road; 303–442–4640; www.flagstaffhouse.com) is the crème de la crème of fine dining. The candlelit dining room, panoramic view, and intimate ambience set the scene for romance. Perched on the ledge of Flagstaff Mountain, the restaurant offers a dramatic evening view of the glimmering lights of Boulder. The restaurant has been owned by the Monette family for more than a quarter-century. Scott Monette manages the dining room with absolute competence, while chef Mark Monette holds reign over the kitchen. Mark Monette, who trained in Paris, Singapore, Tokyo, Thailand, and Hong Kong, creates superb cuisine and shows off his amazing talents in the dishes served. The menu, which changes daily, offers appetizers such as spinach-wrapped poached oysters and pâté of duck, and entrees such as Atlantic salmon, venison fillet, Black Angus New York strip, and Maine lobster. The wine steward advises as necessary while you study the 212-page list of vintages.

While you're splurging, go ahead and order dessert. Chocolate strudel and a crisp hot apple tart with homemade cinnamon ice cream and caramel sauce are among the selections. Robert Redford has dined here, and when the Emperor and Empress of Japan visited the United States in 1994, the entourage chose to eat at Flagstaff House. If it's fit for royalty . . . well, you know the rest. To reach Flagstaff House, drive south from Broadway and Canyon Boulevard to Baseline Road and turn west. Baseline Road curves to the right and eventually becomes Flagstaff Road. Follow the signs to the restaurant. Open Sunday through Friday 6:00 to 9:30 P.M. and Saturday 5:00 to 10:00 P.M. Reservations required.

LODGING: For an especially memorable evening, choose the **Hotel Boulderado** (2115 Thirteenth Street, Boulder; 303–442–4344 or 800–433–4344; www.boulderado.com). Brimming with history and style, this splendid hotel, named after Boulder and Colorado, will impress from the moment you enter the lavishly decorated inn. The graceful, rich cherry-wood staircase and ornate stained-glass ceiling beautify the main lobby. Opening day for the hotel was New Year's Day 1909, and since then this luxury inn has counted among its guests Louis Armstrong, Helen Keller, and Robert Frost.

Rooms are decorated Victorian-style, with floral wallpaper, chenille bedspreads, and period antiques. The **Corner Bar** at Hotel Boulderado is a cozy place for a nightcap. Prices begin at $185 for a standard room. A deluxe room is $225, and a suite is $285.

Day 2 / Morning

BREAKFAST: **Lucile's,** 2124 Fourteenth Street, Boulder; (303) 442–4743. Look for the yellow house between Pine and Spruce, a block from Hotel Boulderado. This Boulder institution has been around for twenty-four years. From zydeco tunes to grits, it's all about the South. Lucile's is famous for its Cajun-style breakfast and lunch. Feast on mammoth homemade biscuits and strawberry-rhubarb jam. Open 7:00 A.M. to 2:00 P.M., Monday through Friday; 8:00 A.M. to 2:00 P.M., Saturday and Sunday. Be prepared to wait on weekends.

It's time for a bike ride. After all, this is Boulder. The 16-mile **Boulder Creek Path** is the main east-west "mixed-use" passage through town and links up with miles of other trails. Shared by bicyclists, in-line skaters, hikers, runners, and dog-walkers, the wide, concrete path is fairly flat to the east and gains more elevation as you head west. Best of all, you won't encounter car traffic. The path continues on to Boulder Canyon and Four Mile Canyon. If you're feeling frisky, keep right on going to **Gold Hill,** a small mining town that is a popular destination for bicyclists. You can maneuver the paths on a mountain bike or a road bike.

Stop at the **Bikesmith** (2432 Arapahoe Avenue; 303–443–1132) to pick up a free *Boulder Greenways Self-Guided Tour Map,* which will give you options for parking, start and stop points, and sights to see on the way. The shop rents bikes and in-line skates and offers a full-service repair department. The Bikesmith is open year-round, from 9:00 A.M. to 6:00 P.M. Closed Sunday and Tuesday.

Rental bikes are also available at **University Bicycles** (839 Pearl Street; 303–444–4196). It's open year-round during the week from 10:00 A.M. to 7:00 P.M., Saturday from 10:00 A.M. to 6:00 P.M., and Sunday from 10:00 A.M. to 5:00 P.M.

LUNCH: Boulder Dushanbe Teahouse, 1770 Thirteenth Street; (303) 442-4993. This beautiful structure was a gift from Boulder's sister city of Dushanbe, Tajikistan. Handcrafted by Tajik artisans, it arrived in boxes and had to be assembled. The teahouse is owned by the city and operated by Lenny Martinelli, who says, "The sister-city project is about bringing cultures together." He and his wife, Sara, have put their hearts and souls into this place. The menu changes monthly, but you can count on an exotic selection, which might include Persian lamb kabob, Thai curry noodle, Bengali curried fish, or Mediterranean flatbread pizza. Persian music plays in the background as you sip a cup of mango ceylon blend or Tibetan Tiger. If you can't schedule lunch, stop in for tea (or espresso). The teahouse is open Monday through Friday from 8:00 to 11:00 A.M. for continental breakfast; 11:00 A.M. to 3:00 P.M. for lunch; and 5:00 to 9:00 P.M. for dinner. On weekends, brunch is served from 8:00 A.M. to 3:00 P.M., and dinner is served from 5:00 to 10:00 P.M.

There's More

Boulder Museum of Contemporary Art, 1750 Thirteenth Street, Boulder; (303) 443–2122. This nonprofit facility offers works by local and national artists. Open Tuesday through Saturday from 10:00 A.M. to 6:00 P.M.; closed Sunday and Monday.

Boulder's Leanin' Tree Museum of Western Art, 6055 Longbow Drive, Boulder; (303) 530–1442. The museum has an extensive collection of Western art and sculpture, as well as a gift shop that sells greeting cards produced at Leanin' Tree. Take the Diagonal Highway (Colorado Highway 119) north to Sixty-third Street; turn right and proceed to Longbow Drive. Admission is free, and the museum is open Monday through Friday from 8:00 A.M. to 4:30 P.M. and Saturday and Sunday from 10:00 A.M. to 4:00 P.M.

Eldora Mountain Resort (P.O. Box 1697, Nederland, CO 80466; 303–440–8700) is 21 miles from Boulder. Take Canyon Road to Nederland, turn south on Colorado 119, and follow the signs to the ski area. This friendly resort, with its forty-three downhill ski runs and nine lifts, offers what the big boys may not: no waiting in lift lines. The Nordic Center has 45 kilometers of cross-country trails.

Fiske Planetarium. Located on the University of Colorado campus, on Regent Drive. For some real celestial viewing, join university astronomers on Friday evening for stargazing, a star talk, and glimpses through the observatory's 16- and 24-inch telescopes. For information call (303) 492–5001.

National Center for Atmospheric Research, 1850 Table Mesa Drive, Boulder; (303) 497–1174. Take Table Mesa Road west from Broadway and follow the signs to NCAR (pronounced N-Car). Admission is free, and you can take a self-guided or a guided tour. Check out the mammoth computer system, the robots, and the weather station where scientists contemplate and study such occurrences as wind shear and the ozone.

Special Events

January. Polar Bear Club Ice Plunge at Boulder Reservoir; (303) 441–3461. Held New Year's Day. It will cost you $15, but you can dip into the icy lake, let out a shriek, then cavort onshore until you warm up. Spectators watch the fun for free.

May. Kinetic Conveyance Challenge, Boulder Reservoir. Usually held the first Saturday in May. Watch as locals and college kids use their resources and wits to race across land and water on anything from beds to human-powered contraptions. It's silly and tons of fun for spectators and competitors alike.

Bolder Boulder 10K Race. Held Memorial Day. Walk, run, or just watch this fun event, but if you're in town, don't miss it. This 10K race features world-class runners but is also open to the public. In addition to a workout, you'll get a cool T-shirt and lunch.

June–August. Chautauqua Auditorium hosts international musicians and guest artists who perform in a festival that is a Boulder summertime favorite. Picnic on the vast lawn before the concert.

Colorado Shakespeare Festival. The performances take place at the outdoor theater on the CU campus. Call (303) 492–0554.

Other Recommended Restaurants and Lodgings

Briar Rose, 2151 Arapahoe Avenue, Boulder; (303) 442–3007; www.briar rosebb.com. As Boulder's first B&B, this graceful inn offers such niceties as feather-bed comforters (during cold weather), afternoon tea and shortbread cookies, and a pleasant courtyard. The B&B is conveniently located about a mile from the Pearl Street Mall. Breakfast of fresh-squeezed orange juice, homemade granola, and croissants can be delivered to your room, or you can enjoy breakfast on a lace tablecloth in the dining room.

Dolan's, 2319 Arapahoe Road, Boulder; (303) 444–8758. Owner Mike Dolan loves wine and it shows with the two wine cellars and a selection of "about 5,000 bottles." Hardwood floors, a great bar, a patio, and early-bird specials make Dolan's a favorite with locals. Entrees vary from pan-seared salmon and ruby-red trout to prime rib of beef. A tip: When you make your reservation, request a booth (much cozier than the tables). Dolan's serves lunch Monday through Friday 11:00 A.M. to 2:00 P.M. and dinner Monday through Saturday 5:00 to 10:00 P.M. Closed Sunday. Located 3 blocks from the Quality Inn and Suites.

Limbo Restaurant & Lounge, 2719 Iris Avenue (across from Laudisio's), Boulder; (303) 544–1464. Swanky but reasonable and decorated in "1930s contemporary" complete with leopard-print bar stools, this restaurant oozes charisma. Try one of the gourmet pizzas such as the basil pesto with grilled chicken, roasted vegetables, goat cheese, and mozzarella; or order an entree such as Caribbean-style, slow-roasted half chicken with fruit salsa. You'll find thirty wines available by the glass. Open Tuesday through Friday from 11:30 A.M. to 10:00 P.M. and weekends from 5:00 to 10:00 P.M. Closed Monday.

Quality Inn and Suites Boulder Creek, 292 Arapahoe Avenue, Boulder; (303) 449–7550 or (800) 228–5151; www.qualityinnboulder.com. The exterior of this lodge looks average, but it's hard to beat the location and price. The family-owned motel is within walking distance of restaurants and Pearl Street Mall. Daddy Bruce's barbecue is right next door. A picture of the owner's dog, a short-haired Wheaten Terrier named Samantha, hangs in every room. (Highway 36 turns into Twenty-eighth Street. Turn left onto Arapahoe to get to Quality Inn and Suites.)

For More Information

Boulder Convention and Visitor Bureau, 2440 Pearl Street, Boulder, CO 80302; (303) 442–2911; (800) 444–0447; www.bouldercoloradousa.com.

Estes Park and Rocky Mountain National Park

The Great Outdoors

1 Night

Estes Park is so accessible from Denver that you can leave the city Friday afternoon and in an hour and a half be sipping a glass of cabernet by the fireplace in the elegant lobby of the historic Stanley Hotel.

The village of Estes Park is at 7,522 feet above sea level and is surrounded by towering mountains. Picturesque and tourist-friendly, Estes Park swells with travelers during summer, but spring, fall, and winter are also great times to visit.

Rocky Mountain National Park, which is the main show in the neighborhood, borders the town of Estes Park. President George W. Bush visited the area in August 2001. The park traces its history to after the turn of the twentieth century,

- ☐ Trail Ridge Road
- ☐ Aerial tramway
- ☐ Shopping
- ☐ Dramatic views
- ☐ Historic landmark hotel
- ☐ Fishing, hiking, golf
- ☐ Enos Mills Cabin

when a hardworking, devoted group of naturalists fought for the area to be granted national park status. The region officially became Rocky Mountain National Park in 1915.

The park flaunts its rugged beauty with columbine-covered meadows, shimmering turquoise lakes, inviting streams, and awesome views of craggy, snowcapped peaks. During the fall, elk mating season at Rocky Mountain National Park fascinates visitors. At dusk, bulls bugle and battle as they compete for rank. Observers may also see mule deer or the occasional bear.

Summer brings out alpine wildflowers, campers, backpackers, and outdoor enthusiasts in general. Serious climbers may want to attempt Longs Peak, the highest mountain within the boundaries of Rocky Mountain National Park. At 14,255 feet, Longs Peak is one of Colorado's more difficult "fourteeners" to scale.

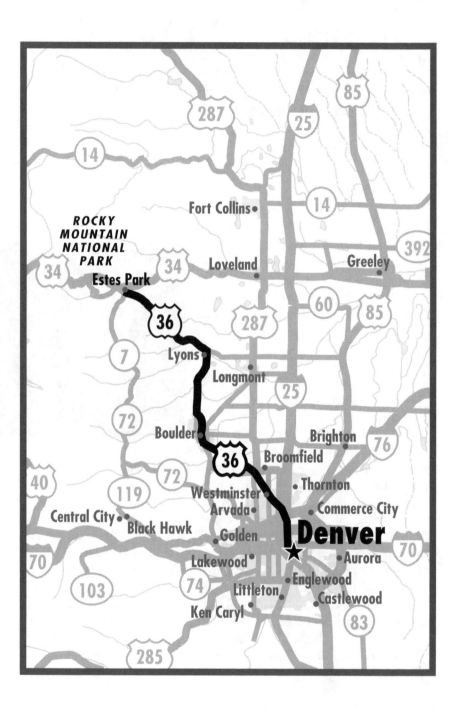

Ponderosa pines, grand peaks, majestic elk, and emerald terrain create a wondrous place. Meander down a quiet trail, loaf beside a clear mountain lake, or get a workout by gaining elevation on one of the climbs. With more than 350 miles of hiking trails, you could spend a lifetime exploring the park's paths and woods.

Day 1 / *Afternoon*

Estes Park is 65 miles northwest of Denver. From Denver, travel north on I–25 and connect with U.S. Highway 36 through Boulder. Head north on 36 to Lyons and northwest to Estes Park. The driving is effortless, and you don't have to cross any mountain passes.

Explore some of the 300 shops and galleries of Estes Park on **Elkhorn Avenue.** You'll discover everything from fine crystal to Old West–style clothing. Several of the shops have been owned and operated for generations by the same family. **Craftsmen in Leather** (135 West Elkhorn; 970–586–2400) is a great place to try on hats. **Rocky Mountain Connection** (141 East Elkhorn; 970–586–3361) has a good selection of outdoor gear.

DINNER: Estes Park Brewery (470 Prospect Village Drive; 970–586–5421). Taste a couple of the complimentary samples, such as Longs Peak Raspberry Wheat or Estes Park Pale Ale. This restaurant-bar is a popular spot for locals and visitors. Freshly brewed root beer is on the menu, as are appetizers such as Jalapeño Poppers and entrees that include thick-crust pizza, burgers, and the Beer Brat Sandwich, made with the brewery's porter beer. Guests share the upstairs dining room with customers playing pool and video games. If the weather cooperates, sit outside at a picnic table on the upstairs deck, which is quieter than the restaurant and has mountain views. Estes Park Brewery is open daily from 11:00 A.M. until late evening.

LODGING: The **Stanley Hotel,** 333 Wonderview, P.O. Box 1767, Estes Park, CO 80517; (970) 586–3371 or (800) 976–1377; www.stanley hotel.com. Remember the hair-raising movie *The Shining,* in which Jack Nicholson spooked theatergoers everywhere? Contrary to what you may have heard, the movie was not filmed here, but the hotel did inspire Stephen King to draft the novel on which the film was based. The television miniseries, which aired in 1997, was shot at the Stanley; King was executive producer. Not only can you overnight in this grand old hotel as a guest, but you can tour the history-filled site as well.

The historic Stanley Hotel overlooks the town of Estes Park.

This regal old inn, with its attractive white clapboard exterior, over-looks the town of Estes Park and was known as one of the most glamorous hotels of its day when it first opened in 1909. In those days the Stanley offered its boarders luxuries such as billiards and stables. Today guests delight in the elegant lobby and comfortable rooms. Summer rates range from $159 to $269, and winter rates range from $129 to $219.

Day 2 / Morning

BREAKFAST: You'll feel oh so elegant sipping coffee on the expansive veranda of the Stanley with glorious views of Longs Peak. Then put on comfortable shoes, pack a picnic lunch, fill your water bottle, and prepare for a day in the great outdoors.

Head straight to **Rocky Mountain National Park.** From Estes Park, take U.S. 34 or U.S. 36. The entrance fee is $10 per car and is valid for a week.

There are lots of activities for kids, and park rangers go out of their way to educate youngsters in an informative and entertaining way. The staff at Park Headquarters (970–586–1206), at the south entrance on the eastern side of the park, can recommend a hiking trail and provide other information. Summer hours are 8:00 A.M. to 9:00 P.M.

The **Kawuneeche Visitor Center** (970–627–3471), on the west side of the Continental Divide, has some nice displays on the history of the park. Summer hours are 8:00 A.M. to 6:00 P.M. Winter hours for both Kawuneeche and Park Headquarters are 8:00 A.M. to 4:30 P.M.

LUNCH: Enjoy a picnic at one of the outdoor tables, or spread a blanket on the ground and take in the views.

Afternoon

Hiking opportunities abound in the park, and you can essentially name your distance, difficulty level, and terrain preference. Easy walks include those around **Sprague Lake** and **Bear Lake,** both of which are wheelchair accessible. For both walks, take the Beaver Meadows (south) entrance (U.S. 36) and follow the signs to Bear Lake.

If fishing is on your agenda, check with rangers for a copy of the park rules. The staff at **Scot's Sporting Goods,** 1.5 miles west of Estes Park on U.S. 36 (870 Morraine Avenue, Estes Park; 970–586–2877), can set you up with gear and a guided trip. They'll tell you where the fish are biting, too.

Colorado Bicycling Adventures (184 East Elkhorn Avenue, Estes Park; 970–586–4241) rents bikes, helmets, and other gear for any biking adventure you have in mind. Ask the staff for information about guided mountain-bike tours. You can rent camping, fishing, climbing, snowshoeing, and cross-country skiing equipment at **Estes Park Mountain Shop** (358 East Elkhorn Avenue, Estes Park; 970–586–6548 or 800–504–6642).

During summer, drive to Grand Lake via **Trail Ridge Road** (Highway 34), which climbs over the Continental Divide in Rocky Mountain National Park. To get to Trail Ridge Road, enter the park at either Beaver Meadows or Fall River. This route, which is usually open from Memorial Day until mid-October, weather permitting, is the highest continuous paved highway in the country. The road stretches between Estes Park and Grand Lake and climbs to 12,183 feet in elevation. Trail Ridge Road was an immediate tourist pleaser when it opened in 1932.

The best way to appreciate the incredible views is to stop at one of the scenic overlooks, get out of your car, take a deep breath, and admire the lofty peaks of the Continental Divide. For a short but strenuous hike, follow the 1-mile, round-trip path to **Toll Memorial.** Rock Cut Trailhead, where the path begins, is located about 6 miles east of the Alpine Visitor Center. For additional information call the visitor center at (970) 586–1206.

There's More

Climbing. For information about technical climbing or hiking, call the Colorado Mountain School (Estes Park; 970–586–5758).

Enos Mills Cabin and Gallery. Located 8 miles south of Estes Park on Colorado Highway 7; (970) 586–4706. Enos Mills, photographer, naturalist, and author of many books that describe his escapades and adventures in the region, first visited this area in 1884 as a young boy. Mills resided and worked in a one-room log cabin for many summers during his life. Today you can visit the home of this man, who was devoted to writing about the wonders of the Rockies. The Enos Mills Cabin and Gallery is open from Memorial Day to Labor Day from 11:00 A.M. to 5:00 P.M. Tuesday through Saturday, and during the winter by appointment only. Donations requested.

Estes Park Aerial Tramway, 420 East Riverside Drive, Estes Park; (970) 586–3675. You'll see extensive views of the Continental Divide, Rocky Mountain National Park, Longs Peak, and the village of Estes Park. At the top you can hike, picnic, or browse the gift shop and snack bar.

Estes Park Area Historical Museum, 200 Fourth Street at U.S. Highway 36; (970) 586–6256. This small but well-appointed museum caters to kids. Children will get to experience hands-on activities while parents browse the gallery. Open May through October, Monday through Saturday from 10:00 A.M. to 5:00 P.M. and Sunday from 1:00 to 5:00 P.M.; November through April, Friday and Saturday from 10:00 A.M. to 5:00 P.M. and Sunday from 1:00 to 5:00 P.M.

Estes Park Golf Course, 1080 South Saint Vrain; (970) 586–8146. This eighteen-hole course stretches through the woodland and is wonderfully scenic. The course is one of the oldest in Colorado.

Special Events

June. Wool Market is a two-day event that includes demonstrations, seminars, spinning and weaving contests, and the display and sale of wool-related items. This is the largest llama and alpaca show in the country. The event takes place at Stanley Park Fairgrounds on U.S. Highway 36. For information call (970) 586–6104.

June–mid-August. SummerFest Concert Series, sponsored by the Estes Park Center/YMCA, features everything from jazz to classical. Call (970) 586–3341.

July–early August. Estes Park Music Festival presents the Colorado Music Festival Orchestra in a series of six concerts on Monday evenings. For details call the Cultural Arts Council of Estes Park at (970) 586–9203.

September. Longs Peak Scottish Irish Festival takes place the weekend after Labor Day. The festival features a parade and contests such as the hammer throw and tin whistle and fiddle competition. You'll hear bagpipes a-playin' during this three-day Celtic event, which attracts about 40,000 visitors and is one of the town's favorite celebrations. For more information call (800) 903–7837.

Other Recommended Restaurants and Lodgings

Estes Park Center/YMCA, 2515 Tunnel Road, Estes Park; (970) 586–3341. This self-contained facility sits on 860 acres near Rocky Mountain National Park. The Estes Park Center offers a choice of lodge-style accommodations or cabins, and you can stay here for a fraction of the price it would cost to stay in resorts around the state. The cabins, some of which have a fireplace, offer either two or four bedrooms and come with an equipped kitchen. This is an ideal family location, and the entire brood can choose from cross-country skiing, horseback riding, swimming, tennis, hiking, snowshoeing, or exploring the backcountry. Take U.S. Highway 36 west to Colorado 66 southwest to the center. To book accommodations, call (970) 586–3341, extension 1010. Visit their Web site at www.ymcarockies.org. Reservations are recommended.

Marys Lake Lodge, 2625 Marys Lake Road, Estes Park; (970) 586–5958 or (877) 442–6279; www.maryslakelodge.com. This historic hotel was nearly destroyed by fire twenty-five years ago but has recently been restored to its former grandeur. Located 2 miles south of Estes Park on Colorado 7.

Romantic Riversong Bed and Breakfast Inn, P.O. Box 1910, Estes Park, CO 80517; (970) 586–4666; www.romanticriversong.com. You'll mellow out almost instantly after you arrive at this country inn with nine guest rooms, tucked away in the backwoods near the Big Thompson River. Relax, kick back, and appreciate your homey bedroom and roaring fire. For directions and reservations contact the inn directly.

Wapiti Bar & Grill, 247 West Elkhorn, Estes Park; (970) 586–5056. Locals recommend the fajitas at this cozy cafe. The menu also offers buffalo stew, halibut steak, and burger baskets.

For More Information

Estes Park Chamber Resort Association, 500 Big Thompson Avenue, Estes Park, CO 80517; (970) 586–4433 or (800) 443–7837; www.estespark resort.com.

Rocky Mountain National Park; (970) 586–1206.

Grand Lake

Snowmobile Capital of Colorado

1 Night

From its wooden boardwalks to the hitching post in front of the Lariat Saloon, Grand Lake overflows with rustic charm. Here you can two-step the night away to a Western band or curl up in the comfort of your cabin.

From approximately 400 full-time residents during winter, Grand Lake expands to several thousand visitors during the height of the summer travel season. Situated a little more than a mile from the western entrance of Rocky Mountain National Park, this is a choice location in which to set up base camp. You can drive from Grand Lake on Trail Ridge Road from May through late fall. The narrow, curving 50-mile route crosses the Continental Divide and provides spectacular views of snowcapped peaks.

At an elevation of 8,369 feet, Grand Lake has pure mountain air,

- ☐ Dogsledding, cross-country skiing, snowshoeing, snowmobiling, ice fishing
- ☐ Mountain biking, golf
- ☐ Colorado's largest natural lake
- ☐ Fishing, boating, waterskiing on Grand Lake
- ☐ Dude ranches
- ☐ Arapaho National Forest

exceptional outdoor recreation, and Colorado's largest natural lake. Surrounded by forested shoreline in a splendid alpine setting, the town's namesake lake offers endless year-round activities.

The entire area is a sportsperson's paradise, boasting hunting, hiking, skiing, and most water sports. Late autumn brings a quiet existence to the village, when many businesses shut their doors. Trail Ridge Road closes, which cuts off traffic through Rocky Mountain National Park, leaving only one entrance into town.

When winter arrives, the area becomes a glorious snow-covered mecca for sports enthusiasts. Locals snowmobile or cross-country ski down Grand Avenue. You've just got to love a town with that kind of gusto.

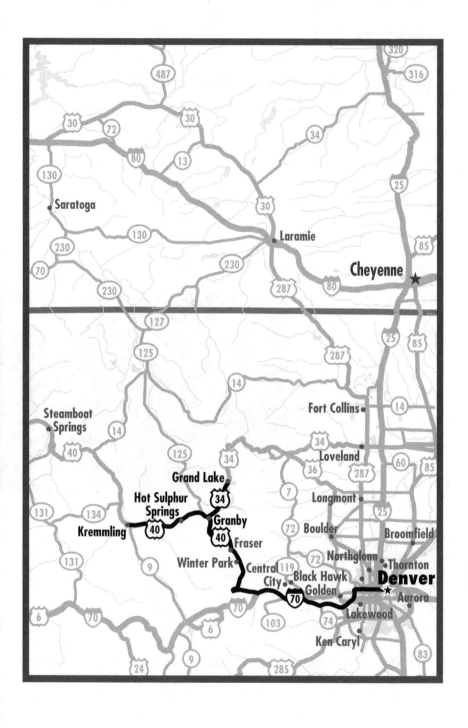

Day 1 / *Morning*

Grand Lake is approximately 100 miles northwest of Denver. Travel via I–70 west to U.S. Highway 40 and turn north. Follow Highway 40 over Berthoud Pass through the towns of Winter Park, Fraser, and Granby.

BREAKFAST: Remington's Restaurant, 52 Fourth Street, Granby; (970) 887–3632. Try the Remington's Benedict, served with country gravy and hashbrowns, at this family dining establishment. Open Monday through Saturday from 6:30 A.M. to 9:00 P.M. Closed Sunday. To get to Remington's, go 1 block north on Fourth Street off Highway 40.

After you leave Granby, travel north on U.S. 34 to Grand Lake. Park on Grand Avenue and spend time browsing the shops. You'll notice the Western atmosphere immediately as you stroll along the wooden boardwalk of this down-home mountain town.

The Grand Lake area was once home to the Native American Ute and Arapaho tribes. Judge Joseph Wescott settled in 1867 and trapped and fished the bounteous wilderness. Prospectors arrived in 1879 after gold was discovered, and by the end of the year the town had its first hotel, general store, and residential area. Today you'll find shops, cafes, galleries, and the occasional saloon along Grand Avenue.

LUNCH: Grand Pizza (717 Grand Avenue; 970–627–8390) serves awesome pizza. Try the Greek pizza, topped with feta cheese, tomatoes, and artichoke hearts, or the Mexican or Cajun pizza. The restaurant is open daily from 11:00 A.M. to 10.00 P.M. Winter hours and days vary.

Afternoon

Stop at **Grand Lake Art Gallery** (1117 Grand Avenue; 970–627–3104) and browse the selection of paintings, sculpture, pottery, stained glass, wood products, jewelry, and textiles, all crafted by Colorado artists. The gallery is open daily, May through October, from 10:00 A.M. to 6:00 P.M.; and during the winter on weekends only, from 10:00 A.M. to 5:00 P.M.

The **Kauffman House** (407 Pitkin; 970–627–9644) is a restored log house that was built by Ezra Kauffman in 1892 and was operated as a hotel until the early 1920s. You'll get a feel for life as it was in the late 1800s and early 1900s in this pioneer museum. Admission is free, and the house is open for tours during summer from 11:00 A.M. to 5:00 P.M. daily.

Boaters Choice (1246 Lake Avenue; 970–627–9273) offers boat tours of Grand Lake that last from forty-five minutes to an hour. The cost is $9.00 for adults and $5.00 for children ten and older; kids under ten tour free. Dinner cruises are also available.

DINNER: E.G.'s Garden Grill (1000 Grand Avenue; 970–627–8404) is a charmingly rustic cafe owned and run by two brothers. E. G. is the creative chef, and Stanton manages the dining room just as well as his brother runs the kitchen. For starters, try the steamed New Zealand greenlip mussels. Entrees include E.G.'s cowboy steak, a twenty-two-ounce, bone-in rib eye steak served with red chile onion rings; and tortilla-crusted salmon, as well as other choices. Dessert selections include Key lime pie and brownie a la mode.

The restaurant is open daily from 11:00 A.M. to 9:00 P.M.; the hours extend to 10:00 P.M. June through September. Winter hours vary. During summer, catch live music in the beer garden from noon to 4:00 P.M. weekends. Reservations are recommended for parties of eight or more and on weekends.

LODGING: Spirit Mountain Ranch, P. O. Box 942, Grand Lake, CO 80447; (970) 887–3551. This secluded bed-and-breakfast, located 6 miles south of Grand Lake, offers four spacious guest rooms, each with private bath, a king bed, and views of the Never Summer Range. Traveling on County Road 41 to reach the ranch is a spectacular drive, especially for visitors who arrive on a crisp September day as fields of golden aspen are ablaze with color. The Great Room is decorated in a whimsical blend of the owners' cherished antiques, modern art, and Western furniture.

Day 2 / Morning

BREAKFAST: Spirit Mountain Ranch. A full breakfast is included in the price of the room and might include a chili cheese frittata, homemade biscuits or muffins, or the inn's signature dish: blue corn–piñon waffles served with fresh fruit.

To see the mountains in all their splendor, drive the **Colorado River Headwaters Scenic and Historic Byway,** which starts at the Kawuneeche Visitor Center in Rocky Mountain National Park. The route follows U.S. Highway 34 through Grand Lake to Granby, then turns west along U.S. Highway 40 to Hot Sulphur Springs and Kremmling. The route is marked by signs with Colorado's state flower, the blue columbine.

Tour **Grand County Historical Museum,** located at the east end of Hot Sulphur Springs on U.S. Highway 40 (970–725–3939). This is an unusually fine museum for such a small community. Housed in a 1924 schoolhouse, the museum reflects Grand County life in the early days, including displays and photographs on skiing. The museum also has a good selection of regional books for sale. Admission is $4.00 for adults, $3.00 for seniors, and $2.00 for students. The museum is open during summer daily from 10:00 A.M. to 5:00 P.M. and in winter Wednesday through Friday from 10:00 A.M. to 5:00 P.M.

Visit the newly renovated **Hot Sulphur Springs Resort and Spa** (800–510–6235), located at the west end of Hot Sulphur Springs. Follow the signs off Highway 40 to reach the resort. Soak in one of five outdoor pools, treat yourself to a massage, or relax in the solarium. The resort is open from 8:00 A.M. to 10:00 P.M. daily. Prices are $15.50 for adults and $11.50 for kids.

LUNCH: The **Moose Cafe** (Highway 40 at the west end of Kremmling; 970–724–9987) is nothing fancy but serves great meat-and-potatoes-style meals and good burgers. The restaurant is open daily from 6:00 A.M. to 2:00 P.M. year-round.

There's More

Fishing, Grand Lake, Shadow Mountain Reservoir, and Lake Granby offer cutthroat, brown, and rainbow trout, as well as spectacular scenery. Try ice fishing in the winter. Check with Boaters Choice, 1246 Lake Avenue, Grand Lake; (970) 627–9273 (summer) or (970) 627–8918 (winter).

Grand Lake, Spirit Lake Rentals, Inc. (970–627–9288; www.spiritlake rentals.com) rents not only snowmobiles but also personal watercraft. Rates are $200 for eight hours, $135 for four hours, and $45 for one hour. Transportation to the lake, instruction, a life vest, and gas are included. Wet suits are available for $5.00 a day.

Grand Lake Golf Course, This challenging 18-hole course has views of the Continental Divide, and at 8,420 feet your ball is sure to travel farther. Follow Highway 34 from Grand Lake north for 0.25 mile, turn left onto County Road 48 for 1 mile, and follow the signs to the course. For information call (970) 627–8008.

Snowmobiling, The Grand Lake area, with more than 150 miles of groomed trails, is known as the Snowmobile Capital of Colorado. Rev up your machine, take off into the backcountry, and glide along the trails in the woods of Arapaho National Forest. Grand Adventures (800–726–9247) rents equipment. Helmet, trail map, and gas are included in the rates, and you can rent an insulated suit, boots, and gloves for $5.00 a day. You'll be glad to know that the snowmobiles have heated hand-warmer grips.

Special Events

March. High Altitude Sled Dog Championships. This event attracts more than a hundred teams from Canada and the United States as they compete in the final event of Grand County's Triple Crown of sled-dog racing. The mushing commences midmorning, and the races are exciting to watch. Wander the grounds and visit with owners of the Alaskan huskies, Siberian huskies, and Samoyeds. For dates call the Grand Lake Chamber of Commerce at (970) 627–3402 or (800) 531–1019. For more information visit www.grandlakechamber.com.

July 4. Independence Day brings spectacular fireworks over Grand Lake and a rollicking good time in the county. For specifics call (800) 531–1019.

August. Grand Lake Regatta and Lipton Cup Races. This is a lively spectator sport, and you'll enjoy cheering on members of the Grand Lake Yacht Club as they vie for the distinguished solid sterling-silver cup, donated by English tea baron Sir Thomas Lipton. The Grand Lake Yacht Club's claim to fame is holding the title as highest yacht club in the world.

October. Kremmling hosts its annual Roadkill Supper during hunting season. A fundraiser for the local chamber of commerce (970–724–3472), this dinner attracts mainly hunters and locals, and it features a selection of wild game that may include venison, elk, moose, or antelope. Buy a roadkill T-shirt with the menu printed on the back. Bundle up—the unique feast is served outside in the town square, 213 Park Center Avenue. For more information visit www.kremmlingchamber.com.

Other Recommended Restaurants and Lodgings

Granby

C Lazy U Ranch, P.O. Box 379, Granby, CO 80446; (970) 887–3344; www.clazyu.com. This ranch manages to pull off being luxurious and Western at the same time. You'll get personal pampering if you so desire (the staff-to-guest ratio is almost one to one), and you'll dine on superb meals. Horseback riding, tennis, racquetball, fishing, and cross-country skiing are available, and if you still have energy, there's an exercise room. Book well in advance.

Grand Lake

Caroline's Cuisine, 9921 U.S. Highway 34, 5 miles south of Grand Lake; (970) 627–9404. Locals say that this French-American restaurant is "consistently excellent." Try the escargot sautéed in garlic butter or the pan-seared salmon served with corn bread. Steaks and pasta are also available. Caroline's is open for dinner only, daily from 5:00 to 9:00 P.M.

Grand Lake Lodge, 1 mile north of Grand Lake on Highway 34, is a historic lodge with character and charm. Built in 1925, the lodge offers striking views of Shadow Mountain Reservoir and Grand Lake. Take a break on the inn's porch or relax by the pool. Contact Grand Lake Lodge, P.O. Box 569, Grand Lake, CO 80447 (970–627–3967), for a reservation. The lodge is open from the first weekend in June through mid-September.

Grand Lake Lodge Restaurant, (north of Grand Lake on Highway 34; 970–627–3967) has a selection of entrees that include buffalo burger, grilled rainbow trout, and Norwegian salmon. The restaurant follows the lodge's schedule and is open June through mid-September. The restaurant is open daily and serves champagne brunch Sunday from 9:30 A.M. to 1:00 P.M.

Kremmling

Latigo Ranch, P.O. Box 237, Kremmling, CO 80459; (800) 227–9655; www.latigotrails.com. Secluded, authentic, and cozy, this family-run dude ranch offers incredible views of the Indian Peaks. The ranch cuisine is marvelous. Join a cattle roundup or settle in with a favorite book. Snowshoeing and cross-country skiing are superb in winter.

Silver Creek

The Inn at Silver Creek, P.O. Box 4222, Silver Creek, CO 80446; (800) 926–4386; www.silvercreeklodging.com. This resort has suites (some with fireplaces), studios, and standard rooms. Facilities include a hot tub, an exercise room, a sauna, an indoor/outdoor pool, racquetball courts, and a restaurant.

Latigo Ranch, near Kremmling.

For More Information

Colorado Dude and Guest Ranch Association, P.O. Box 2120, Granby, CO 80446; (970) 887–3128; www.coloradoranch.com.

Grand County Colorado Tourism Board, P.O. Box 208, Winter Park, CO 80482; (800) 729–5821; www.grand-county.com.

Grand Lake Area Chamber of Commerce, P.O. Box 57, Grand Lake, CO 80447; (800) 531–1019 or (970) 627–3402; www.grandlakechamber.com.

Greater Granby Area Chamber of Commerce, P.O. Box 35, Granby, CO 80446; (800) 325–1661; www.rkymtnhi.com/granbycoc.

Kremmling Area Chamber of Commerce, P.O. Box 471, Kremmling, CO 80459; (970) 724–3472 or (877) 573–4263.

Central City and Black Hawk

Opera in a Mountain Setting

1 Night

With nearly thirty casinos in Central City and nearby Black Hawk, this area has returned to the lively atmosphere that existed in the 1860s when Central City thrived as a booming mining town. In 1859 John Gregory discovered gold here. The site is marked by the Gregory Monument, near the city limits. Shortly after his strike, several thousand people, hoping to unearth riches, moved into the area known as Gregory Gulch.

Completed in 1878, the gorgeous Central City Opera House opened its ornate doors for the first time with a gala event that attracted dignitaries, theater lovers, and members of society.

Both Central City and Black Hawk became nearly deserted as a result of the dwindling gold production at the beginning of the twentieth century. The beautiful opera house was boarded up until 1932, when the Central City Opera Association restored the building to its former glory.

☐ Opera

☐ Historic mining town

☐ Museums

☐ Gold mine

☐ Jazz festival

☐ Victorian B&B

The Central City Opera House, one of the West's most distinguished, reigns as the area's majestic prize. The lovingly restored structure is a beautiful example of early architecture. Appreciate a true opera with its silvery sounds and incredible costumes in this 1878 setting. Performances, which are sung in English, will delight the most discriminating fan and may even convert the nonenthusiast into an opera lover.

Day 1 / Afternoon

Take I–70 west out of Denver and continue past the Evergreen/El Rancho exit about 8 miles. Take the Golden/Central City exit (number 244). Turn right on Highway 6 and follow the signs for Central City. Travel about 3

miles to the intersection with Highway 119; turn left and follow the signs for Central City and Black Hawk. Driving time from central Denver is approximately an hour.

Depending on your interests, you can begin rolling the dice or choose other activities. Even if gambling isn't your thing, you'll want to at least peek into the casinos, some of which have been built in mansions. One is in a former jail. Slot machines are generally the favorite, but gambling enthusiasts can try their luck at blackjack or poker. The age limit of twenty-one for gambling is strictly enforced at all casinos.

To learn some interesting tidbits about the area, take a self-guided Historic Walking Tour of Central City. Thanks to the Central City Opera House Association, the State Historical Fund, and the Gilpin County Historical Society, you can read about the history of the area. Ask at the Teller House, 120 Eureka Street, for details and a map.

The **Teller House** (120 Eureka Street, Central City; 303–582–3200) was once one of the classiest hotels in the area. Completed in 1872, the hotel was said to be the most elegant building in Colorado. Rooms rented for $2.00 a night and a suite was $3.00, excessive amounts for the times. Visitors flocked to the lavish hotel to enjoy running water, fine furnishings, and excellent cuisine. The Teller House was the gathering place for Central City society. On the first floor in what is now the Face Bar, inspect the famous *Face on the Barroom Floor,* painted by a Denver journalist in 1936. Although the Teller House has undergone a $15-million restoration, overnight accommodations are not available. During the summer, the opera crowd still gathers at the Face Bar for cocktails before the performance.

DINNER: Black Forest Restaurant, 24 Big Springs Drive, Nederland; (303) 279–2333 or (303) 582–9971; www.blackforestrest.com. Since the Black Forest moved from Central City to Nederland, nothing has replaced this popular restaurant. In fact, there are no "stand-alone" restaurants in Central City, only the eateries located in the casinos. The Black Forest has changed its name from Inn to Restaurant because they do not rent rooms, but otherwise it's the same dependable menu and service. And it's worth the extra 19-mile drive from Central City to Nederland. Many customers still dine here before attending the opera. The restaurant serves authentic German dishes, including Wiener schnitzel and sauerbraten, as well as steak and seafood. Enjoy elk steak, a bottle of wine from the extensive selection, and exquisite pastries. Open year-round, Monday through Saturday from

11:00 A.M. to 10:00 P.M. and Sunday from 11:00 A.M. to 9:00 P.M. From Central City, continue north on Highway 119 for 19 miles to Nederland.

Evening

Central City Opera (124 Eureka Street, Central City) is the best attraction in town. The opera runs from late June through mid-August. Call the box office at (303) 292–6700 or (800) 851–8175 or go online at www.centralcityopera.org for tickets. Prices range from $42 to $72, depending on where you wish to sit in the opera house. Ask about bus transportation from Denver to Central City on the Express Charter Opera Bus. Parking in Central City can be a challenge, and the bus offers a relaxing ride, classical music, and convenience.

The Central City Opera House shines as the jewel of the area. Patrons are treated to an elegant matinee or evening in this magnificent setting. Restored to reflect its original grandeur, the opera house today seats 550 patrons. Productions include such classics as *Madame Butterfly, The Merry Widow,* and the opera's signature presentation, *The Ballad of Baby Doe.* Enjoy the flawless acoustics, ornate ceiling, splendid performance, and luxurious seats. During intermission, check the back of your chair for the name, carved in the wood, of a Colorado citizen, performer, or pioneer. Opera supporters and other special persons have been honored by this tradition since the early days. If you wish to introduce yourself to one of the singers or get an autograph after the performance, linger on the patio just outside the opera house, where the performers exit. They are generally pleased to oblige.

When you call for reservations, inquire about special events such as salon recitals, presented Saturday and Sunday at 11:45 A.M. Artists perform a thirty-minute solo as guests dine on a gourmet lunch in the Victorian beauty of the Teller House. Reservations are essential. There is also a thirty-minute cabaret opera, *The Face on the Barroom Floor,* that details the tale of the face painted on the floor of the Teller House. The short production takes place across the street from the Teller House in the historic Williams Stables on selected days throughout the season. Check the schedule at www.centralcityopera.org.

LODGING: Chateau L'Acadienne (325 Spring Street, Central City; 303–582–5209 or 800–834–5209) is a restored nineteenth-century home located within walking distance of the opera and casinos. The name *Chateau L'Acadienne* translates to "big house of the Cajun," and the entire house is decked in Victorian and Louisiana French decor. Built in the 1870s during the gold-mining boom, the house features grand bay windows, 10-foot-high ceilings, antique crystal chandeliers, and three well-appointed guest rooms.

The Victorian Room is decorated with period furniture, an antique crystal chandelier, and a large bay window that overlooks Central City. This room offers a king bed and a daybed and accommodates up to four persons.

The Emerald Room offers a queen canopy bed and an antique dresser and was named for its view of Central City. The New Orleans Room features French decor and a marble-top dresser. Room rates are $75 to $125, and reservations are recommended. The guest parking is especially convenient.

Day 2 / Morning

BREAKFAST: Chateau L'Acadienne. You'll eat family-style on weekends (continental breakfast is served Monday through Friday) as owners James and Shirley Voorhies share stories of Central City and the history of their home. Ask about Gwendolyn, the friendly resident ghost; the stories flourish come Halloween. Full breakfast served on weekends may include Grand Marnier French Toast, Crispy Potato Quiche, or Baked Eggs L'Acadienne—Shirley's own slightly spicy creation, which includes eggs, cayenne, and oregano.

Drive through Central City on Eureka Street about 2 miles west (the road becomes dirt) to the century-old cemeteries that stretch over the horizon. Wander the area and spend time reading the aged tombstones. The grounds are unkempt but interesting, and you'll no doubt avoid crowds.

There's More

Gilpin County Historical Museum (228 East High Street, Central City; 303–582–5283) is located in a restored 1870 schoolhouse. The museum chronicles the area's rich history, and you'll get a sense of what life was like in the late 1800s by browsing through the chambers, which include mining memorabilia and an antique doll collection. Open daily from 11:00 A.M. to 4:00 P.M. Memorial Day through Labor Day. Admission is $3.00. *The* ***Operatique,*** across Eureka Street from the Opera House (both

303–582–5202), has a nice selection of special books about the Central City Opera House, along with T-shirts and other merchandise.

Special Events

June. Madam Lou Bunch Days, Central City. Held the third weekend in June. Ladies dress in "Sporting House Girl" and "Madam" costumes (the Madam outfits are the more conservative) and gentlemen wear Western attire for the Parade of Madams and Dandy Dans. The weekend includes bed races down Main Street and the traditional Madams and Miners Ball.

August. Central City Music Fest. Jazz and contemporary musicians from around the country perform during the third weekend in August. Main Street closes, and the town parties with street dancing and celebrating.

Other Recommended Restaurants and Lodgings

Dostal Alley, 1 Dostal Street, Central City; (303) 582–1610. This restaurant has homemade pizza and is also a favorite gathering place for opera singers after Central City Opera House performances.

Harvey's Wagon Wheel Casino and Hotel, 321 Gregory Street, Central City; 800–HARVEYS. Harvey's is conveniently located near the opera house. Suites and nonsmoking rooms are available. Shuttle service to Black Hawk available.

Isle of Capris, 401 Main Street, Black Hawk; (303) 998–7777; www.isleof capriscasino.com. This hotel/casino offers 237 rooms and three restaurants, shuttle service around Black Hawk, and several levels of parking.

O's Steak and Seafood Restaurant, 10600 Westminster Boulevard, at the Westin Westminster; (303) 410–5066. O's Restaurant is open for lunch and dinner and has a superb selection of fresh seafood.

Westin Westminster, 10600 Westminster Boulevard, Westminster; (303) 410–5000; www.westin.com. This resort offers an alternative to staying in Central City or Black Hawk. Ask about the hotel's welcoming pet policy. Here, Fido can stay in luxury and you don't even have to sneak him in. The Westin Westminster is located at Church Ranch Road off the Boulder Turnpike.

For More Information

Central City Information; (800) 542–2999 or (303) 582–5251; www.centralcitycolorado.net.

Central City Opera House Association, 621 Seventeenth Street, Suite 1601, Denver, CO 80293; (303) 292–6700; www.centralcityopera.org.

Fort Collins

Brewing Up a Good Time

1 Night

Even with its population of 118,000, Fort Collins retains that small-town feeling. Residents here indulge in the good life with magnificent outdoor recreation and enough restaurants, galleries, and microbreweries to enjoy a night on the town.

- ☐ Historic Old Town Square
- ☐ Colorado State University
- ☐ World-famous Clydesdales
- ☐ Horsetooth Reservoir
- ☐ Cache la Poudre River
- ☐ Flower farm

Established in 1864 as a post to protect settlers and travelers along the Overland Trail, the city was once an active military fort. Today the mixture of lifestyles—students, farmers, ranchers, professors, and retirees—helps create the community's charm.

As the home of Colorado State University, Fort Collins has the attractions that every good college town should: excellent bookstores, outdoor cafes, and that youthful intellectual edge found in a university setting.

Day 1 / Morning

From Denver, take I–25 north for 60 miles to Fort Collins. Plan on a one-hour drive.

BREAKFAST: Silver Grill Cafe (218 Walnut Street, Fort Collins; 970–484–4656) has a history that traces back to 1912. Today this restaurant is a favorite among locals and a "must" for visitors. You'll find marvelous cinnamon rolls and menu items such as homemade sausage gravy served over fresh biscuits. Silver Grill Cafe opens at 6:00 A.M. Monday through Saturday and at 7:00 A.M. Sunday. The cafe serves breakfast until 2:00 P.M. and also serves lunch from 11:00 A.M. to 2:00 P.M. Lunch selections include burgers, a BLT and a BOLT (*o* is for onion), homemade chili, and Lois's cranberry chicken salad.

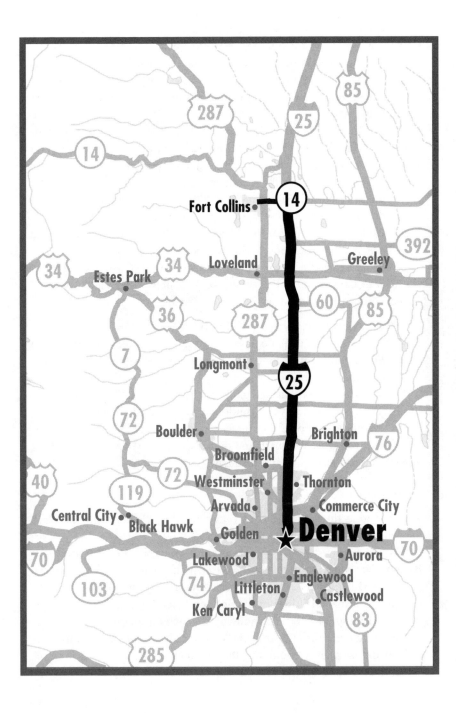

Whether you want to tool around town or head into the wilderness, Fort Collins and the surrounding area offer both. Stroll College Avenue and the renovated **Historic Old Town Square,** which extends in a triangle from the intersection of College and Mountain Avenues. Many of the shops and restaurants are frequented by students, which makes exploring all that much more interesting.

For a unique selection of Western-style furniture and accessories, visit **Rocky Mountain Home Collection** (128 South College Avenue; 970–482–8608). Hand-carved wooden coffee tables and fishing-motif decor are for sale here. The birdbaths, fountains, and books at the **Perennial Gardener** (154 North College Avenue; 970–224–3987) are interesting for nongardeners as well as those with a green thumb. The **Cupboard** (152 South College Avenue; 970–493–8585) is another wonderful store filled with kitchen accessories, pots and pans, cookbooks, and specialty foods.

When you need a break, stop at **Starry Night Coffee Company** (112 South College; 970–493–3039) for an espresso drink and a slice of coffee cake as you linger over the local newspaper.

LUNCH: Austin's American Grill (100 West Mountain Avenue, Fort Collins; 970–224–9691) is a contemporary restaurant that has attracted a local following. Big-band swing music plays in the background as you look over the menu with choices such as baby back ribs, served with the house barbecue sauce, ranch beans, and garlic mashed potatoes. The restaurant has a full-service bar and a relaxing outdoor dining area. The chef will prepare any of the meals "to go" if you prefer to picnic in one of the local parks. Austin's is open daily for lunch and dinner from 11:00 A.M. to 10:00 P.M.; open to 11:00 P.M. Friday and Saturday.

Afternoon

Referred to as the Napa Valley of Breweries, Fort Collins is a great place to spend the afternoon brewery-hopping.

You don't need to be a beer lover to enjoy a tour of **Anheuser-Busch Brewery.** Located at 2351 Busch Drive (970–490–4691), Anheuser-Busch offers a free tour, which lasts an hour and twenty minutes. You'll hear the Budweiser theme song, smell hops, and see the high-speed packaging lines that fill thousands of cans and bottles every minute as you are guided through this immense facility. Guests may sample the beer in the hospitality room, but the real highlight is a visit to the eye-catching barn to see the world-famous Clydesdales.

To get to Anheuser-Busch Brewery, take I–25 to Mountain Vista Drive and turn right onto Busch Drive. Tours are available from 10:00 A.M. to 4:00 P.M. Thursday through Monday, October through May; from 9:30 A.M. to 5:00 P.M. daily, June through August; and from 10:00 A.M. to 4:00 P.M. daily, September. There is a special Budweiser Clydesdale Camera Day the first Saturday of each month, year-round, from 1:00 to 3:00 P.M. For more information visit www.budweisertours.com

Next, stop at the more down-home **Odell Brewing Company** (800 East Lincoln; 970–498–9070), a much smaller operation than Anheuser-Busch. At Odell's your guide may be one of the owners of the company. Sample the popular 90 Shilling or Cutthroat Porter Ale. Free tours are available weekdays 11:00 A.M. to 3:00 P.M. and Saturday from 1:00 to 3:00 P.M. on the hour. The retail store and tasting room are open from 9:00 A.M. to 6:00 P.M. weekdays and from 10:00 A.M. to 6:00 P.M. Saturday.

To see where Fat Tire Ale is brewed, visit **New Belgium Brewing Company** (500 Linden Street; 970–221–0524). In keeping with the "fat tire" theme, the tasting room has several 1950s-style bicycle replicas. Employees are given a bike—with fat tires, of course—after a year of service. The hand-crafted regional beers include not only Fat Tire Amber Ale, but Sunshine Wheat Beer, Blue Paddle Pilsener Lager, Abbey Belgian Style Ale, and Trippel Belgian Style Ale. Employees compete in a contest to name new additions. You can take a self-guided tour from 10:00 A.M. to 5:30 P.M. Monday through Saturday. Guided tours are available at 2:00 P.M. weekdays and from 11:00 A.M. to 4:00 P.M. Saturday on the hour.

DINNER: **Bisetti's Italian Restaurant,** 120 South College Avenue, Fort Collins; (970) 493–0086. This family-owned Italian restaurant consistently wins awards for being one of the best in the city. A favorite dining area is the room with a grapevine-covered ceiling. Try the baked penne with roasted garlic or the smoked salmon lasagna. The restaurant is about 5 blocks from your lodging at the Edwards House. Bisetti's is open for lunch Monday through Friday from 11:00 A.M. to 2:00 P.M. and for dinner daily. Call for a reservation.

LODGING: The **Edwards House** (402 West Mountain Avenue, Fort Collins; 970–493–9191 or 800–281–9190; www.edwardshouse.com) may be the most upscale lodging in Fort Collins. This Victorian-era B&B, conveniently situated within minutes of Historic Old Town District, is the kind of tastefully decorated house where every nook and cranny holds discoveries. You'll find an antique typewriter in the well-stocked, inviting library and a yellow rubber duckie near the tub in your room. Each of the eight rooms has cable television with VCR, telephone, bathrobes, and a shower or clawfoot tub. Guests gather in the afternoon for conversation and a glass of wine in the elegant parlor.

The Avery Suite, named for its view of the historic Avery House across the street, is decorated with floral wallpaper, lace curtains, a pine armoire, a queen-size canopy bed, and a claw-foot tub. The Montezuma Fuller Suite is the room requested most often by honeymoon couples. This spacious, third-floor bedroom has a gorgeous mahogany sleigh bed, separate sitting room, fireplace, and hot tub. Rates at the Edwards House range from $89 to $159.

Day 2 / Morning

BREAKFAST: You'll dine in the formal dining room of the Edwards House at an oval antique table once owned by actor Adolphe Menjou. Breakfast includes fresh fruit, home-baked scones, and an entree such as crepes, quiche, or eggs florentine. Order an espresso or cappuccino to top off the feast.

It would be a shame to not take advantage of the beauty and adventure of the great outdoor attractions that lie just beyond the city. Located fifteen minutes west of Fort Collins, **Horsetooth Reservoir** is a 6.5-mile-long body of water named for the nearby rock that resembles a horse's tooth. Popular with anglers, boaters, swimmers, campers, and picnickers, this lake attracts crowds during summer months for good reason: The scenic setting remains unspoiled and beautiful.

Nearby **Horsetooth Mountain Park** offers acres of public land available to hikers, mountain bikers, and horseback riders. To get to Horsetooth Reservoir and Horsetooth Mountain Park, take Taft Hill Road south; 0.5 mile south of Horsetooth, turn right on County Road 38E. That road takes you directly to the southern end of Horsetooth Reservoir; if you continue past the reservoir, you will arrive at Horsetooth Mountain Park's parking lot. For more information contact Larimer County Parks Department at (970) 679–4570.

LUNCH: Picnic at one of the many sites at **Lory State Park,** which borders Horsetooth Reservoir. This park is another fantastic area for exploration. Watch for deer and the occasional rattlesnake. During winter, cross-country skiers will find a network of relatively undisturbed trails. For information on horseback riding, contact **Double Diamond Stables**

(710 Lodgepole Drive, Bellvue; 970–224–4200); open Memorial Day through Labor Day. For additional information contact Lory State Park (708 Lodgepole Drive, Bellvue; 970–493–1623).

River-rafting enthusiasts will want to float the **Cache la Poudre River,** which, according to legend, got its name, meaning "hide the powder," when early French traders stashed their gunpowder barrels next to the river. Today rafters, kayakers, and canoeists maneuver the significant white water of this twisting, scenic river that eventually flows into the South Platte. To arrange a guided raft, kayak, or fly-fishing trip, contact **Rocky Mountain Adventures** (1117 North Highway 287, Fort Collins; 970–493–4005 or 800–858–6808) or **Wanderlust Adventure** (3500 Bingham Hill Road, Fort Collins; 800–745–7238). For kayak instruction and rentals, call **Poudre River Kayaks** at (970) 484–8480. To get to Poudre Canyon, take College Avenue (Highway 287) north out of Fort Collins and turn left on Highway 14, the entrance to Poudre Canyon.

There's More

Avery House (328 West Mountain Avenue, Fort Collins; 970–221–0533) is a historic house museum that was home to Franklin Avery, who founded First National Bank and was instrumental in developing water projects in northern Colorado. Today the Victorian house, gazebo, fountain, and carriage house are listed on the National Register of Historic Places. Tours of Avery House are available from 1:00 to 3:00 P.M. Sunday and Wednesday. Free admission, donations accepted.

Discovery Center Science Museum (703 East Prospect Road, Fort Collins; 970–472–3990) is a nonprofit institution devoted to science and technology. Kids love the hands-on exhibits, which include the opportunity to make arcs and sparks in the Electricity Room. StarLab Planetarium is another favorite. The museum is open Tuesday through Saturday from 10:00 A.M. to 5:00 P.M. and Sunday from noon to 5:00 P.M. Admission is $6.50 per adult and $4.50 for ages three through twelve; children two and under are admitted free.

The *Farm Heritage Museum and the Farm at Lee Martinez Park* (600 North Sherwood Street; 970–221–6665) offer visitors the chance to view farm animals in a rural setting. You'll see antique farm machinery, a barbed-wire collection, and a large horseshoe used by one of the Anheuser-Busch Clydesdale horses. Admission is free. The farm is open from 10:00 A.M. to 5:00 P.M. Monday through Saturday and from noon to 5:00 P.M. Sunday.

The **Fort Collins Museum** (200 Mathews Street; 970–221–6738) emphasizes the local history of the area and its natural environment. The biggest attractions at the museum are the three historic cabins located in the courtyard. One of these, Auntie Stone's Cabin, is the only remaining building from the time when the fort was in operation. Admission is free. The museum is open Tuesday through Saturday from 10:00 A.M. to 5:00 P.M. and Sunday from noon to 5:00 P.M.; the facility is closed Monday.

Swetsville Zoo (4801 East Harmony Road, Fort Collins; 970–484–9509) doesn't boast a single live animal, but this sculpture park offers more than 150 animals and flowers constructed from scrap metal and old car parts. Swetsville Zoo is located 0.5 mile east of I–25. Admission is free, but donations are accepted. The zoo is open daily from dawn to dusk.

Windswept Farms (5537 North County Road 9, Fort Collins; 970–484–1124) is a family-owned flower farm that visitors can tour Monday through Saturday, June through September. Stroll through the herb garden or watch the staff create dried floral arrangements.

Special Events

July. Rendezvous and Skookum Day. The history of Fort Collins is re-enacted with demonstrations of blacksmithing, milking, quilting, branding, trapping, weaving, and more.

August. New West Fest celebrates the city's birthday in a long-weekend event with music, food booths, and arts and crafts for sale.

Fall. "Make it a Ram Weekend." Call the Fort Collins Convention and Visitor Bureau at (800) 274–3678 for a brochure listing events and lodging options to consider during the CSU football season.

Other Recommended Restaurants and Lodgings

Ciao Vino, 126 West Mountain Ave., Fort Collins; (970) 484–8466. This fine Italian restaurant offers forty-seven wines by the glass, live music every evening, marble walls, vaulted ceilings, and a superb menu. Ciao Vino is open daily. Wine tastings every Saturday evening.

Jay's American Bistro (135 West Oak Street, Fort Collins; 970–482–1876) serves Italian-style pastas and a variety of seafood, wild game, and pizzas. Open daily.

Positano's Pizzeria, 3645 South College Avenue, Fort Collins; (970) 207–9935. The thin-crust pizzas are hand tossed at this authentic pizzeria. Try the Quattro Formaggio with four cheeses or the Sicilian. Positano's is open from 10:30 A.M. to 9:30 P.M. Monday through Saturday and from 2:00 to 8:00 P.M. Sunday.

For More Information

Fort Collins Convention and Visitor Bureau, 3745 East Prospect Road, Suite 200, Fort Collins, CO 80525; (800) 274–3678; www.ftcollins. com.

Saratoga, Wyoming

Wild, Wild West

2 Nights

Rugged, vast, and beautiful, the Cowboy State evokes images of Western novels and an untamed landscape.

- ☐ Blue-ribbon trout fishing
- ☐ Golf, tennis, horseback riding
- ☐ Western lodge
- ☐ Scenic highways
- ☐ Wide-open spaces

Wyoming doesn't aspire to glitz and glamour. Here jeans and cowboy boots are appropriate attire anytime, anywhere. Saddle up and ride off into the lush canyons or snag a trophy-size trout from the crystal-clear Upper North Platte River. Waterfalls, streams, and lakes are abundant with fish. Golf the spectacular 9-hole course at Saratoga Inn, or set off on a mountain bike to explore this uncrowded haven.

Surrounded by sprawling ranches, acres of national forest, and the Sierra Madre and Snowy Range Mountains, the town of Saratoga (population 1,950) offers a permanence and personality that fast-paced resorts may be missing. Here, the American Legion advertises "Happy hour from 5 to 6," the daily fire whistle blows at noon in small-town tradition, and the local Chevrolet dealer shows more trucks than cars. Don't expect to buy the *New York Times* or even the *Denver Post*. There's not a Starbucks for miles, and you won't find parking meters or stoplights. Plan to kick back, soak in the hot springs, and listen to fish tales by the outdoor fireplace at Saratoga Inn. This rural area has what many people want in a weekend retreat: peace and quiet, pristine wilderness, pleasant accommodations, excellent food, and a long list of outdoor activities.

Day 1 / Morning

From Denver, take Interstate 25 north to Cheyenne and Interstate 80 west to Laramie, where you follow Wyoming 130 (Snowy Range Road) west to where the road splits. Then take 130 to Saratoga. You might consider

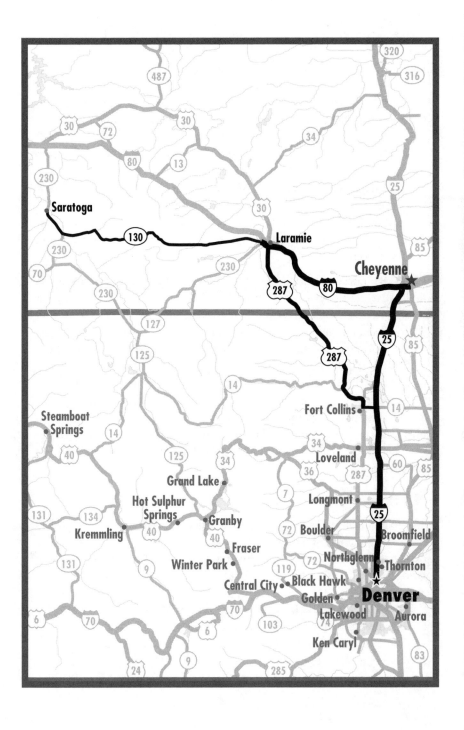

spending the night in Cheyenne. Another option is to take I–25 north to Fort Collins, U.S. Highway 287. From Fort Collins head northwest to Laramie. Snowy Range Road is closed in the winter, so you must follow the route on I–80 west. Saratoga is about 240 miles from Denver.

For a history of Cheyenne Frontier Days and the West, visit **Cheyenne's Old West Museum** (4501 North Carey Avenue, Cheyenne; 800–778–7290), which also has one of the nation's largest carriage collections. The museum is open Monday through Friday from 9:00 A.M. to 5:00 P.M. and weekends from 10:00 A.M. to 5:00 P.M.

The **Historic Governor's Mansion** (300 East Twenty-first Street, Cheyenne; 307–777–7878), built in 1904, is open year-round to visitors. Take a self-guided tour of this lovely two-and-a-half-story house. Admission is free, and the mansion is open Tuesday through Saturday from 9:00 A.M. to 5:00 P.M.

LUNCH: Located in the oldest brick home in Cheyenne, **Lexie's Mesa Grill** (216 East Seventeenth Street; 307–632–9119) is located next door to the elegant Nagle Warren Mansion Bed and Breakfast (see "Other Recommended Restaurants and Lodgings" at end of the chapter). Lexie's Mesa Grill serves a delicious mango mint shrimp salad. Open daily from 11:00 A.M. to 9:00 P.M.

From Cheyenne, continue west on I–80. Plan on a two-hour drive from Cheyenne to Saratoga. At Laramie, follow Highway 130 on the Scenic Byway through the Snowy Range Mountains, and continue north on Highway 130 to Saratoga. The route winds across the grand Medicine Bow Mountains and past several crystalline lakes, including picture-perfect Lake Marie.

Afternoon

The individualistic, frontier spirit that ruled the West of the 1800s still thrives in Saratoga. Shop for a new pair of waders and get the latest scoop on where the fish are biting at **Fishpaw Trading Company** (120 East Bridge Street; 307–326–5000). The store also sells antiques, art, and Western collectibles.

Visit the **Hat Creek Saddlery & Trading Post** at First and Bridge Streets, downtown Saratoga. There you can order your own custom-built saddle or shop for horseshoes, saddlesoap, a canteen, chaps, a cowboy hat, a branding iron, silver jewelry, or a Patsy Cline CD.

Join other guests in the **Lounge at Saratoga Inn** (601 East Pic Pike

Road) for social hour, from 4:30 to 5:30 P.M. daily, and sample the inn's beer. The Rodeo Pale Ale and the Winkin' Willy's Wild Wheat are especially good. Or sip a glass of wine and nibble cheese and crackers as you admire the Western wild mounts in the Trophy Room. Stroll outside to the terrace, which has an oversize hand-carved chess set. One set of pieces represents the Native Americans; the other, the Cavalry. Guests are welcome to play a game.

DINNER: The **Wolf Hotel Restaurant,** 101 East Bridge Street, Saratoga; (307) 326–5525. This casual restaurant has an excellent reputation. The menu includes prime rib, the Wolf Burger, and a soup-and-salad bar. Open daily for lunch and dinner.

Evening

LODGING: Saratoga Inn (601 East Pic Pike Road, P.O. Box 869, Saratoga, WY 82331; 307–326–5261 or 800–594–0178; www.saratoga inn.com) is a rare find. This classic Western lodge has recently undergone a multimillion-dollar renovation. Each of the fifty-six guest rooms and suites has a feather bed, a Pendleton blanket, Western art, and custom-made lamps with cowhide shades. Warm chocolate chip cookies are delivered to your doorstep nightly, and you can choose from more than 400 movies to watch in the privacy of your room. Relax on the porch next to the outdoor fireplace, or lounge in the lobby with its soft leather couches, bull-hide rugs, and grandfather clock.

Saratoga Inn offers a 70-foot mineral-springs pool, three private teepee-covered hot-springs pools, a giant chess arena and terrace, and a spa. The inn is open year-round, and rates range from $98 to $218, depending on the season and your choice of rooms.

Day 2 / Morning

BREAKFAST: Mom's Kitchen, 402 South First (307–326–5842) serves great biscuits and sausage gravy. Service can be a bit slow, but keep in mind that the unhurried pace is one of the attractions of this getaway. Read the *Casper Star Tribune* or the *Saratoga Sun* and plan a day of fishing, golfing, or just soaking and relaxing.

After you've had your fill, head for the great outdoors. Ask at the front desk of the Saratoga Inn for an outfitter for a fly-fishing or horseback-riding trip.

Wide-open spaces and scenic landscape welcome you to Wyoming.

Afternoon

LUNCH: Dine on a burger and fries at Saratoga Inn's **Silver Saddle Restaurant** (307–326–5261), or request a box lunch to go.

With three "over-the-river" shots and a cliff tee-off, the scenic 9-hole course at Saratoga Inn is a golfer's dream. Clubs are available for rent at the pro shop. There's also mountain biking, tennis, and horseback riding.

DINNER: Bubba's Barbecue, 119 North River Street (you can walk from the Saratoga Inn); (307) 326–5427. Bubba's serves outstanding ribs with "sauces made daily from an old Southern recipe." They *don't* serve beer or liquor, but diners are welcome to bring their own. Bubba's is the epitome of casual and easygoing dining. You might see a handwritten note on the blackboard congratulating someone on the birth of a new baby (complete with time, date, and weight) or a Happy Anniversary greeting.

Open Tuesday through Sunday from 11:00 A.M. to 8:00 P.M. Closed Monday. Another choice is the dining room at the Saratoga Inn, the **Silver Saddle Restaurant,** offering chicken, steaks, seafood, and pasta.

LODGING: Saratoga Inn.

Day 3 / Morning

BREAKFAST: Lollypops, 107 East Bridge, Saratoga; (307) 326–5020. Eggs Benedict, Belgian waffles, and espresso are on the menu. Breakfast is served from 7:00 to 11:00 A.M. daily from mid-May through September. The remainder of the year, Lollypops opens at 8:00 A.M. and is closed Thursday.

Return to Denver via Highway 287 from Laramie. Connect with I–25 south at Fort Collins.

To tour the restored, nineteenth-century prison where Butch Cassidy served time in the late 1890s for grand larceny (stealing horses), stop at **Wyoming Territorial Prison & Old West Park,** 975 Snowy Range Road, Laramie; (307) 745–6161 or (800) 845–2287. Cassidy was originally sentenced to two years of hard labor but was pardoned by Governor William A. Richards in return for a pledge to "do no further thieving in Wyoming." Cassidy—reportedly a model prisoner—served eighteen months. The large black-and-white photographs of Cassidy and others who served time here give this place an eerie feel. Lighten the mood by watching Calamity Jane crack her whip or ride her horse around the grounds. The woman who portrays this legend is Calamity Jane's great-great niece. Open May through September. **National U.S. Marshals Museum** (975 Snowy Range Road, Laramie; 307– 745–3733), located on the grounds of the Wyoming Territorial Prison, is a fascinating museum that chronicles the first 200 years of the U.S. Marshals.

LUNCH: Coal Creek Coffee Company (110 Grand Avenue, Laramie; 307–745–7737) has coffee drinks and a "Light Food" menu that includes an Italian garden pita sandwich and a bagel melt.

There's More

Historic Atlas Theatre, 211 West Sixteenth Street, Cheyenne; (307) 638–6543. Hiss, boo, and cheer as much as you want at this old-fashioned melodrama. During July and August, performers entertain in this theater, which is on the National Register of Historic Places.

Prairie Rides, 190 Sprague Lane, Laramie; (307) 745–5095. Enjoy a horse-drawn wagon ride or an all-inclusive package complete with chuckwagon dinners and a weekend of cattle drives, branding, and roping.

River rafting. The Class III and IV rapids of the North Gate Canyon on the North Platte will get your heart pounding. Half-day, full-day, and overnight white-water trips are available through **Great Rocky Mountain Outfitters** (P.O. Box 1677, 216 East Walnut Street, Saratoga, WY 82331; 307–326–8750). You'll see petroglyphs and may catch a glimpse of a bald eagle or some mountain sheep as you float down the river. **Brush Creek Ranch** guides fishing trips. Call (800) 726–2499 or make reservations at the front desk of the Saratoga Inn.

The **University of Wyoming Art Museum,** 2111 Willett Drive, Laramie; (307) 766–6622. This excellent museum is located in the Centennial Complex on the university's main campus. The museum's diverse and extensive collections may surprise you. Works by artists such as Charles M. Russell, Albert Bierstadt, and Thomas Moran are on display. Nine formal galleries house the hundreds of paintings, sculptures, and photographs. Take time to browse the exceptional gift shop. Admission to the museum is free. Summer hours are Monday through Friday from 10:00 A.M. to 7:00 P.M.; Saturday from 10:00 A.M. to 5:00 P.M.; and Sunday from noon to 5:00 P.M.

Special Events

July. Cheyenne Frontier Days, Cheyenne, is a ten-day event with rodeos, parades, stage shows, square dancing, a world-class Western art show, and some of Nashville's big-name entertainers. Attend a free pancake breakfast, watch bronco busting and steer wrestling, and see a melodrama, all in the same day. For ticket information contact Cheyenne Frontier Days, P.O. Box 2477, Cheyenne, WY 82003; (307) 778–7222 or (800) 227–6336.

August. Saratoga is home to Wyoming's Official State Microbrewery Competition, the "Steinley Cup," and is limited to Wyoming brewers. A $10 fee will buy a souvenir glass, unlimited sampling, and the chance to decide for yourself who has the best brew in the state. For further information call Saratoga/Platte Valley Chamber of Commerce at (307) 326–8855.

Other Recommended Restaurants and Lodgings

Nagle Warren Mansion Bed and Breakfast (222 East Seventeenth Street, Cheyenne; 307–637–3333 or 800–811–2610; www.naglewarrenmansion .com) is a magnificent, 9,300-square-foot Victorian home with eleven antiques-filled rooms. Ornate fireplaces, parquet floors, and stained-glass windows grace this lovely B&B, which is listed on the National Register of Historic Places. Innkeeper Jim Osterfoss has endeavored to restore the mansion to its original elegance of the late 1800s. Afternoon tea and pastries are served daily, and breakfast may include eggs Benedict, quiche, or raspberry–chocolate-chip pancakes.

For More Information

Cheyenne Convention and Visitor Bureau, 309 West Lincolnway, Cheyenne, WY 82001; (800) 426–5009; www.cheyenne.org.

Saratoga/Platte Valley Chamber of Commerce, P.O. Box 1095, 106 North First Street, Saratoga, WY; (307) 326–8855 or toll-free 866–828–8855; www.saratogachamber.info.

Wyoming Division of Tourism, I–25 at College Drive, Cheyenne, WY 82002; (307) 777–7777; www.wyomingtourism.org.

Steamboat Springs

Hats Off to Real Cowboys

2 Nights

- ☐ Mountain biking, golf, hiking
- ☐ Strawberry Park Natural Hot Springs
- ☐ Wacky winter festival

Summer in Steamboat Springs is bliss. When all that snow melts, delicate wildflowers emerge in lush valleys and the landscape flourishes. Here you can soar in a hot-air balloon, climb steep rock faces, or trek backcountry trails by llama. Anglers rave about fishing for rainbow trout in the more than eighty lakes and streams in the area. Take in the rodeo, dancing, or golf, or kick back and soak in the Rocky Mountain views and mellow atmosphere.

During winter, Steamboat Springs will win you over—even if you're not a skier. And if you are a downhill enthusiast, this schussing paradise will delight to no end. Not into tackling those moguls? Check this out: You can slip and slide through "winter driving" school, tour the hot springs, or cozy up under a wool blanket on an evening sleigh ride.

Steamboat labels itself Ski Town, USA, and the title fits. We're talking mega-snow: 300-plus inches of fluffy white stuff. According to locals, the expression *Champagne Powder* was born on these mountains. The area also prides itself on its Western lifestyle. One skier who personified this was Billy Kidd, a 1964 Olympic Silver Medalist ski racer. Living in Steamboat Springs, Kidd took to wearing a cowboy hat.

Today he directs the Billy Kidd Performance Center, a facility that provides training for promising young skiers. Steamboat Springs has produced more Olympians (Fifty-four winter and four summer) than any other town in the country.

Steamboat Springs traces its history to the Native American Utes and later to the grizzled fur trappers who arrived in the early 1800s and found the area perfect for hunting and fishing. Legend has it that Carl Howelsen, who was nicknamed "the Flying Norseman," introduced skiing to the local townspeople in 1913 by flinging himself off a homemade ski jump. Howelsen originated the town's first Winter Carnival in 1914.

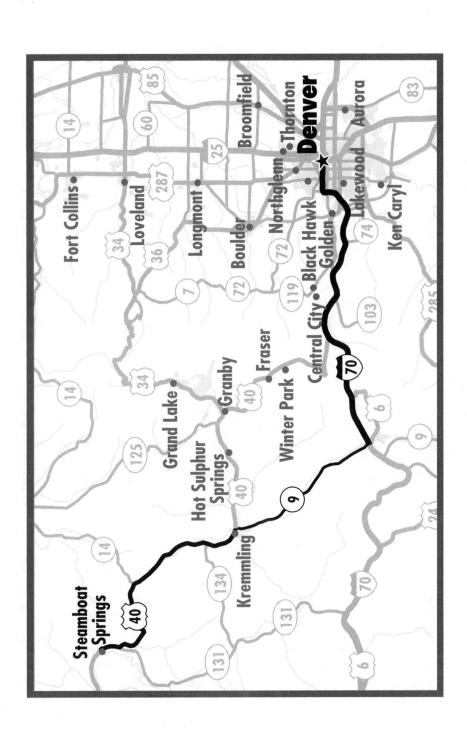

Steamboat still holds the annual weeklong festival, which includes ski-jump competitions, ski races, shovel races, and merrymaking in general. The best event of all occurs when the local high school marching band takes to the streets on skis. The lucky person who plays tuba gets to march in snowshoes!

Day 1 / Morning

Steamboat Springs is located 160 miles northwest of Denver. Take I–70 west through the Eisenhower Tunnel to the Silverthorne exit. Continue north on Colorado Highway 9 to Kremmling, then west on U.S. 40 to Steamboat Springs. Plan on about a three-hour drive from Denver.

LUNCH: Steamboat Yacht Club (804 Yampa Avenue, Steamboat Springs; 970–879–4774) is the ideal place to park yourself on the patio, order lunch, and watch people of all ages leisurely float by on inner tubes down the Yampa River. In the winter, sit by the roaring fireplace in the dining room. The Yacht Club serves salads, sandwiches, and soup. Dinner entrees include mango salmon, orange pecan trout, elk, and Colorado lamb.

Afternoon

After seeing the thirty-seven road signs advertising everything from cowboy boots to overalls along the highway between Kremmling and Steamboat Springs, you'll be curious about the Western store **F. M. Light & Sons** (830 Lincoln Avenue, Steamboat Springs; 970–879–1822 or 800–530–8908). Frank Light moved to Steamboat Springs in the early 1900s with his wife and seven children and opened the store in 1905, selling merchandise brought in by freight wagon. Over the years this classic store has expanded, succeeded, and become a legend in the area. In 1928 more than 250 signs were erected within a 150-mile radius of Steamboat Springs.

Today many of the 1905 fixtures remain in this historic store. You'll also find stuffed jackalopes, old wagon wheels, bearskin rugs, and a life-size John Wayne cardboard cutout. Shop for the latest in cowboy boots, spurs, cowboy hats, jeans, and dusters. F. M. Light & Sons has an excellent reputation for quality merchandise and friendly service. Kids like to have their photo taken sitting on Lightning, the life-size horse in front of the store. F. M. Light & Sons is open daily. For more information visit www.fmlight.com.

Don't miss **Into the West Furniture & Art Gallery** (807 Lincoln Avenue; 970–879–8377), a well-designed store that sells elk-antler chandeliers, leather furniture, and fine art.

DINNER: Antares, 57½ Eighth Street, Steamboat Springs; (970) 879–9939. Ask owner Doug Enochs how he named his popular restaurant, and you're in for a yarn. We don't want to spoil the story, but the tale has to do with things celestial (and maybe a bottle of wine or three). Cuisine and service at Antares are the equal of anything you'd find in the city. Diners could pick from the menu blindfolded and no doubt be pleasantly surprised. One local, who is a weekly regular, swears by the Thai chili prawns. Top off this spicy dish with a Fat Tire on tap and a mango and avocado salad. For dessert, try the fresh blueberries sautéed in Frangelico and poured over Mexican vanilla ice cream, and you'll thank your lucky stars. Check out the antiques throughout the restaurant and the sunken bar that puts seated customers at eye level with the bartender. Antares is open for dinner only at 5:30 P.M. daily. Closed Monday during the fall.

LODGING: Steamboat Grand Resort Hotel, 2300 Mount Werner Circle, Steamboat Springs; (970) 871–5500 or (877) 269–2628; www.steamboatgrand.com. This $80-million upscale mountain lodge opened in October 2000, to superb reviews. Guests enter the grand lobby, complete with an indoor stream, two-story stone fireplace (with a roaring fire year-round), and Western-style chandeliers and lamps created from rawhide and wrought iron. Known as "The Grand," the lodge offers a year-round heated pool, ski valet service, and a beautifully appointed spa. After a day on the slopes or the trails, pamper yourself with a massage, smoothing fruit acid facial, or one of many treatments available. The Steamboat Grand recently received the AAA Four Diamond designation.

Day 2 / Morning

BREAKFAST: You may have to wait in line at the **Shack Cafe** (740 Lincoln Avenue; 970–879–9975), but that's a good endorsement for any restaurant. The Shack has an Old West, log-cabin decor. Take note of the colorful mural that depicts life in the early days of the town and also the photo of the Steamboat Springs band skiing down the street. The Shack Cafe is open from 6:30 A.M. to 2:00 P.M. weekends and from 6:00 A.M. to 2:00 P.M. weekdays.

Winter visitors will want to hit the slopes early, and summer visitors can pack a picnic lunch and head to **Fish Creek Falls** for a spectacular

The countryside near Steamboat Springs offers acres of beautiful hills to explore.

hike. Fish Creek Falls is 4 miles from Steamboat Springs. Take Third Street north to Fish Creek Falls Road, turn right, and follow the signs. There is an admission fee of $3.00 per car. You'll get a workout as you climb the short but steep trail to the awesome 280-foot waterfall. Continue up the trail to a second set of falls. This is a popular hike, but the crowds thin out the farther you go. You'll eventually reach **Long Lake,** about 5 miles from the lower falls.

LUNCH: There are numerous places along the trail to eat your picnic lunch as you gaze at the majestic setting.

Afternoon

Opened in 1997, **Haymaker Golf Course,** located in the heart of the lush Yampa Valley, is a challenging 18-hole course designed after the Scottish-style links. *A warning:* Stay on the fairway or your ball will end up in the native grasses of this spectacular 233-acre course. Haymaker Golf Course is located at the corner of Highway 131 and U.S. 40. Call (970) 870–1846 for information. Another option is **Sheraton Steamboat Golf Club** (970–879–2220), an 18-hole mountain course that offers challenges as well as views of the Yampa Valley and Mount Werner.

During winter, steer your way through the **Bridgestone Winter Driving School.** Professional instructors teach the safest ways to navigate difficult driving conditions on an ice- and snow-covered private circuit. Choose a half-day, full-day, or two-day program. Contact the Bridgestone Winter Driving School, P.O. Box 774167, 1850 Ski Time Square Drive, Steamboat Springs, CO 80477; (970) 879–6104; or visit www.winter-drive.com.

DINNER: The **Cabin,** at the Steamboat Grand Resort Hotel. Executive Chef Chris Wyant created a dinner menu that offers wild game, Midwestern prime beef, and Routt Country trout. Dine in the faux aspen grove and enjoy the extensive wine list, impeccable service, and cozy fireplace. The Cabin also offers breakfast daily and a brunch buffet on Sundays. Awarded *Wine Spectator* Award of Excellence for second consecutive year.

LODGING: Steamboat Grand Resort Hotel.

Day 3 / Morning

BREAKFAST: Winona's (617 Lincoln Avenue; Steamboat Springs; 970–879–2483) serves awesome blueberry pancakes, as well as breakfast burritos, waffles, and eggs Benedict. Breakfast is served from 7:00 A.M. to 1:00 P.M. daily, and lunch hours are from 11:15 A.M. to 3:00 P.M. Monday through Saturday.

The **Tread of Pioneers Museum** (800 Oak Street, Steamboat Springs; 970–879–2214) features a firearm collection that includes weapons owned by Steamboat Springs's founding family, the Crawfords. You'll also see a collection of chairs crafted from bighorn sheep, moose, and elk antlers. The museum is open Tuesday through Saturday from 11:00 A.M. to 5:00 P.M. Admission is $5.00 for adults, $4.00 for seniors, and $1.00 for children; kids six and under get in free. During summer, the museum offers a walking tour of town on Wednesday. Meet at 9:30 A.M. on the front porch of the museum for this hour-long, guided tour.

LUNCH: **Coyote Springs** (425 Lincoln Street, Steamboat Springs; 970–879–4443) serves a luscious Mexican/Southwest lunch at an everyday price. Menu items range from $4.95 to $6.95. Try the pork chili verde or the chicken enchiladas. Coyote Springs is open daily for lunch and dinner.

Afternoon

In the earlier days, visitors skied into **Strawberry Park Natural Hot Springs,** but today you can reach the springs via auto. Located 7 miles north of Steamboat on County Road 36 (Strawberry Park Road), Strawberry Park Natural Hot Springs is a natural rock-lined spring fed by source and creek water to create the perfect-for-soaking, 102-degree temperature. Hold on to the railing when getting in—steps are slippery. For additional information contact Strawberry Park Natural Hot Springs, P.O. Box 773332, Steamboat Springs, CO 80477; (970) 879–0342; www.strawberryhotsprings.com.

There's More

Gondola. Ride on Steamboat's eight-passenger gondola to get a grand view of the area. At the top you'll find mountain dining, a souvenir shop, and a fabulous panorama.

Hot-air ballooning. Pegasus Balloon Tours (P.O. Box 882091, Steamboat Springs, CO 80488; 970–879–9191 or 800–748–2487) offers early-morning rides in summer and morning or afternoon rides during colder months. Drift in a balloon over the Yampa Valley for a bird's-eye view of Steamboat Springs and the Flat Tops Wilderness Area.

Llama trekking. Pyramid Llama Ranch (P.O. Box 1167, Hayden, CO 81639; 970–276–3348) offers day hikes and overnight camping trips. Llamas carry the gear as you enjoy the scenery.

Mountain biking. State-of-the-art mountain bikes, maps, and helmets are available for rent at the base area. Mountain bikers who ride on Steamboat Ski Area trails are required to wear helmets. There are 50 miles of mountain bike trails to accommodate beginners and more advanced riders. Call the Ski Area (970–879–6111) for information.

Tour the springs. Take a two-hour, 2-mile walking tour of the springs of Steamboat. Considered sacred by the Native Americans who soaked in the springs after battles to rejuvenate their strength, the hot springs remain effervescent and even somewhat mysterious today. Pick up a map at the Steamboat Springs Chamber Information Center (1255 South Lincoln Avenue; 970–879–0880), and follow directions for a self-guided tour of seven springs.

Special Events

February. Winter Carnival. Steamboat throws an awesome party in the doldrums of winter. Inaugurated in 1914, this festival is billed as the oldest continuous winter festival west of the Mississippi.

June. Yampa River Festival. Celebrate spring runoff in a grand style with amateur and advanced canoe and kayak competition and a "white-water" rodeo.

June–August. Strings in the Mountains Festival of Music features renowned musicians performing classical music, chamber music, jazz, country, or rhythm and blues in the Strings Music Tent, located near the base of the ski area. For more information on Strings in the Mountains, call (970) 879–5056 or visit www.stringsinthemountains.org.

Mid-June–mid-August. Steamboat Springs PRCA ProRodeo Series. On weekends, professional cowboys show their stuff as they compete in bull riding, steer wrestling, and barrel racing. Begin the evening with a plateful of barbecue served at the booth near the stands and then settle in for a night of real rodeo entertainment.

July. Steamboat Cowboy Roundup Days. Held July 4, this is an authentic Western celebration, with parades, fireworks, rodeos, and partying.

Rainbow Weekend. The Annual Hot Air Balloon Rodeo is a marvelous gala, featuring more than fifty brilliantly colored hot-air balloons. Request a wake-up call for 6:00 A.M. because you'll want to be in the middle of the action as crews inflate the balloons. On the west side of the Steamboat Grand Resort Hotel is a small hill perfect for watching the balloons launch. (Coffee lovers may wish to first pick up a latte at Starbucks, in the Sheraton across the street.) One event calls for the pilot to maneuver close enough to pop a helium-filled weather balloon tethered above the ground. Admission is free.

September. Steamboat's Fall Foliage Festival and Mountain Brewfest. Polka bands, autumn hues, and beer highlight this fun-filled weekend.

Other Recommended Restaurants and Lodgings

Clark

The Home Ranch, P.O. Box 822, Clark, CO 80428; (970) 879–1780 or visit the Web site at www.homeranch.com. This Relais & Chateaux property defines Western hospitality. Wranglers teach guests to ride horses and conduct classes on topics such as saddling and grooming. Join wranglers on a cattle round-up or spend the morning learning to fly fish. During winter, guests cross-country ski, downhill ski at nearby Steamboat, or may climb on the horse-drawn sleigh and help toss hay bales to the horses. Meals, which are included with your stay, are occasions to be remembered.

The ranch offers eight private cabins and six rooms in the lodge. Call for minimum-stay requirements and rates. The Home Ranch is located about 13 miles north of Steamboat Springs on County Road 129, 0.25 mile past the Clark General Store on the west side of the road.

Steamboat Springs

Del's Triangle 3 Ranch (P.O. Box 333, Clark CO 80428; 970–879–3495 or www.steamboathorses.com) is a family-run operation that has been in the valley for six generations. Sign on for an hourly horseback ride or a summer pack trip in the Mount Zirkel wilderness. Horseback rides are available year-round.

Slopeside Grill, in the Torian Plum Plaza in Ski Time Square; (970) 879–2916. In the summer dine outside on the patio before attending the Strings in the Mountains concert. This casual restaurant is a favorite with locals. It serves such dishes as pesto primavera, blackened mahi, and baby back barbecued pork ribs. Open for lunch and dinner.

Torian Plum, 1855 Ski Time Square Drive, Steamboat Springs; (970) 879–8811 or (800) 228–2458. The slope-side location offers ski-in/ski-out convenience, hospitality, and a European ambience. Torian Plum also rents one-, two-, and three-bedroom condominiums with an outdoor swimming pool and underground parking. Best of all, it's steps away from the action. Visit www.torianplum.com.

Vista Verde Guest & Ski Touring Ranch (P.O. Box 770465, Steamboat Springs, CO 80477; 800–526–7433 or 970–879–3858) is located 25 miles north of Steamboat Springs and offers gourmet meals, a secluded environment, and personalized service.

For More Information

Steamboat Ski & Resort Corporation, 2305 Mount Werner Circle, Steamboat Springs, CO 80487; (970) 879–6111; www.steamboat.com.

Steamboat Springs Chamber Information Center, 1255 South Lincoln Avenue, P.O. Box 774408, Steamboat Springs, CO 80477; (970) 879–0880; www.steamboat-chamber.com. For lodging information call (800) 922–2722.

DENVER AND
POINTS EAST

Denver

Urban Getaway

1 Night

Denver is perfect for an in-town getaway. If you're a local, try being a tourist for a couple of days and take in the sights you've been meaning to visit for years. Tour the Denver Art Museum, the Botanic Gardens, and the Colorado State Capitol. If you're an out-of-towner, check out places locals frequent. Spend an afternoon lounging in an overstuffed chair at the Tattered Cover Book Store or cheering the Colorado Rockies from a bargain seat in the "Rockpile" at Coors Field.

- ☐ Art museum
- ☐ Fine dining
- ☐ Live theater
- ☐ First-class shopping
- ☐ Butterfly Pavilion and Insect Center
- ☐ Denver Zoo
- ☐ Colorado's Ocean Journey

Located 5,280 feet above sea level, the Mile High City offers not only views of the towering Rocky Mountains but also professional sports, performing arts, extraordinary museums, and great shopping.

Since the 1850s, when Denver was home to a dozen or so theaters, the city has had a love affair with the arts. Today the Mile High City boasts the Denver Performing Arts Complex, a 4-square-block network that is home to several performing arts organizations.

The following three Denver-getaway chapters focus on culture, history, and sports. Don't worry about finding things to do in Denver; rather, concern yourself with how you'll have time to do them all.

Day 1 / Morning

BREAKFAST: Begin your day with a latte or cappuccino at **Starbucks** (303–388–7565), located at the corner of Second Avenue and Fillmore. Sitting in the heart of the action of Cherry Creek North Shopping District, this particular Starbucks is an ideal location for people-watching. Join other java lovers outside on the patio.

23rd St.

18th Av.
17th Av.

Denver Zoo

Denver Museum of Nature and Science

City Park

Civic Center Park

Colfax Av.

40

Denver Art Museum

14th Av.
13th Av.

Corona St.

Downing St.

Cheesman Park

11th Av.

Denver Botanic Gardens

Congress Park

8th Av.

6th Av.

Speer Blvd.
Speer Blvd.

Cherry Creek North

Cherry Creek Shopping Center

3rd Av.

1st Av.

Broadway

Lincoln St.

Alameda Av.

Washington St.

Clarkson St.

Downing St.

University Blvd.

Washington Park

25

You could spend days or weeks exploring the boutiques and unique shops in **Cherry Creek North.** The streets of this trendy neighborhood are lined with fashionable restaurants and snazzy stores. Begin at the coolest of the cool, the **Wizard's Chest** (230 Fillmore; 303–321–4304), north of Starbucks. This one-of-a-kind toy store sells more than toys. You'll find computerized chess games, the latest in new and trendy playthings as well as old standbys like marbles and jacks, and an entire floor of costumes, masks, and makeup for children and adults. You *won't* find video games. The facade of the store looks like a castle.

For a truly unforgettable shopping experience at one of the best bookstores in the country, visit the **Tattered Cover Book Store** (2955 East First Avenue; 303–322–7727 or 800–833–9327). As Denver's premier bookstore, the Tattered Cover is famous for its superb service and extensive selection. Browsing and reading are encouraged, so sink into one of the comfy couches and curl up with a stack of books or magazines. The Tattered Cover is open daily from 9:00 A.M. to 11:00 P.M. and on Sunday from 10:00 A.M. to 6:00 P.M. **Fourth Story Restaurant and Bar** (303–322–1824), located on the fourth floor at the Tattered Cover, is a great spot for budding writers and authors to meet for lunch or dinner.

With world-class shopping, stores such as Neiman Marcus, and Saks Fifth Avenue, and more than one hundred shops and numerous restaurants, it's no surprise that **Cherry Creek Shopping Center** (3000 East First Avenue) ranks among Denver's top tourist destinations, attracting sixteen million visitors a year.

LUNCH: Mel's Restaurant and Bar, 235 Fillmore Street; (303) 333–3979 or www.melsbarandgrill.com. There is no better place to have lunch on a sunny Colorado day than the outside patio under the colorful awning at Mel's (and yes, there really is a Mel). Opened in 1995 as Mel's Bar and Grill, this exceptional restaurant has established itself in Denver's culinary scene. For lunch, try Mel's cobb salad or the penne with rock shrimp, roasted tomatoes, asparagus, white wine, basil pesto, and capers. Open Monday through Saturday for lunch from 11:30 A.M. to 2:30 P.M., and for dinner from 5:00 to 10:00 P.M.

Another option for lunch is **Palettes,** adjacent to the Denver Art Museum (100 West Fourteenth Avenue Parkway, Denver; 303–629–0889). Palettes is the perfect place to meet a favorite aunt for lunch. The music of Yo-Yo Ma playing in the background, a bottle of French wine and fresh flowers on each table, crisp white linens, outside seating, and excellent service and cuisine make this tasteful restaurant a good choice. Palettes was named "Best Power Lunch—Ladies' Division" by *Westword* newspaper in 1999. The menu changes with the seasons, but selections might include charbroiled salmon with mashed potatoes or vegetarian tomato basil risotto with grilled vegetables. Palettes is open 11:00 A.M. to 3:00 P.M. Tuesday through Sunday, 5:00 to 9:00 P.M. Wednesday. Closed Monday and most major holidays.

Afternoon

Featuring a large collection of Native American, Western, and American art, the **Denver Art Museum** (100 West Fourteenth Avenue Parkway, Denver; 720–865–5000) is a must-see. The twenty-eight-sided, two-towered building is a work of art in itself. Windows are designed so visitors inside can look out onto framed city landscapes. Sign the guest book and take a quick glance to see where other visitors are from. You'll no doubt see places listed such as Israel, Switzerland, Ohio, New York, and Littleton, Colorado. Families will especially like the backpacks chockful of activities—the Japanese pack includes some plastic sushi and chopsticks—to help the exhibits come to life. Packs are available every day during the summer and weekends year-round. The Denver Art Museum is open Tuesday through Saturday from 10:00 A.M. to 5:00 P.M., Wednesday from 10:00 A.M. to 9:00 P.M., and Sunday from noon to 5:00 P.M.; the museum is closed Mondays and major holidays. Admission is $6.00 for adults and $4.50 for seniors and students; $4.50 for ages 13–18; children twelve and under are admitted free. Price does not include entrance to ticketed exhibitions. On Saturday, admission to the museum is free for Colorado residents.

See where "money is made," at the **U.S. Mint** (320 West Colfax Avenue; 303–405–4761). The mint stamps forty million coins a day, adding up to eight billion coins a year. Walk-in tours are not presently available. Tours must be arranged through your Congressperson's office with three weeks' advance notice. The mint is closed on legal holidays.

DINNER: **Tamayo** (1400 Larimer Square; 720–946–1433) occupies the former location of Cadillac Ranch, but that's where the similarities end. Gone are the Western bar stools, cowboy pictures, and mostly meat menu. A colorful tile mosaic behind the bar sets a sleek and contemporary tone. Tamayo serves "modern Mexican cuisine," including pan-seared tuna tacos, salmon Azteca, and molé poblano (grilled chicken breast with cilantro rice, plantains, and molé poblano sauce). Open daily for dinner 5:00 to 10:00 P.M. (11:00 P.M. on weekends). Lunch hours are 11:30 A.M. to 2:00 P.M., Monday through Friday.

Evening

To see an unparalleled blend of performing artists in a multifaceted facility, attend a production at the **Denver Performing Arts Complex,** a 4-block network located in the heart of downtown Denver that houses the Denver Center for the Performing Arts, the Colorado Symphony Orchestra, the Colorado Ballet, and Opera Colorado.

Boettcher Concert Hall, where the Colorado Symphony Orchestra and Opera Colorado perform, seats 2,634 and is the nation's first concert-hall-in-the-round. The **Temple Hoyne Buell Theatre,** which opened in 1991, is the second-largest theater in the complex. The **Helen G. Bonfils Theatre Complex** encompasses four smaller theaters, including the Stage, the Space, the Source, and the Ricketson. The **Garner Galleria Theatre** produces cabaret-style theater. For additional information on the Denver Center for the Performing Arts, call (303) 893–4000. For ticket information call (303) 893–4100. The Center Box Office is located at Fourteenth and Curtis.

To see premieres of New York Broadway and off-Broadway productions on a regional scale, attend a performance at **Theatre on Broadway** (13 South Broadway) or the **Phoenix Theatre** (1124 Santa Fe Drive). The Theatre Group (303–860–9360), which runs both, has brought new energy into the Denver theater scene. Productions run the gamut from cutting edge and sometimes scandalous to heartwarming and hilarious. The Theatre Group has received accolades and awards for its designers, directors, actors, and actresses. The 120-seat theaters sell out often, so call in advance for tickets.

LODGING: Loews Giorgio (4150 East Mississippi Avenue, Denver; 303–782–9300 or 800–345–9172) is located in a contemporary black-glass structure. The hotel offers European charm and 183 guest rooms that are spacious and inviting. The lobby features original art, a hand-sculpted fireplace, and fresh-cut flowers. In the afternoon you'll find a tray of Italian cookies and wine available to guests in the Library Room next to the lobby.

Day 2 / Morning

BREAKFAST: For a hearty meal at an affordable price, begin your day at **Zaidy's Deli of Cherry Creek** (121 Adams, Denver; 303–333–5336). Black-and-white photographs on the wall of this light-filled cafe show Denver in the early 1900s. This family-owned, neighborhood deli serves fresh corned-beef hash, steak and eggs, and a Reuben omelet, along with plenty of other selections.

The **Denver Zoo,** located in Denver's City Park (East Twenty-third Street between York Street and Colorado Boulevard; 303–376–4800; www.denverzoo.org), is home to more than 2,500 animals. **Tropical Discovery,** a state-of-the-art rain forest housed in two glass pyramids, takes you down a winding pathway past waterfalls and along a tropical riverbank to a muggy marsh and a cypress swamp. The hot, humid climate and the sight of vampire bats or a Siamese crocodile make you feel as though you're exploring an equatorial jungle. **Primate Panorama** extends over seven acres and is home to howler monkeys, gorillas, and a six-ounce pygmy marmoset. With thick vegetation, thatched-roof huts, and waterfalls, the zoo offers an extensive and beautiful habitat for its more than 600 species.

LUNCH: Hungry Elephant, located near the Denver Zoo entrance, serves hamburgers, hot dogs, corn dogs, and tacos.

Afternoon

To see what's blooming, visit the **Denver Botanic Gardens** (1005 York Street, Denver; 303–331–4000). No matter what time of year it is, you'll find this outdoor garden and tropical conservatory a serene spot. The Japanese Garden is particularly peaceful and is an excellent location for photographs. The Botanic Gardens are open daily from 9:00 A.M. to 5:00 P.M.; from May 1 through the end of September, hours extend to 8:00 P.M. Saturday through Tuesday. During the Christmas season the Botanic Gardens feature **Blossoms of Lights,** a spectacular display of colorful lights in the shape of flowers.

There's More

Butterfly Pavilion and Insect Center, (6252 West Tenth Avenue, Westminster; 303–469–5441) is just fifteen minutes from downtown Denver. This incredible sanctuary is home to more than fifty species of butterflies.

You'll feel as though you're exploring a rain forest bursting with brilliantly colored butterflies due to the tropical temperature and lush foliage of the pavilion. The Insect Center provides a close-up look at tarantulas, cockroaches, mealworms, and other creepy-crawly things. The Butterfly Pavilion is open daily year-round from 9:00 A.M. to 6:00 P.M. Visit www.butterflies.org.

Colorado's Ocean Journey, U.S. West Park, 700 Water Street (exit 211 off I–25), Denver; (303) 561–4450. This $93-million aquarium on the South Platte River opposite downtown Denver opened in June 1999 to marvelous reviews. Sumatran tigers, live coral, rainbow trout, sea otters, and make-believe flash floods are part of the journey that takes visitors through exhibits designed to look like the real thing. Colorado's Ocean Journey is open daily (closed Christmas) from 10:00 A.M. to 6:00 P.M.

FlatIron Crossing, located between Boulder and Denver along Highway 36 (One West FlatIron Circle, Broomfield; 720–887–9900; www.flatiron crossing.com). This immense structure offers nearly 200 shops and restaurants.

Hudson Gardens, (6115 South Santa Fe Drive, Littleton; 303–797–8565) is a superb, thirty-acre display garden located along the South Platte River in Littleton. Here you'll see rock gardens, colorful wildflowers, native shrubs, roses, waterfalls, and cacti in a setting so tranquil that you'll forget you're in the city. Don't miss the Secret Garden, located off the main pathway. Hudson Gardens is open—weather permitting—from 9:00 A.M. to 5:00 P.M. daily, May through October. The remainder of the year it's best to call ahead to check hours. Concerts (held every Sunday, rain or shine, beginning at 6:30 P.M.) are a fun summer event. Visit www.hudsongardens.org.

Park Meadows. Billed as a "retail resort," this dynamic center, with its Colorado mountain-lodge atmosphere, will thrill shopping connoisseurs. Stone fireplaces, natural wood-beam ceilings, and more than $2 million in artwork create the total shopping experience. You'll find the area's largest Foley's, as well as more than one hundred specialty shops and restaurants. Park Meadows is located at the intersection of I–25 and C–470.

Special Events

Late May–October. Every Saturday at 10:00 A.M. sharp, tours of LoDo depart from the front of Union Station, located on the corner of Seventeenth and Wynkoop. The two-hour walk around the historic Lower

Downtown District is a fun way to learn more about some of Denver's most historic and beautiful buildings. Cost is $5.00 per person. No reservations required. For more information call (303) 628–5428.

July. Cherry Creek Arts Festival, held Fourth of July weekend. This successful outdoor event is becoming one of the finest shows of its kind in the nation. Nearly 200 artists, who are chosen from 2,000-plus applicants, sell paintings, sculpture, photography, jewelry, and crafts. The arts festival takes place on the closed streets north of Cherry Creek Shopping Center and draws huge crowds, so be prepared to share the viewing venue with other festival-goers.

October. Denver International Film Festival, 1430 Larimer Square, attracts film lovers, actors, directors, and critics. This is an extremely popular event for locals, so call well in advance for a schedule and tickets. For information call the Denver Film Society at (303) 595–3456 or visit www.denver film.org.

Other Recommended Restaurants and Lodgings

Castle Marne (1572 Race Street, Denver; 303–331–0621) describes itself as a luxury urban inn. As one of Denver's most imposing mansions, this B&B is furnished in authentic period antiques, yet it also offers modern amenities for business and pleasure travelers. Visit www.castlemarne.org.

Cherry Cricket (2641 East Second Avenue, Cherry Creek North, Denver; 303–322–7666) is a lively local bar, with nineteen beers, including Guinness, on tap. The Cricket Burger and the chicken wings are all-time favorites, or you can order a No-Tofu sandwich (cream cheese and veggies) or a grilled meat loaf sandwich.

Cielo (1109 Lincoln Street; 303–597–2435) is located in the space formerly occupied by the Buffalo Company. That's where the similarities end. Cielo (translated by the manager as *sky*) describes its cuisine as Mexican/French. Entrees include items such as salmon, strip steak, and chicken, but you'll still find traditional chips, salsa, and margaritas. The patio—complete with palms—is fabulous in the summertime. When temperatures drop, the outdoor patio is still pleasant thanks to heaters and a fireplace.

Hotel Teatro (1100 Fourteenth Street, Denver; 303–228–1100) displays some fabulous costumes and props from productions by the Denver Center Theatre Company. Ask to see the wine cellar, which doubles as a dining room for private parties. The hotel's Restaurant Jou Jou is open for breakfast, lunch, and dinner, and Restaurant Kevin Taylor (named for the well-known chef) offers formal dining.

The Swan, at Inverness Hotel & Golf Club, 200 Inverness Drive West, Englewood; (303) 799–5800. The Inverness is such a class act that they have a private florist who comes in daily. Save the Swan for a special occasion. The intimate setting is perfect for a romantic dinner, and the menu is superb. Begin with the portobello mushroom ravioli appetizer; the Caesar salad (prepared table-side for two) is excellent. Outstanding entrees include Colorado rack of lamb and Chilean sea bass fillet. Open Tuesday through Saturday 6:00 to 9:00 P.M.

The Tuscany Room, Loews Giorgio (4150 East Mississippi, Denver; 303–782–9300), features an excellent Northern Italian menu in a romantic setting. The luxury decor, elaborate floral displays, crisp white linen tablecloths, and fine china and stemware of this candlelit room are matched by superb service and outstanding cuisine. Begin with an appetizer such as Calamari Fritti or focaccia, followed by Caesar salad or Tuscan White Bean Soup. Entrees include Spicy Chicken Linguine, Grilled Fillet of Salmon, and Spicy Orange Marinated Duck Breast, in addition to other selections. The Tuscany Room is open for breakfast, lunch, and dinner daily. Brunch is served Sunday.

The Westin Hotel (1672 Lawrence Street, Denver; 303–572–9100 or 800–228–3000) deserves special mention. This fine hotel is beautifully decorated, is conveniently located in the heart of Denver, and offers theater and opera packages. The Augusta Restaurant at the Westin offers a spectacular view of the city, as well as an excellent breakfast and a superb Sunday brunch. The Augusta is open from 6:00 to 10:00 A.M. Monday through Saturday, to 1:00 P.M. Sunday.

For More Information

Denver Metro Convention and Visitor Bureau, 1555 California Street, Denver, CO 80202; (303) 892–1112 or (800) 645–3446; www.denver.org.

Downtown Denver

A Capital Excursion

1 Night

For history buffs, Denver is the ideal place to delve into the Western past. The city is full of local lore and excellent museums. Denver's Museum of Nature and Science ranks as the fifth largest of its kind in the country. Specialized museums include the Denver Firefighters Museum and the Molly Brown House Museum.

In addition, visitors will find historic homes in residential neighborhoods, lovely old B&B inns brimming with tales of the past, and the grande dame of them all: the elegant, more-than-a-century-old Brown Palace Hotel. Royalty, celebrities, and politicians have spent the night at the Brown, but you don't need to be famous to be treated regally at this renowned

- ☐ State-of-the-art library
- ☐ Museums
- ☐ Brown Palace Hotel
- ☐ Historic Larimer Square
- ☐ State capitol

hotel. From the magnificent lobby, with its shining marble floors and fresh flowers, to the genteel cigar room, with its leather chairs and rich atmosphere, the Brown Palace is gracious by any account.

Day 1 / Morning

BREAKFAST: Dozens (236 West Thirteenth Avenue; 303–572–0066) packs them in for breakfast. Rock-bottom prices, a creative menu, and the casual atmosphere of this earthy restaurant appeal to the masses. Popular items include the Here's Your Aspen Omelet, served with avocado, tomato, and goat cheese; and Eggs Arnold, Dozens's version of eggs Benedict. Dozens is open from 6:30 A.M. to 2:00 P.M. daily.

An extravaganza of architecture, the **Denver Public Library** (10 West Fourteenth Avenue Parkway; 720–865–1111; www.denverlibrary.org) is one of the most distinctive buildings in the city. Add to that the extraordinary collection of more than five million items and the result is a superior facility. The library was recognized in 2000 and 2001 as the "Number One" library in the nation. The library is open Monday and Tuesday from

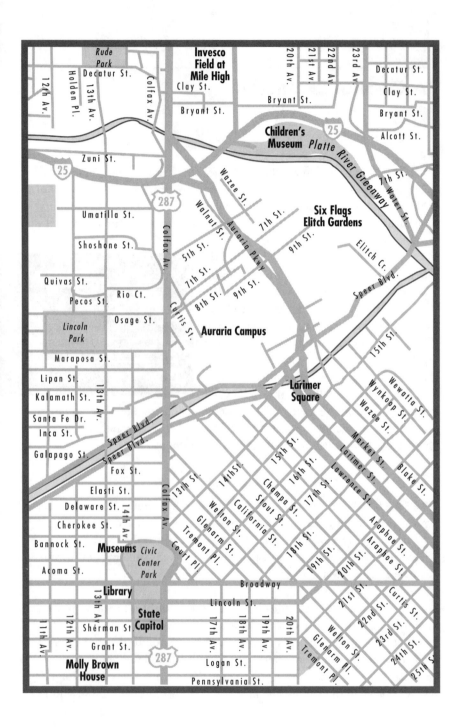

10:00 A.M. to 9:00 P.M., Thursday through Saturday from 10:00 A.M. to 5:30 P.M., and Sunday from 1:00 to 5:00 P.M. Closed Wednesday. Free tours are available.

Restored by the Colorado Historical Society, the **Byers-Evans House** (1310 Bannock Street; 303–620–4933) was formerly occupied by two prominent Denver families. William N. Byers, who founded the *Rocky Mountain News,* built the home in 1883. Six years later William Gray Evans, the son of Colorado's second territorial governor, John Evans, bought the home. The Evans family owned the home for ninety-five years before donating it to the Colorado Historical Society. Today you can tour the two-story house, which exhibits furniture from the period 1912–24. The Byers-Evans House is open Tuesday through Sunday from 11:00 A.M. to 3:00 P.M. and is closed Monday.

Colorado History Museum (1300 Broadway; 303–866–3682) tracks the past of fur trappers, miners, and pioneers of Colorado. Western photographs, dioramas, and old mining equipment are among the displays. The museum is open Monday through Saturday from 10:00 A.M. to 4:30 P.M. and Sunday from noon to 4:30 P.M.

LATE LUNCH: "Take tea" at Denver's exquisite **Brown Palace Hotel** (321 Seventeenth Street; 303–297–3111). Afternoon Tea takes place in the atrium lobby, where the entire scene brims with grace, charm, and the nostalgia of yesterday. Sip properly steeped Earl Grey in a bone china teacup; nibble on dainty sandwiches, pastries, and scones with Devonshire cream; and listen to the soft tones of live harp and piano music. Afternoon Tea is served daily from 2:00 to 4:00 P.M. Reservations are a must, especially during the holidays. A Luncheon Tea, which includes a choice of entree salads, is also available Monday through Friday, from noon to 2:00 P.M.

Afternoon

When it was completed in 1908, the **Colorado State Capitol** (200 East Colfax Avenue; 303–866–2604) was arguably the most impressive building downtown. Today, the capitol, with its gold-plated dome, remains a striking sight, especially as the light reflects off its 200 ounces of pure gold in the afternoon sun. The building's interior is a work of art, with rose onyx, brass banisters, stained glass, and a spiral staircase. People from around the world come to see the Women's Gold Tapestry, which honors women in Colorado history. Free tours of the capitol are available every forty-five minutes, weekdays from 9:15 A.M. to 2:30 P.M. Don't miss the step located outside the building that marks the mile-high point, although the exact measurement continues to be a debate.

Train buffs and history enthusiasts will want to visit Denver's **Union Station** (1701 Wynkoop Street), a historic landmark that still functions with daily Amtrak service and has several shops and restaurants.

DINNER: If pizza is your idea of comfort food, you'll love **Josephina's Ristorante** (1433 Larimer Square; 303–623–0166). The National Champion Pizza, with spicy pepperoni, sausage, sweet red peppers, roasted garlic, fresh basil, red onion, and mozzarella, took first place in a national contest in Chicago in 1991. Or create your own pizza with items such as artichoke hearts, avocados, caramelized onions, and asparagus. The menu also features Italian favorites such as grilled eggplant marinara. For dessert, try tiramisu, espresso-soaked ladyfingers garnished with chocolate sauce and strawberries. Josephina's serves lunch and dinner daily Monday through Friday from 11:00 A.M. to 11:00 P.M. and on weekends from noon to midnight. The bar stays open later and features live music nightly.

Evening

Before turning in, retreat to the **Churchill Bar,** located just off the atrium lobby of the Brown Palace Hotel (321 Seventeenth Street), for an after-dinner cocktail. Designed primarily as a cigar bar, this intimate room has enough atmosphere, appeal, and efficient ventilation that even nonsmokers will enjoy its rich ambience. Dark red leather wingback furniture, walls lined with books, soft lighting, and fine art create a library setting that's perfect for quiet conversation.

LODGING: The Brown Palace Hotel, 321 Seventeenth Street; (303) 297–3111; www.brownpalace.com. The Brown Palace Hotel is one of the oldest, most distinguished hotels in the region. Well-heeled travelers of the early 1900s were pampered at the Brown, and today there's no skimping on indulgence either. Business or pleasure travel becomes utterly enjoyable in the sophisticated environment of this classy hotel. With its graceful nineteenth-century architecture, its more than one hundred years of history, and its reputation for excellence, the Brown attracts celebrities, politicians, and Denver's avant-garde. President George W. Bush stayed here in 2001. Treat yourself to luxury and surround yourself with elegance at this fine hotel.

Denver's Union Station is a historic landmark.

Day 2 / *Morning*

BREAKFAST: You'll be treated royally at **Ellyngton's** in the Brown Palace Hotel (303–297–3111). The waitstaff here doesn't overlook a single detail. Selections from the menu include eggs Benedict, crab Benedict, and coffee brewed with water from the hotel's private well. Sunday brunch at Ellyngton's is famous for live jazz, good food, and Dom Pérignon.

If you can't get an overnight reservation at the Brown Palace, you'll want to at least walk through the exquisite lobby, or better yet, take a tour. Complimentary guided tours are available Wednesday and Saturday at 2:00 P.M. You can take a self-guided tour at any time. Stop at the concierge desk to pick up a brochure or call for more information.

To savor a taste of true Denver history, scout out historic **Larimer Square,** located between Fourteenth and Fifteenth Streets on Larimer. As Denver's oldest block, Larimer Street was at one time a disreputable and run-down area. Today Larimer Square thrives with unique shops, upscale restaurants, and refurbished brick Victorian buildings. Hanging flower baskets, open courtyards, and classical music playing from outdoor speakers add to Larimer Square's charm. From here you can take a horse-drawn carriage ride up the 16th Street Mall or through Lower Downtown.

For Western furniture, cowboy stuff, and "cowkid" clothes, don't miss **Cry Baby Ranch** (1422 Larimer Square; 303–623–3979). This store is a great place to browse and remember the good old days when Roy Rogers was a superstar.

LUNCH: Il Fornaio, 1631 Wazee Street; (303) 573–5050. Il Fornaio (say "eel-for-NIGH-oh") bakes bread from scratch daily and pours its own extra-virgin olive oil, imported from Italy. The restaurant periodically features a different region of Italy—such as Tuscany or Sicily—with a special dinner menu. For lunch, try the seafood ravioli or the rigatoni.

Afternoon

For a close-up look at dinosaurs, visit the **Denver Museum of Nature and Science** in City Park (2001 Colorado Boulevard; 303–322–7009 or 800–925–2250; www.dmns.org). **Prehistoric Journey,** the $7 million permanent exhibit at the museum, chronicles prehistoric life in an animated process complete with life-size dinosaurs and bellowing sound effects. The presentation captivates visitors as they learn about the several-billion-year history of life on Earth. On the other museum floors, you'll see dioramas depicting animals in their habitats. The Denver Museum of Nature and Science is open from 9:00 A.M. to 5:00 P.M. daily. Admission is $9.00 for adults, $6.00 for seniors, children, and students with photo identification. A visit to **Gates Planetarium** is included in the museum price. **IMAX Theater,** located next to the museum, features films so realistic on its four-and-a-half-story screen that you'll feel as though you're in the middle of the action.

There's More

Black American West Museum and Heritage Center (3091 California Street; 303–292–2566) chronicles the lives of African-Americans who settled the West, through an excellent collection of photographs, books, and artifacts. The museum is open weekdays from 10:00 A.M. to 5:00 P.M. and weekends from noon to 5:00 P.M. Admission charged.

Denver Firefighters Museum (1326 Tremont Place; 303–892–1436) has antique fire engines and firefighting equipment. You'll also learn the history of firefighting in Denver. The museum is open Monday through Saturday from 10:00 A.M. to 2:00 P.M. and until 4:00 P.M. during summer. Admission charged. For more information visit www.denverfire fightersmuseum.org.

Molly Brown House Museum (1340 Pennsylvania Street; 303–832–4092) was once the residence of the colorful character known as the "Unsinkable Molly Brown," whose place in history was firmly established when she survived the *Titanic* disaster of 1912. Today women clothed in 1900s period dress will escort you through this gorgeous Victorian mansion and historical landmark. The museum is open Monday through Saturday from 10:00 A.M. to 3:30 P.M. and Sunday from noon to 3:30 P.M. A forty-five-minute guided tour is available during museum hours; the last tour of the day begins at 3:30 P.M. The museum is closed Monday during winter. For more information visit www.mollybrown.org.

Special Events

July. During Buffalo Bill Days in Golden, celebrate the life and times of Western hero Buffalo Bill with a Wild West show, burro races, a parade, and games. For information call (303) 279–3113.

September. Oktoberfest in Larimer Square highlights include beer, brats, strudel, oompah bands, and dancers decked in lederhosen. For more information call (303) 607–1276.

December. Denver boasts one of the world's largest outdoor Christmas displays when the City and County Building (1460 Cherokee Street) becomes an illuminated showpiece with thousands of multicolored lights. The decorations have been a Denver tradition for more than seventy years, and the lights have become a cherished custom for locals.

Other Recommended Restaurants and Lodgings

Adam's Mark Hotel (1550 Court Place, Denver; 303–893–3333) features more than 1,200 rooms. The hotel offers three ballrooms, convention facilities, and banquet space.

Assignments Restaurant (675 South Broadway, Denver; 303–778–6625; www.assignmentsrestaurant.com) gets an "A plus." Students from the Culinary Arts School operate this cozy cafe. Everything, from the escargot with goat cheese appetizer, to the vichyssoise, to the espresso, is perfection. Service, presentation, and cuisine are all superlative. Call and ask to be put on their mailing list so you can take advantage of the coupons. Reservations are essential. Assignments is tucked a bit off Broadway.

Embassy Suites (1881 Curtis Street, Denver; 303–297–8888) has more than 300 luxury guest suites and access to the adjacent Athletic Club at Denver Place, which offers racquetball, squash, and basketball courts; an indoor swimming pool; and an indoor running track.

Hotel Monaco (1717 Champa, Denver; 303–296–1717 or 800–397–5330) offers a fantastic location in the heart of downtown Denver, rooms customized for tall persons (with 9-foot-long king-size beds and raised showerheads), and a pet goldfish to keep you company.

Lumber Baron Inn (2555 West Thirty-seventh Avenue, Denver; 303–477–8205 or visit www.lumberbaron.com) was voted Denver's best place for a romantic night. Restored to the tune of $1 million, this ornate three-story house is located minutes from downtown Denver. Rates begin at $145, but check the Web site for Internet specials as low as $49 per night.

Pint's Pub (221 West Thirteenth Avenue, Denver; 303–534–7543) has a serious beer menu. Choose from twenty-five draught beers and a huge selection of single-malt scotch whisky. Wine lovers may be disappointed at the choice of two wines: "red or white." The food menu offers broiled fish-and-chips, bangers and mash, and sheepherder's stew.

Strings (1700 Humboldt Street, Denver; 303–831–7310) has plenty of clout and cachet on the Denver restaurant scene. Come any night and you're likely to see businessmen in dark suits and women in cocktail dresses. The menu offers appetizers such as crab cakes and roasted mussels and entrees that include black pepper linguine and pan-seared mahimahi.

For More Information

Denver Metro Convention and Visitor Bureau, 1555 California Street, Denver, CO 80202; (303) 892–1112 or (800) 645–3446; www.denver.org.

Lower Downtown (LoDo)

Sports Town and Microbrew City U.S.A.

1 Night

Even seasoned travelers delight in this vibrant area that is the heartbeat of the city. Visitors to Denver's redeveloped Lower Downtown (LoDo) will find much to praise: art galleries, first-class dining, lively brewpubs, and a sophisticated yet easygoing charm.

☐ Professional football, hockey, baseball, basketball, soccer

☐ Bicycling, golf

☐ Brewpubs and billiards

☐ Tour of Coors Field

☐ Hot jazz

As sports fans, Coloradans rank among the most loyal in the country. Denver is one of ten cities in the United States with all four major league sports: NFL Broncos, NBA Nuggets, NHL Avalanche, and MLB Colorado Rockies. Denverites are devoted sports participants as well as spectators. On any given day you'll see joggers, in-line skaters, bicyclists, and walkers.

Beer connoisseurs will have a field day in LoDo. As home to the largest brewpub in the United States (the Wynkoop Brewing Company), Denver boasts more than forty microbrews to sample.

Day 1 / Morning

As you travel north on I–25, exit Auraria Parkway and follow the signs to **Lower Downtown.** Traveling south on I–25, exit Speer Boulevard South. Once you arrive downtown, let the valet at the Oxford Hotel (your lodging for this evening; 1600 Seventeenth Street) park your car. Then forget about it for the weekend. You can walk, take the free Sixteenth Street Shuttle, or have the hotel's limousine take you where you want to go.

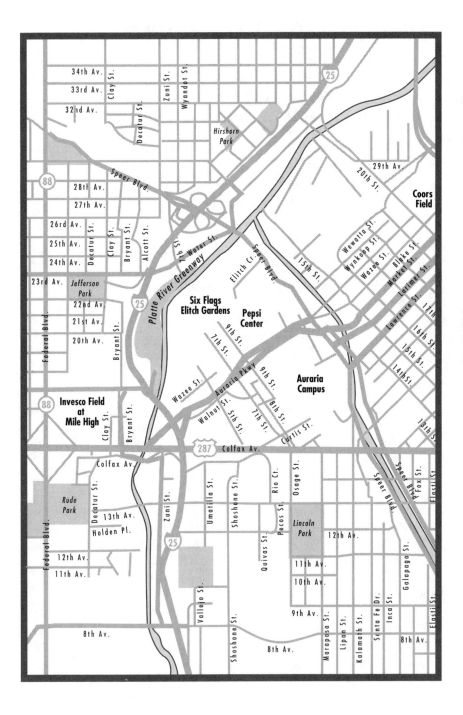

LUNCH: Beer is serious business at **Wynkoop** (that's WIN-koop) **Brewing Company,** located on the corner of Eighteenth and Wynkoop (that's WINE-koop); (303) 297–2700. Stop in and hoist a pint of Railyard Ale, have lunch, and relax in this trendy local favorite. Just don't plan on having an intimate conversation during Friday-evening happy hour, when this popular pub really gets lively. Laying claim to the titles of being Denver's first brewpub and North America's largest, the Wynkoop brewed and sold more than 4,000 barrels in 2003. When the business opened in 1988, founders pronounced the name "Win-Koop" rather than "Wine-Koop," like the street, and with a tongue-in-cheek attitude explained that they make beer, not wine. The pronunciation and the brewery's excellent reputation have stuck.

The Wynkoop chalks up another victory with its consistently excellent food. The menu ranges from basics such as fish-and-chips (dipped in Railyard Ale batter) to baked Atlantic salmon. Burgers, shepherd's pie, salads, and soup are also good selections. Billiards on the second floor attracts a huge pool-playing crowd, as well as a fair share of spectators. The handsome mahogany tables, exposed brick walls, and low lighting create the perfect ambience for an afternoon or evening game. You can also opt for shuffleboard, darts, or Foosball.

Afternoon

Walk to the **Tabor Center,** located at Sixteenth and Lawrence, and check out the stores and the architectural design of this unique, glass-enclosed, three-level shopping center. You'll find interesting vendor carts throughout the Tabor Center, as well as specialty shops and major retailers.

Cruise the **16th Street Mall,** an outdoor shopping district filled with cafes, food vendors, and clothing and souvenir stores. The mile-long mall has fountains, flowers, benches, and a passing parade of shoppers, business executives, and the occasional street entertainer. A free shuttle bus runs up and down the mall. You can't miss the larger-than-life **Denver Pavilions** marquee, located on the 16th Street Mall. This complex houses a movie theater, restaurants the likes of the Wolfgang Puck Cafe, and trendy boutiques and specialty shops.

Get a behind-the-scenes look by touring **Coors Field,** home of the Colorado Rockies Baseball Club. Located on the corner of Twentieth and Blake Streets, this ballpark is not only handsome but also user-friendly. Tours are offered year-round and include visits to the club level, suite level,

The larger-than-life marquee at the Denver Pavilions, 16th Street Mall.

press area, visitors' clubhouse, and visitors' dugout. Call (303) 762–5437 to purchase tickets in advance.

DINNER: Morton's of Chicago (1710 Wynkoop; 303–825–3353) has perfected the formula of fine dining. Genteel, classy, and intimate, this restaurant tops the list. You'll find professional service, exquisite cuisine, and elegant surroundings at this first-class establishment, which attracts the city's elite.

Start with an appetizer such as smoked Pacific salmon or sautéed wild mushrooms. The specialty of the house is beef, although the menu includes whole baked Maine lobster, lemon oregano chicken, and domestic rib lamb chops. Choose from entrees such as porterhouse steak, double filet mignon, and tenderloin brochette, cooked precisely to your liking. Save room for the Godiva hot chocolate cake with a liquid chocolate center, served with Häagen-Dazs vanilla ice cream. Morton's is open for dinner only.

Evening

For late-night conversation in a chic cigar room, stop in at **Trios Enoteca** (1730 Wynkoop Street; 303–293–2887). *Enoteca* is a Greek word that means "wine library." This spot has a selection of more than sixty wines served by the glass as well as live jazz and rhythm and blues five nights a week.

Jive the night away at **El Chapultepec** (1962 Market Street; 303–295–9126), the dive where President Bill Clinton stopped in to play a few notes on a borrowed saxophone when he was on the campaign trail in Denver. This funky, smoky bar is the coolest place in town to hear hot jazz. El Chapultepec has live music nightly from 9:00 P.M. to 1:00 A.M. and is open daily from 9:00 A.M. to 2:00 A.M.

LODGING: The **Oxford Hotel** (1600 Seventeenth Street; 303–628–5400 or 800–228–5838; www.theoxfordhotel.com) offers a congenial retreat from the hustle and bustle of the city, and you'll find every amenity necessary for a secure and pleasant stay. Located in historic Lower Downtown Denver, the Oxford is within walking distance of Larimer Square, Coors Field, and numerous galleries and restaurants. Built in 1891 and renovated in 1983, this classic hotel is listed on the National Register of Historic Places. The lobby features marble floors, a gorgeous marble fireplace, and Baby Doe Tabor's piano. Enjoy a complimentary afternoon glass of sherry as you lounge in a wingback chair in the lobby. Rooms are decorated with English and French antiques, and the triple-sheeted beds are sheer indulgence. The hotel offers complimentary limousine service in the downtown area. Visit the full-service Oxford/Aveda Spa and Salon for a massage, or stop at the Oxford Club to work out with a personal trainer.

A walk through the **Cruise Room,** the restored bar next to the hotel's lobby, is a must. If you can find a seat, order a cocktail and enjoy the ambience of this local landmark, which is art deco at its finest.

Day 2 / Morning

BREAKFAST: **McCormick's Fish House** (303–825–1107), located in the same building as the Oxford, changes its menu daily, but you'll find entrees such as Denver omelets and Idaho rainbow trout from which to select. This popular restaurant, with its warm, wooden decor and comfortable streetside booths, is the perfect place to meet with friends or dine on your own. McCormick's is open daily from 7:00 to 10:00 A.M. for breakfast, from 11:00 A.M. to 2:00 P.M. for lunch, and from 5:00 to 10:00 P.M. for dinner. Brunch is served Sunday from 10:00 A.M. to 2:00 P.M.

At any time of the day, expect to find lots of action at the **Market** (1445 Larimer Street; 303–534–5140), an ideal spot for a midmorning cup of coffee and a pastry. Read the newspaper or people-watch at this Denver institution that buzzes.

If you're a literature lover, look no further. The **Tattered Cover Book Store** (1628 Sixteenth Street; 303–436–1070) has it all. This location is not as busy as the Tattered Cover Book Store in Cherry Creek, but it's just as wonderful. You can spend hours browsing the three floors of this incredibly well-stocked store. Don't miss the Travel Alcove on the first floor, which has a comprehensive selection of maps, globes, books, and comfortable couches. The Tattered Cover in LoDo is open from 7:00 A.M. to 9:00 P.M. Monday through Friday, from 9:00 A.M. to 11:00 P.M. Saturday, and from 10:00 A.M. to 6:00 P.M. Sunday.

LUNCH: You don't have to be a sports nut to enjoy the **Denver ChopHouse and Brewery** (1735 Nineteenth Street; 303–296–0800). Located next door to Coors Field, the Denver ChopHouse is a great stop before going to a Colorado Rockies game, or any other time, for that matter. The microbrews are fresh, the potatoes are hand mashed, and the pizzas are piled high. Call early for a reservation if you go on game day. Colorado Avalanche players celebrate here.

There's More

Basketball. The Denver Nuggets professional basketball team plays at the Pepsi Center and regularly hosts family evenings with special package deals. The season runs November through April. For ticket information call (303) 405–1111 or (303) 830–8497. For more information visit www.nba.com/nuggets.

Bicycling. Denver has an excellent trail system, with 415 miles of trails for bicyclists, walkers, and in-line skaters. Try the Cherry Creek Trail, which runs from Confluence Park through downtown Denver to Cherry Creek Reservoir. You can access the bike trail from ramps situated along Speer Boulevard and First Avenue.

Football. Coloradans love their Denver Broncos, the 1998 and 1999 Super Bowl Champions. If you're lucky enough to find a ticket to a game, you'll know why. Cheer the Broncos at the new *Invesco Field at Mile High*. For information call (720) 258–3333 or go to www.invescofieldatmile high.com.

Golf. Denver's city golf courses are a bargain. Reservations can be made by calling (303) 784–4000.

Hockey. Winner of the 1996 and 2001 Stanley Cup, the Colorado Avalanche has also won the hearts of fans here. Hockey season runs from October through mid-April. Playoffs run through mid-June. For tickets call (303) 405–1111 or (303) 830–8497.

Major league baseball. As one of two expansion teams added to the National League in 1993, the Colorado Rockies continue to have a loyal following. Coors Field, at Blake and Twentieth Streets, has been described as one of the best ballparks in the country. For Rockies ticket information, call (303) 762–5437 or (303) ROCKIES. Ask about bargain seats in the "Rockpile." For more information visit www.coloradorockies.com.

REI, 1416 Platte Street, Denver; (303) 756–3100; www.rei.com. This outdoor-recreation store is a tourist attraction all by itself. Located on the Platte River at Confluence Park, west of downtown Denver, REI offers an indoor climbing route designed to resemble Boulder's Flatirons, an outdoor single-track trail to test a mountain bike, and other interactive shopping options.

Six Flags Elitch Gardens (299 Walnut Street; 303–595–4FUN), near downtown Denver, has sixty-seven fun-filled acres with flower gardens, a 300-foot-tall tower with views of Denver, and the Twister II roller coaster. Admission to the theme park is $35.99 for persons 48 inches and taller; $20.99 for children four years of age, up to 48 inches tall; and free for kids three years of age and under as well as seniors seventy years and older.

Soccer. Since its arrival in 1995, the Colorado Rapids has established a loyal following. The Rapids play from April through September. For ticket information call (303) 299–1599 or (800) 844–7777. For more information visit www.coloradorapids.com.

Special Events

January. The National Western Stock Show and Rodeo brings out the cowboy or cowgirl in everyone. Rodeos, cattle auctions, livestock exhibitions, and horse shows attract locals and visitors from around the country.

Dress in your Western duds and join in the fun. The stock show takes place at the Denver Coliseum, off I–70. Call (303) 297–1166 for information.

March. The St. Patrick's Day Parade in Denver is the city's largest annual parade. Marching bands, horses, floats, and stagecoaches take to the streets of downtown Denver to celebrate.

October. The Great American Beer Festival attracts beer lovers and beer makers from around the world. Experts judge the top brews and award gold, silver, and bronze medals in thirty-two categories. Taste a one-ounce sample of nearly 1,000 different beers, including lagers, ales, porters, and stouts. For information call (303) 447–0816 or visit www.beertown.org.

Other Recommended Restaurants and Lodgings

Blue Sky Grill (Pepsi Center, 1000 Chopper Circle; 303–405–6090) is open only when events, such as Avalanche and Nuggets games and concerts, are happening at the Pepsi Center. Luckily, this averages about 200 nights a year. Located on the ground floor at the south entrance to the Pepsi Center, Blue Sky Grill feels like a comfy Western lodge with its rustic iron and antler chandeliers, historic paintings, and Western artifacts. The floor is made of wooden planks reclaimed from historic barns. Hearty cuisine includes bison chili with cheddar cheese; Gore Range prime rib; and mountain trout. Visit www.pepsicenter.com to find out when Blue Sky Grill is open. To make a reservation, leave a message at 303–405–6090. You will receive a response generally within the day. Blue Sky Grill is so exceptional, you'll want to plan your vacation to include a visit.

The Buckhorn Exchange (1000 Osage Street, Denver; 303–534–9505) is legendary for its display of elk, buffalo, and bear trophies. As Denver's oldest restaurant, the Buckhorn Exchange offers choice beef, barbecued pork ribs, and the occasional rattlesnake appetizer. Each February the restaurant celebrates Buffalo Bill's birthday with a look-alike contest.

Fado Irish Pub (1735 Nineteenth Street, between Coors Field and the ChopHouse, Denver; 303–297–0066) is an authentic Irish pub that will make any Guinness lover swoon. Fado has an outdoor patio and live Irish music every Sunday evening.

Hyatt Regency Denver (1750 Welton Street, Denver; 303–295–1234 or 800–233–1234) offers spacious accommodations.

Queen Anne Inn (2147 Tremont Place, Denver; 303–296–6666 or 800–432–4667), fashioned in the Queen Anne style, offers both posh surroundings and convenient access to downtown Denver.

Wazee Lounge and Supper Club (at the corner of Fifteenth and Wazee Streets, Denver; 303–623–9518) has an atmosphere worthy of its steady stream of clientele, whose members include artists, theatergoers, and social gatherers. The black-and-white tile floor, mahogany bar, and stained-glass windows above the bar create a classic 1930s mood. The Wazee claims to be the "Source of the Best Pizza in the Civilized World." You can also choose from items such as a Philadelphia steak sandwich or a hot tuna sandwich on rye.

For More Information

Denver Metro Convention and Visitor Bureau, 1555 California Street, Denver, CO 80202; (303) 892–1112 or (800) 645–3446; www.denver.org.

Stratton

The Eastern Plains

1 Night

If you've never considered heading east of Denver to vacation, the elegant Claremont Inn in Stratton may change your mind. As you motor through the vast flatland stretches, a couple of hours east of Denver, you will see an impressive mansion standing tall on the prairie.

Luxurious, quiet, and classy, the Claremont can best be described as a destination B&B. This stylish inn offers all the amenities you could want and more. Rooms are private hide-aways, and guests can retreat here in grand comfort. Kick back in the sumptuous, red brocade chairs in the private Claremont Theater, or relax with a glass of cabernet and listen to classical music in the

☐ Luxury B&B

☐ Golf

☐ Old-fashioned carousel

☐ Bike riding

☐ Cooking Class Getaway Weekends

☐ Murder Mystery Weekends

well-stocked, cozy wine cellar. Every inch of this inn is tastefully decorated, and you'll want to indulge in its sophistication.

When you're ready to explore, borrow a bicycle from the inn for a spin around town (population 650) or play a few holes of golf at the Stratton Municipal Golf Course. Ride the restored 1905 carousel and visit historic Old Town in nearby Burlington.

It doesn't take long to settle into a relaxed mood. You may want to simply admire the sunset from the inn's terrace or stroll the grounds. The peace and quiet of the wide open spaces are a prescription for urban stress, and before you know it you'll be scheduling a return trip.

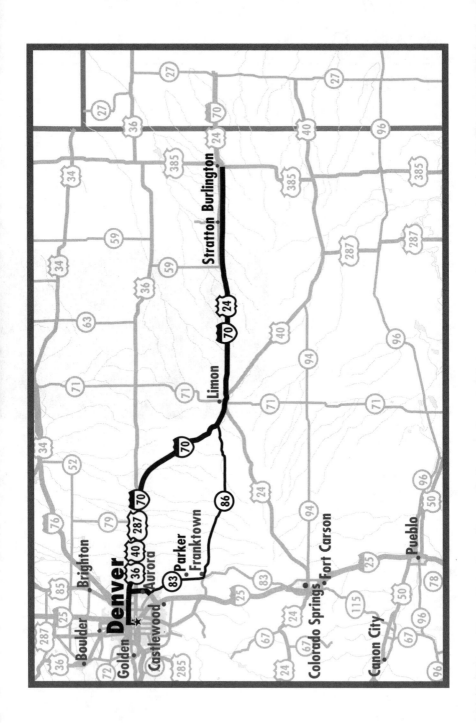

Day 1 / *Morning*

Stratton is 137 miles east of Denver (exit 419 off I–70) and about 30 miles west of the Kansas/Colorado border. Take the **scenic route** from Denver south on Parker Road (Colorado Highway 83), in the midst of rolling meadows and ponderosa pines.

BREAKFAST: Tailgate Tavern, 19522 East Mainstreet Parker (next to the Warhorse); (303) 841–7179. Don't let the name scare you away. The Tailgate has the best steak and eggs in the Denver metropolitan area, according to one local. Open for breakfast weekends only, 8:00 A.M. to noon, and for lunch and dinner daily. The menu includes pasta, burgers, ribs, fajitas, and more.

Mountain Man Nut and Fruit Company (19565 Mainstreet, Parker; 303–841–0915) has a nice selection of nuts and fruits, candies, trail mixes, dried fruits, and chocolates. The store is open Monday through Friday from 9:00 A.M. to 6:00 P.M. and Saturday from 9:00 A.M. to 5:30 P.M. Closed Sunday except during the Christmas season.

Continue south on Highway 83 until you reach Colorado Highway 86. Turn east at Franktown. You'll drive through the scenic Black Forest on a two-lane highway and pass through the small towns of Elizabeth and Kiowa before intersecting with I–70 about 10 miles north of Limon.

Continue east on I–70 to Burlington (17 miles east of Stratton).

LUNCH: Interstate House, 415 South Lincoln Street, Burlington; (719) 346–9406. Join locals at the best lunch spot in town—the truck stop. The all-you-can-eat salad bar offers a good selection, and you can top it off with a piece of homemade coconut cream pie. Breakfast is served all day. Open from 6:00 A.M. to 9:00 P.M. daily. Interstate House is located on the west side of Lincoln Street about one block north after exiting I–70.

Afternoon

Visit the **Kit Carson County Carousel and Old Town** in Burlington. From the Burlington exit, take Lincoln Street to Rose Avenue; continue north on Fourteenth Street, and signs will direct you to the carousel.

The carousel was carved in 1905 by the Philadelphia Toboggan Company and is now a National Historic Landmark. A Wurlitzer Monster Military Band Organ plays tapes of marches, waltzes, and polkas. Rides are 25 cents per person, and the fully restored carousel operates from 1:00 to 8:00 P.M. daily, Memorial Day to Labor Day.

Old Town, just off I–70 in Burlington, is a collection of historic buildings filled with antiques. During summer you'll find cancan shows, melodramas, and a soda fountain that serves floats and hand-dipped sundaes. Old Town is open year-round from 9:00 A.M. to 6:00 P.M. Monday through Saturday and from noon to 6:00 P.M. Sunday. For additional information call (800) 288–1334.

Return to Stratton via I–70 west.

DINNER: Claremont Inn, 800 Claremont Drive, Stratton; (719) 348–5125 or (888) 291–8910; www.claremontinn.com. Dinner at the Claremont, available for overnight guests, is served in the wine cellar and includes an Italian entree, focaccia bread, wine, and dessert. The kitchen is supervised by innkeeper Dave Dischner, who trained at the Cooking School of the Rockies in Boulder, as well as in France and New York. Weather permitting, the staff will serve you on the terrace, which overlooks the plains of eastern Colorado.

Guests may call ahead for a gourmet picnic-style dinner complete with a bottle of wine and fresh-baked bread. Available in the summer season. Ask about the Fine Dining Dinners held the first Saturday of the month. Special dinners feature a regional menu from France, Italy, or Germany.

LODGING: Claremont Inn. Host Dave Dischner seems to have a sixth sense about his guests' interests, whether those be privacy, chatting about eastern Colorado, or needing a recommended route for a bicycle ride. This establishment is a class act, and guests will delight in any one of its seven lavishly decorated suites. Each room comes with a whirlpool tub and walk-in shower, thick bathrobes, a television, and a VCR.

The Colorado Room has expansive views of the wide-open spaces to the west and is decorated in a perfect blend of whimsy and good taste. Fish and bear accessories enhance this large suite, decorated in a fishing-lodge motif. The headboard of natural hickory graces the queen-size bed, and the fabric covering the deep-seated sofa (which turns into a queen sleeper) features fishing and hunting scenes. The hand-carved, hand-painted rainbow trout that hangs on the wall reads CLAREMONT INN, WORMS 5 CENTS.

The Secret Garden Suite is the room most often requested by honeymooners. Couples will find homemade cookies, a gas fireplace, and a wildflower garden outside the window. This room offers a private entrance, queen-size sleigh bed with down comforter inside a delicate cream-colored duvet, and a whirlpool tub for two. Fresh red roses with baby's breath; monogrammed towels; and a pedestal sink are special touches in the larger-than-life bathroom. Two Adirondack chairs outside the back entrance provide the perfect place to enjoy a glass of wine and the peaceful garden view.

The Out of Kansas Suite is decorated in a British Colonial motif with a four-poster bamboo queen bed, a sea-grass carpet, and a fanciful monkey lamp. The bathroom has a wooden cheetah standing guard and white mosquito netting over the tub.

The Waverly Room, once featured in *Country Inns* magazine, is a favorite with guests. The room is so named because of the Waverly fabrics and wallcoverings. This suite has a blend of rose-colored florals, stripes, and plaids and includes a combination of antique and contemporary furnishings.

Ask about the wine tastings that take place in the Claremont's garden-level wine cellar. Here you can relax in the comfortable surroundings as you sip wines from around the world. The Claremont also hosts Murder Mystery Weekends, when guests dress in character and solve a whodunit plot. Each weekend features a different focus, such as a 1920s theme. Props, a script, and costumes are provided, and guests vote on their favorite actor, who is then awarded a complimentary night at the inn.

Rooms at the Claremont start at $119 Sunday through Friday and $199 Saturday. Prices include a full breakfast.

Day 2 / Morning

BREAKFAST: Claremont Inn. A pot of coffee and a newspaper will arrive at your doorstep in the early morning. Breakfast is served from 7:00 to 10:00 A.M. in the light-filled dining area near the kitchen. Huge windows provide prairie views as you enjoy fresh fruit, coffee, juice, muffins, and croissants. The entree may be an egg frittata with sausage or bacon; French toast; or scrambled eggs with fresh herbs and cheese. The Hearth Room, decorated in a floral and country motif, is a great breakfast location. Weather permitting, breakfast may be served on the terrace.

Take a spin through Stratton on the inn's unique side-by-side bicycle-built-for-two. Locals wave and smile as you pedal your way down Colorado Avenue.

LUNCH: Stop in at the Stratton Super Valu (216 Colorado Avenue; 719–348–5518) to stock up on picnic items. Then head to **Stratton City Park,** several blocks north of the Claremont. The park has a pool, tennis courts, a gazebo, and lots of areas in which to picnic or explore.

There's More

Golf. The 9-hole course at the Stratton Golf Club (719–348–5412) is a fairly flat course, with views that stretch for miles.

Weekend cooking classes are offered at the Claremont. Check in Friday evening and enjoy cocktails and a buffet supper. After breakfast Saturday morning, culinary techniques are taught in the state-of-the-art kitchen. You'll sample your efforts during a leisurely two-hour lunch and then return to class. A formal dinner is served in the evening. For information contact Claremont Inn Bed and Breakfast, 800 Claremont Drive, Stratton; (719) 348–5125 or (888) 291–8910.

Special Events

September and October. Fall Cooking Classes (featuring holiday menus and recipes). The Cooking Class includes hands-on participation, lecture, discussion of the recipes, and a demonstration. These fun-filled weekends include accommodations and dinner Friday and Saturday nights, and breakfast Saturday and Sunday. Cooking Weekend Getaway package is $499 per couple. Call Claremont Inn Bed and Breakfast at (719) 348–5125 or (888) 291–8910.

December. The Claremont goes all out to welcome the holiday season with an 18-foot-tall Christmas tree, covered with 10,000 lights and countless ornaments. The dazzling creation stands in the center of the Great Hall. The entire house is decked for the holidays.

Other Recommended Restaurants and Lodgings

Parker

Hickory House, 10335 South Parker Road; (303) 805–9742. This restaurant is known for its barbecue ribs, but there is also a veggie burger on the menu. Try the award-winning dish, Pork Danish Baby Back Ribs—they're really brought in from Denmark. This restaurant has a second site in Aspen.

Junz Restaurant, 11211 Dransfeldt Road; (720) 851–1005. This new restaurant has become known for its superb sushi. Junz has an excellent selection that includes sea bass, halibut, salmon, and steak teriyaki. Open daily for lunch, 11:30 A.M. to 2:30 P.M., and dinner from 5:00 to 9:00 P.M.

For More Information

Burlington Chamber of Commerce, 415 Fifteenth Street, Burlington, CO 80807; (719) 346–8070.

Parker Chamber of Commerce, 19201 East Mainstreet, Parker, CO 80134; (303) 841–4268.

Stratton Chamber of Commerce, 700 New York Avenue, P.O. Box 419, Stratton, CO 80836; (800) 777–6042.

WESTERN
ESCAPES

Winter Park and the Fraser Valley

The Perfect Mountain Getaway

1 Night

Getting to Winter Park via the gorgeous mountain drive or the popular Ski Train may be, as the saying goes, half the fun.

- [ ] Snowshoeing, snowtubing
- [ ] Nordic skiing
- [ ] Bicycling, hiking
- [ ] Snowboarding camp
- [ ] Four-wheel-drive tours
- [ ] Spring Splash
- [ ] Music festival
- [ ] Ski Train

At 9,000 feet above sea level, the air is pure, thin, and guaranteed to clear your head. Thanks to the laid-back ambience of Winter Park, big-city stress is sure to take a tumble. Novice skiers are enthusiastically welcomed on the slopes. With runs named Shoo Fly and Moose Wallow, how could a beginner go wrong?

If you're a mogul maniac, the black-diamond Outhouse run may be more your speed. Better yet, head over to Mary Jane, Winter Park's baby sister. Affectionately known as "the Jane," these moguls are wild and woolly, just like the skiers the intimidating slopes attract. Mary Jane's reputation is one of big bumps, abundant powder, and steep terrain. Dubbed the First Lady of Adrenaline, Mary Jane is to be respected.

If you're a nonskier, no problem. Tour the mountain in a heated Sno-Cat and sip a cup of hot chocolate at the mid-mountain Snoasis Restaurant during the tour break. Or strap on a set of snowshoes and take a guided trip just beyond the slopes. You'll pass through silent forests and spectacular backcountry, and you might catch a glimpse of wildlife such as a coyote, porcupine, fox, or snowshoe hare.

Ice skating, sledding, and Nordic skiing are available, and if you want to feel like a kid again, snowtube down the slopes on an inflated rubber tube at Fraser Valley Tubing Hill. Feet-first or head-first, it's a blast. Later,

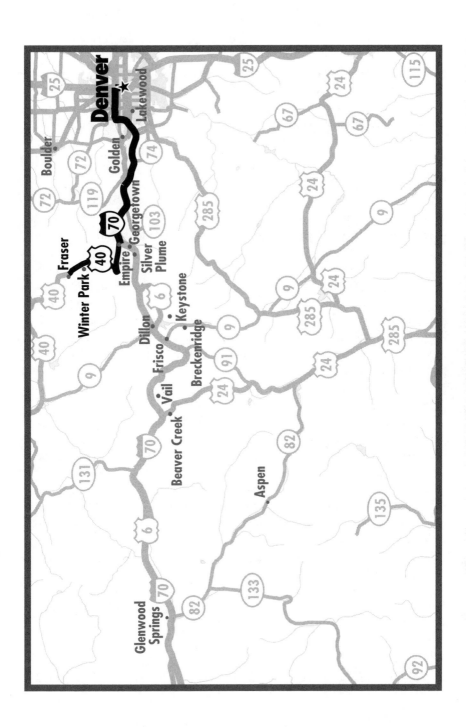

bundle up and steal away for a romantic, horse-drawn sleigh ride under a star-filled evening sky.

Summer in Winter Park rivals ski season. Wildflowers grow in grand style, and hikers and mountain bikers flock to the alpine meadows and lush valleys. Flower boxes overflow with pansies, and the surrounding area is transformed from a winter wonderland into a haven for cyclists, hikers, anglers, and rafters.

Day 1 / Morning

Winter Park is located 67 miles northwest of Denver. Travel west on I–70 for 40 miles and take exit 232 to U.S. Highway 40. Continue on U.S. Highway 40 over Berthoud Pass into the town of Winter Park.

If you prefer, arrive via the Winter Park **Ski Train,** which pulls out of Denver's Union Station (Seventeenth and Wynkoop Streets) on weekends at 7:15 A.M. Two relaxing hours later you'll arrive 50 yards from the foot of the lifts at Winter Park. On the train, sip a cup of coffee and enjoy incredible views that you wouldn't see from the highway. The train departs promptly at 4:15 P.M. the same day and arrives in Denver at 6:30 P.M. If you plan to spend the night in Winter Park, you will need to purchase full-fare tickets for both days.

A round-trip ticket (depart and return same day) is $45 for coach and $70 for club. The coach price offers reclining seats, as well as access to the snack bar and the Cafe Lounge Car, where you can order a breakfast burrito, a bagel, a cinnamon roll, coffee, and juice. Club-car rates include a continental breakfast buffet, a private bar, and après-ski snacks on the return trip. You can purchase discounted lift tickets on the train. The Ski Train operates weekends mid-December through late March (also some Fridays and holidays the months of December, February, and March), and Saturdays from mid-June through mid-August. Reservations are essential. Call (303) 296–4754 or go to www.skitrain.com.

As the closest major ski resort to Denver and with an average snow-fall of nearly 31 feet, Winter Park is one of the most popular in the state. The ski area opened in 1939 with a simple rope tow and a long queue of enthusiastic people. Since then local and destination skiers have streamed to these slopes. With three interconnected mountains, superb snow, and diverse terrain, Winter Park Resort triumphs with outstanding green, blue, and black runs.

If you're not a skier, tour the mountain in comfort by Sno-Cat. You'll get a grand view, stories and interesting tidbits from the driver, and a stopover at the mid-mountain Snoasis Restaurant. Rides depart three times daily from the base of the lifts. Call the resort at (970) 726–5514 for a reservation. The price is $35 for adults and $30 for seniors. Shuttles to the Mountaintop Lodge at Sunspot depart at 10:30 and 11:30 A.M. daily and are the only way for non-skiers to dine at Sunspot. Cost is $30 (does not include meal).

In the winter, guided snowshoe tours are offered twice daily. For $30, snowshoers ride the Gemini Express chairlift and then head into the woods for a two-hour trek through the forest. Equipment is included. Call (970) 726–5514 or (800) 729–7907 for reservations and information. Walk-ins welcome. Meet at the Balcony House near the base of Winter Park Ski area.

LUNCH: Summer visitors can ride the **Zephyr Express Chairlift** to the 10,700-foot summit of Winter Park Mountain and have lunch at the **Lodge at Sunspot.** You'll have views of the Fraser Valley and the Continental Divide as you enjoy a sandwich or salad. Winter visitors can catch the free "Lift" bus in the Winter Park transportation circle to the base of Mary Jane mountain. The **Club Car** (970–726–8105) is a cozy restaurant that offers lunch items such as fried calamari, Mediterranean salad, sesame ginger mahimahi, and an unforgettable and wickedly delicious mud pie for dessert. Enjoy lunch on the outdoor deck and watch the skiers and snowboarders.

Afternoon

Summer visitors will want to stroll, bike, or skate the paved **Fraser River Trail,** an easy-grade 5-mile path between Winter Park Resort and Fraser. You'll cross the Fraser River and travel through lush wooded areas along the way.

To see the countryside by vehicle, sign up for a guided tour with **Mad Adventures** (535 Zerex Street, Fraser; mailing address: P.O. Box 650, Winter Park, CO 80482; 970–726–5290 or 800–451–4844). The company offers a variety of tours, including a four-hour scenic trip to the 11,670-foot summit of Rollins Pass. You'll travel in an open-air, four-wheel-drive vehicle with a licensed guide.

Be sure to visit Winter Park's well-stocked shops and galleries, which offer outdoor clothing, year-round sporting equipment, Southwestern jewelry, Native American art, and Colorado souvenirs.

DINNER: The **Shed Southwestern Grille and Cantina** (78672 U.S. Highway 40, Winter Park; 970–726–9912) offers a punch bowl–sized margarita described as "forty-eight ounces of heaven." Low lighting, cacti painted on the wall, more than twenty tequilas on the menu, excellent service, and creative cuisine set the tone for a fun evening. Open for dinner 4:00 to 10:00 P.M. nightly.

LODGING: **Wild Horse Inn,** P.O. Box 609, Fraser; (970) 726–0456; www.wildhorseinn.com. Western elegance describes this inn. Built of 400-year-old Engelmann spruce logs, the Wild Horse Inn is a gem. Each of the rooms has a private balcony, television and VCR, and private bath and whirlpool. To get to the Wild Horse Inn from Winter Park, follow U.S. Highway 40 for 3 miles northwest of Fraser to County Road 83. The lodge is 1.5 miles north on the right side of the road.

Day 2 / Morning

BREAKFAST: Wild Horse Inn. French toast, fresh-baked maple nut scones, good coffee, pancakes and sausage, or an egg frittata might be on the menu. You won't leave the table hungry.

Depart Winter Park, traveling northwest on Highway 40 headed for Fraser, the town that boasts about its reputation as "Icebox of the Nation." Fraser is the site on the weather map that has pictures of icicles next to its frigid temperature, which can plunge to well below zero. You will see signs on the east side of Highway 40 between Winter Park and Fraser for **Cozens Ranch House and Museum** (970–726–5488). Here you will get a glimpse of how the former sheriff of Central City lived. William Zane Cozens moved to the Fraser Valley in 1874 and operated a complex that included a hotel, dining room, and post office. Thanks to the Grand County Historical Association, today you can tour the restored ranch, which displays Cozens family artifacts. Hours vary, so it's best to call ahead.

LUNCH: **Carver's Bakery** (Cooper Creek Square, Highway 40, Winter Park; 970–726–8202) is tucked behind Cooper Creek Square. This hidden treasure is a locals' favorite. All sandwiches are made with fresh-baked bread. There are plenty of vegetarian options, homemade soups, burgers, and salads. Save room for a dessert pastry. Open 7:00 A.M. to 3:00 P.M. Sunday through Wednesday and 7:00 A.M. to 9:00 P.M. Thursday through Saturday.

Afternoon

Return to Denver via Highway 40 and I–70 east.

There's More

Fly fishing. Don those neoprene waders and insect repellent, grab a fly rod, and claim your spot on the Colorado River. Don't worry if you don't snag a rainbow trout. As the guides say, "Catching isn't everything. If it were we'd call it *catching,* not *fishing.*" For lessons that range from a one-hour introduction to several hours, contact Devil's Thumb Ranch Resort, just outside of Winter Park, at (970) 726–8231.

The **National Sports Center for the Disabled** (NSCD), founded by Hal O'Leary, is Winter Park's greatest gift. Originally created to teach young children with leg amputations to ski, the program has expanded to involve disabilities of many types. Today blind skiers and single and double amputees cruise the slopes. The center also offers a summer program for persons with disabilities. Activities include bicycling, hiking, camping, and rafting. For more information about the program, call the NSCD at (970) 726–1540 or (303) 316–1540.

Snowtubing. Go for it. Pounce onto a custom-made inner tube and soar down the slope. A rope tow will lug you and your tube back to the top so you can do it again. The *Fraser Valley Tubing Hill,* located at the south end of Fraser (970–726–5954), rents tubes weekends from 10:00 A.M. to 10:00 P.M. and weekdays from 4:00 to 10:00 P.M.

Summer skiing and snowboarding camp. Parsenn Bowl, at 12,060 feet above sea level, has snow late into the season. Die-hard skiers see no reason to squander a good snowpack, so Winter Park offers summer ski and snowboard camps, which begin in late May. Call the Winter Park Competition Center at (970) 726–1590.

Special Events

Late March and early April. Spring Splash attracts a big crowd. Spectators cheer as skiers and snowboarders negotiate a zany obstacle course that includes skiing or snowboarding across a 60-foot pond of icy water to reach the finish line. Skiers and snowboarders get discounted late-season ticket prices. An outdoor barbecue takes place daily on the deck of the mid-mountain Snoasis Restaurant. For information call Winter Park Resort Guest Services at (970) 726–5514.

June. Annual American Red Cross Fat Tire Classic. As a major fund-raising event for the Mile High Chapter of the American Red Cross, this popular weekend was in its fourteenth year in 2004. For novices and experts alike, this well-planned bike/walk/hike is an occasion not to be missed. For information and dates call the American Red Cross at (303) 722–7474.

July. KBCO World Class Rock Fest is a two-day festival that features a mixture of sounds from country to alternative to rock. Fans rave about this event, which is a favorite with locals. Bring a blanket and spread out on the grassy slopes. Call the Winter Park and Fraser Valley Chamber of Commerce at (800) 903–7275.

July and August. The High Country Stampede Rodeo in Fraser is held every Saturday evening during July and August. Fill up on barbecue and corn on the cob and watch cowboys rope and ride bulls and broncs.

August. Rocky Mountain Wine, Beer, & Food Festival. Enjoy sampling wine, beer, and gourmet cuisine in the alpine setting of Winter Park Resort. Other activities include winemakers' dinners, mountain biking, and a giant human maze. For more information call (970) 726–1540.

December. The Christmas Eve torchlight parade is one of Winter Park's most enduring traditions. Santa leads a parade of torch-bearing skiers down the slopes of Lower Hughes Trail. A nondenominational service follows.

Other Recommended Restaurants and Lodgings

Tabernash

Devil's Thumb Guest Ranch and Cross-Country Center, east of Fraser at 3530 County Road 83, P.O. Box 750, Tabernash, CO 80478; (970) 726–5633. This facility offers more than 90 kilometers of trails to cross-country ski. The ranch has cozy rooms and woodsy, backcountry charm. The on-site restaurant offers gourmet cuisine. Visit www.devilsthumb ranch.com for more information.

Winter Park

Destinations West—(800) 545–WEST (9378) or (970) 726–8881;

www.mtnlodging.com—offers superior lodging options that include cabins, ski condos, and properties large enough for a family reunion. Condos have amenities that include everything from a private hot tub to a huge flat-screen television. Staff can arrange an entire vacation package with ski lift tickets, a golf package, or a visit to historic Rapids Lodge and Restaurant in nearby Grand Lake. To reach the Destinations West office, take U.S. Highway 40 through Winter Park to Fraser and turn left into the shopping center (across from the Safeway). The office is at the east end of the shopping center on the second floor.

Divide Grill, located at the top of Cooper Creek Square, 78930 U.S. Highway 40; (970) 726–4900. This casual restaurant serves fresh seafood specials, juicy steaks, and a selection of pastas, and also has a great salad bar.

Fontenot's Cajun Café (78711 Highway 40, Winter Park; 970–726–4021) specializes in zesty Cajun specialties such as blackened catfish, étouffée, gumbo, shrimp salad, and a variety of sandwiches served with spicy fries. Fontenot's (say "FON-ten-nose") is open for lunch and dinner daily.

Iron Horse Resort, 100 Winter Park Drive, P.O. Box 1369, Winter Park, CO 80482; (970) 726–8851 or (800) 621–8190; www.ironhorse resort.com. This ski-in/ski-out facility has condominiums that range from studios to two-bedroom luxury units. Amenities include free local shuttle service, an on-site restaurant and lounge, a health club, an indoor/outdoor pool, hot tubs, and a ski shop.

For directions to the Kitchen (970–726–9940), locals will tell you "It's the yellow building that looks like a house next to the Post Office in the center of town." This popular cafe that's been in business for more than a quarter of a century is known for its corned-beef hash and huevos rancheros. You can even get a hamburger or BLT at 8 o'clock in the morning. Open every day from 8:00 A.M. to noon, with some variation in hours, depending on business and the owner's whims. Expect to wait for a table on weekends in winter and summer.

Moffat Market at West Portal Station, located at the base of Winter Park Mountain, has surprisingly fresh affordable cuisine (order a full breakfast of French toast, eggs, bacon, and hash browns for $6.95). An impressive feature of the recently remodeled facility is a replica of the west portal of the famous Moffat Tunnel. Open during ski season only, daily from 8:00 A.M. to 3:00 P.M. Closed summer. Call resort for information, (970) 726–5514.

Mountaintop Lodge at Sunspot; (970) 726–5514. Ride the gondola Friday and Saturday evenings during ski season to this mid-mountain restaurant, indulge in an elegant five-course meal in the spectacular timbered dining room, and gaze at the twinkling lights of Winter Park and the Fraser Valley below.

The Pines Inn, P.O. Box 15, Winter Park, CO 80482; (970) 726–5416 or (800) 824–9127; www.bestinns.net/usa/col/pine.html. One of the nicest things about staying at this cozy B&B surrounded by lodgepole pines is visiting with owners Jan and Lee Reynolds. They cheerfully answer questions about which trail to ski, hike, or bike or where to dine; they know which chef has moved and who serves the best margaritas. Shadow, the resident black lab, also makes friends easily. Room number eight is the choice of honeymooners. Here you will find a wooden sleigh bed, loveseat, antique armoire, and private deck. The B&B is walking distance from the base of the ski area. To get to the Pines Inn, take the first left after the ski area (Old Town Drive) and follow the signs for 0.5 mile.

For More Information

Winter Park and Fraser Valley Chamber of Commerce, 78841 Highway 40, P.O. Box 3236, Winter Park, CO 80482; (970) 726–4221 or (800) 903–7275 or, in Denver, (303) 422–0666.

Winter Park Central Reservations, P.O. Box 36, Winter Park, CO 80482; (970) 726–5587 or (800) 729–5813; www.winterparkresort.com.

Winter Park Resort, P.O. Box 36, Winter Park, CO 80482; (970) 726–5514; www.skiwinterpark.com.

Georgetown

Victorian Charm

1 Night

Georgetown is one of Colorado's most beloved Victorian towns. This attractive, before-the-turn-of-the-twentieth-century village charms at the outset. Gingerbread houses, flagstone sidewalks, and lovingly preserved churches create an elegant, bygone era.

The community traces its roots to the early gold prospectors who were tempted by rumors of fortune. Subsequently, miners unearthed silver deposits not far upriver at Silver Plume in the late 1800s. Shortly following the boom, the Georgetown Loop Railroad was constructed.

Today you'll find a community devoted to the restoration and preservation of its heritage. The area also offers elegant B&B accommodations and hiking, biking, and skiing, all in the stunning setting of Colorado's Clear Creek Valley and the Arapaho National Forest.

- ☐ Narrow-gauge steam train
- ☐ Walking tour
- ☐ Romantic B&B inn
- ☐ Shopping
- ☐ Christmas Market

The first two weekends of December, the town gussies up to greet the Christmas season. Smell the chestnuts roasting, listen to carolers serenade "Silent Night," and visit with Father Christmas.

Day 1 / Morning

From Denver, travel west on I–70 for 45 miles and exit at Georgetown.

BREAKFAST: Save your appetite for a meal at the **Happy Cooker** (412 Sixth Street; 303–569–3166). The restaurant deserves a visit for its clever name, and the chef gets credit for the delicious Belgian waffles and home-made bread. Open 7:00 A.M. to 4:00 P.M. weekdays; 7:00 A.M. to 5:00 P.M. weekends.

Stroll the streets of Georgetown and browse the shops, galleries, book-stores, and cafes. Be sure to visit **Georgetown Mercantile** (614 Rose, on

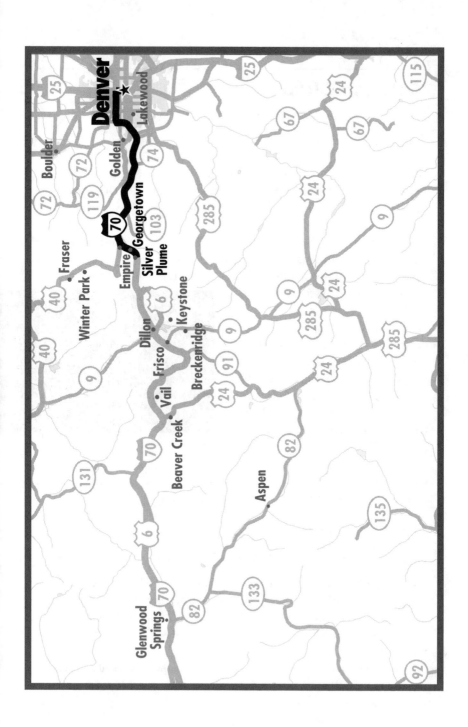

the corner of Seventh and Rose Streets; 303–569–2109). The mercantile is housed in the St. James Hotel Building, which was built in 1875 before Colorado obtained statehood. This well-stocked store is a potpourri of treasures. You'll find old-fashioned tin boxes, candles, greeting cards, and much more. Georgetown Mercantile is open from 10:00 A.M. to 5:00 P.M. daily.

For an outstanding selection of casual and ethnic clothing and hand-made jewelry, shop at **Expeditions** (614 Sixth Street; 303–569–3322), upstairs from the Georgetown Gallery. Expeditions is open daily from 10:00 A.M. to 5:00 P.M.

Take a self-guided walking tour of the 5-square-block downtown. Pick up a map at the Community Center, located at Sixth and Argentine Streets (303–569–2888). Originally the town bakery and later the Clear Creek County Courthouse, today this building houses an excellent visitor information center.

From the Community Center, continue south to the **Hamill House** (305 Argentine Street; 303–569–2840). This restored structure was the home of silver tycoon William Arthur Hamill, who was one of the richest men in the county. The building, which is now operated by **Historic Georgetown, Inc.,** exhibits 1880s furnishings. Admission is $5.00 for adults and $4.00 for seniors and students; children under six are admitted free. Open from 10:00 A.M. to 4:00 P.M. daily, Memorial Day through September; and from noon to 4:00 P.M. on weekends only, October through December. Closed January 1 until Memorial Day. Group tours are available year-round by appointment.

You won't want to miss the grand **Hotel de Paris,** at Sixth and Taos Streets (303–569–2311). The hotel opened in 1875 and today is a museum operated by the National Society of Colonial Dames of America. This lovely old building was modeled after a French inn. The builder, Louis Dupuy, a Frenchman who arrived in Georgetown as a miner, longed to have a bit of his homeland in Colorado. Open from 11:00 A.M. to 4:30 P.M. daily Memorial Day weekend through September and from noon to 4:00 P.M. on weekends during winter. Admission is $4.00 for adults; discounts are available for seniors and children.

Of special note is the **Georgetown Gallery** (612 Sixth Street; 303–569–2218), which features Colorado artists and has an impressive selection of pottery, oils, and pastels. Georgetown Gallery is open from 10:00 A.M. to 5:00 P.M. daily in summer. Winter hours are from 11:00 A.M. to 4:30 P.M., except on Tuesday and Thursday, when the gallery closes.

LUNCH: Panda City, 1510 Argentine Street; (303) 569–0288. Excellent Chinese food is served at this restaurant recommended by locals. The staff and owners are exceptionally friendly and accommodating. Open daily for lunch and dinner.

Afternoon

After lunch it's "all aboard" the **Georgetown Loop Railroad.** Sit back and take in the incredible scenery as you wind through the woods, twist and turn on sharp curves, and cross Clear Creek several times. The 1920s narrow-gauge steam locomotive (restored in 1975) crosses Devil's Gate Bridge and stops at Silver Plume. Here you can visit the Lebanon Silver Mine. Slip on a hard hat and admire the old silver mine as a guide talks about mining methods in the 1800s. The round-trip train ride lasts an hour, and if you tour the mine, the trip will take two and a half hours.

The train departs from both Devil's Gate boarding area and the Silver Plume Depot (exit 226 off I–70). Tickets are available at the Old Georgetown Station and the Silver Plume Depot. The train runs daily, rain or shine, from Memorial Day through the first part of October. For tickets contact Georgetown Loop Railroad, Old Georgetown Station, 1106 Rose Street, P.O. Box 217, Georgetown, CO 80444; (303) 569–2403 or (800) 691–4386. A round-trip ticket is $15.50 for adults and $10.25 for children ages three to fifteen.

Visit the **Georgetown Energy Museum** (600 Griffith Street; 303–569–3557), where you will see waterwheels and generators that were installed in 1906 and still produce electric power. The plant also operates as a museum and is open to the public Memorial Day weekend through September from 10:00 A.M. to 4:00 P.M. daily. The facility is closed except by appointment the remainder of the year.

DINNER: Raven Hill Mining Company, 612 Sixth Street; (303) 569–2209. This restaurant specializes in buffalo prime rib and buffalo burgers, Mexican food, barbecue ribs, and chicken. Dinner specials change nightly and include wild game, fresh salmon, and seafood. Dine on the deck. Open for lunch and dinner; closed Tuesday during the winter.

LODGING: Alpine Hideaway, P.O. Box 788, Georgetown, CO 80444; (800) 490–9011 or (303) 569–2800. This luxuriously peaceful B&B is the ideal place to celebrate a special occasion. The Alpine Hideaway offers privacy and comfort in a sumptuous setting. Each of the three elegant guest rooms has a gas fireplace, a Jacuzzi tub for two, and mountain views. The

"All aboard" for the Georgetown Loop Railroad.

Country Irish Room, located on the second floor, displays photos of innkeeper Dawn Janov's prizewinning Arabian horses. The dreamy Mountain Contemporary Room boasts a romantic four-poster iron bed and private entry to an outdoor garden with a swing, hammock, and waterfall. The bathroom is decorated in black-and-white tile and offers such extras as gold fixtures and a bidet. The Scandinavian Room features a ceramic fireplace.

Day 2 / Morning

BREAKFAST: Janov refers to her B&B as a "bed and basket." Breakfast at the Alpine Hideaway is indeed an occasion. At a prearranged time, a gourmet basket of food and a carafe of coffee, tea, or hot chocolate appear at your doorstep. The basket holds items such as bacon quiche, pistachio banana bread, and a plate of fresh kiwi, grapes, and mango. Presentation is superb. Fresh flowers, cloth napkins, and heart-shaped cheeses help create the detailed array. Dining in the privacy of your room is a relaxed way to begin the day.

Motor along the 22-mile loop on **Guanella Pass Road,** a Scenic and Historic Byway (CRs 381 and 62) that twists through Arapaho National Forest. The byway climbs to 11,600 feet through lush aspen and spruce forests to the broad, windswept tundra. The route gains elevation almost immediately but can be driven with an ordinary vehicle, even though the road is not paved the entire way. Park at the top of Guanella Pass and take in the exhilarating air and dramatic scenery. At Guanella Pass you'll get views of Mount Bierstadt, Grays Peak, and Mount Wilcox. On the descent you'll pass alpine lakes, spruce forests, and, if it's summer or autumn, aspen trees. Schedule two hours for this route.

On your return trip to Denver via I–70, stop at **Tommyknocker Microbrewery & Pub** (1401 Miner Street, Idaho Springs; 303–567–2688). Its Maple Nut Brown Ale is an excellent brew. Order a buffalo burger or the buffalo meat loaf served with mashed potatoes and gravy. Open daily from 11:00 A.M. to 10:00 P.M.; the bar stays open until 2:00 A.M.

There's More

Cross-country skiing. Whatever can be hiked in the summer can usually be skied in the winter. Numerous trails in the Arapaho National Forest welcome Nordic skiers with good snow conditions, well-marked paths, and peaceful touring. Check with the Clear Creek Ranger District Office (303–567–2901) at exit 240 off I–70 for maps, weather conditions, and advice on skiing or hiking. The ranger office is open 8:00 A.M. to 5:00 P.M. Monday through Saturday during the winter and daily during the summer.

Fishing. Georgetown Lake, located at the east end of Georgetown, is packed with cutthroat and rainbow trout. The mountain setting makes this lake an excellent spot to drop a line and contemplate the day away.

Hiking. Pavilion Point, a favorite with railroad buffs, is a historic footpath that follows a portion of the Argentine Central Railroad bed. The easy trail is about 1 mile one-way and is a good picnic spot. You'll get views of the train, Silver Plume, and Georgetown. Drive south from Georgetown on

Guanella Pass Road 2.5 miles to Waldorf Junction (Forest Road 248). Turn right and travel 1.2 miles.

Mountain biking. Bike the 6-mile path to the ghost town of Waldorf. The trail begins 2.5 miles south of Georgetown along Guanella Pass Road.

Special Events

July. Traditional Independence Day celebration includes a parade, a barbecue, bucket brigade races, fireworks, and old-fashioned merrymaking. Drive to Silver Plume for the ice cream social and street dance.

December. The holidays come to life during the first two weekends of December during Christmas Market, a glorious outdoor festivity that celebrates the season in a Victorian fashion. The festival takes place from 10:00 A.M. until dusk.

Other Recommended Restaurants and Lodgings

Silver Plume

Sopp and Truscott, 486 Main Street; (303) 569–3395. This mom-and-pop bakery is worth the visit even if you're on a diet (you won't be for long). The proprietor sets out entire loaves of bread to sample and even provides a toaster and jam. Take exit 226 off I–70 and drive north about 3 blocks to the tiny burg of Silver Plume. Continue east on Main Street (it's dirt and gravel) and follow your nose to the corner bakery on the south side of the street. Here you'll find banana, jalapeño cheddar, sourdough, and sunflower oatmeal bread; cookies; and jams, including the basics such as apricot and strawberry as well as more exotic varieties such as pineapple jalapeño chutney. Sopp and Truscott is named after two gentlemen who had a business at the same location in the 1890s. The bakery is open Thursday through Sunday from 7:00 A.M. to 5:00 P.M. Sales are on the honor system Monday through Wednesday. A sign outside the front door reads, "Look in the bread box."

A few steps from the bakery is the Silver Plume Antique Shop (456 Main Street; 303–569–2358; www.silverplumetearoom.com) where you can enjoy afternoon tea (reservations recommended) or a sandwich. Delicious whole pies such as rhubarb or peach are available.

For More Information

Clear Creek Ranger District Office, P.O. Box 3307, Idaho Springs, CO 80452; (303) 567–2901.

Gateway Information and Visitor Center, Fifteenth and Argentine Streets (off I–70, Georgetown exit), Georgetown, CO 80444; (303) 569–2405.

Georgetown Community Center, 404 Sixth Street, Georgetown, CO 80444; (303) 569–2888 or (800) 472–8230.

Historic Georgetown, Inc., 305 Argentine Street, P.O. Box 667, Georgetown, CO 80444; (303) 569–2840; www.historicgeorgetown.org.

Summit County

It's All Downhill

1 Night

This multimountain, multiresort area offers powder skiing, a renowned culinary school, mountaintop gourmet dining, and much more.

Summit County encompasses four ski areas, four towns, and three resorts. Breckenridge is the oldest settlement, followed by Dillon, Silverthorne, and Frisco. Victorian street lamps and architecture enhance Breckenridge, which was once a one-road community made up of hardy settlers and gold-seeking prospectors. Locals later realized the area's other commodity of "white gold," and ski areas sprouted to accommodate the downhill craze. Summit County soon boasted Breckenridge; Arapahoe Basin (affectionately known as A-Basin, or the Legend); Keystone; and Copper Mountain.

In the summer the area becomes a playground for bicyclists, golfers, and trekkers. When is the last time you took a llama to lunch? Let a llama carry the load as you hike to a beautiful picnic site with 360-degree views of the Rockies. With activities that range from conventional to extraordinary, it's little surprise that visitors flock to this mountain getaway.

- [ ] Skiing
- [ ] Mountain-bike Dirt Camp
- [ ] Llama lunch hike
- [ ] Gondola rides
- [ ] Sailing on Lake Dillon
- [ ] Snowshoe tour
- [ ] Fly fishing
- [ ] Snow Sculpture Championships

Day 1 / Morning

Summit County is located 70 miles west of Denver via I–70. To get to Keystone, take the Dillon/Silverthorne exit (exit 205) and travel 6 miles south on U.S. Highway 6.

Skiers will want to head directly to the slopes. The area offers choices for beginners, intermediate skiers, and experts.

Arapahoe Basin tops out at 13,050 feet above sea level. A-Basin is a favorite with die-hard skiers, thanks to its late season (usually ending July Fourth) and festive atmosphere. With only 10 percent of the terrain

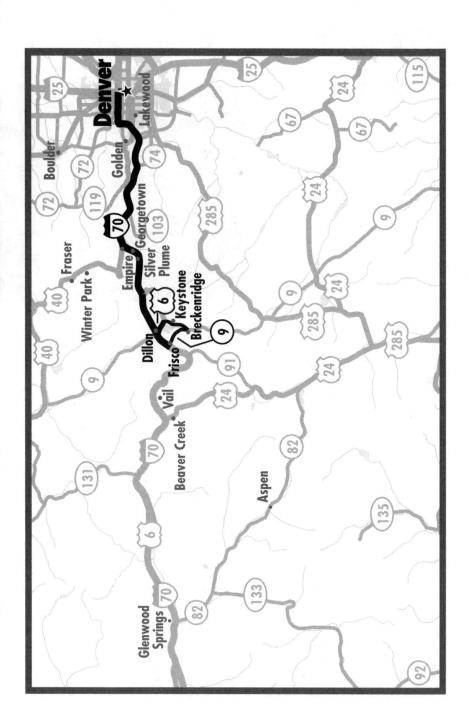

designated as easy, A-Basin may not be the place for a beginner, but it's pure enchantment for the intermediate to expert skier. Nearly vertical terrain and long chutes (not to mention an outdoor barbecue at the top of Exhibition Lift) are enough to satisfy hard-core mogul-seekers. A-Basin is located east of Keystone on Highway 6, at the base of Loveland Pass. For information call (888) 272–7246.

With more than 2,000 acres of skiable terrain, **Breckenridge Ski Area** offers moguls for the advanced skier and nearly horizontal slopes for the rookie. Beginners may wish to avoid Hades and Devil's Crotch runs and stay on Flapjack. Peaks 8, 9, and 10, which are part of the Ten Mile Range, may have lackluster titles, but the high-altitude mountains are anything but boring. Skiers will find plenty of opportunities to break into high speed on the steep slopes. Breckenridge Ski Area is 70 miles west of Denver via I–70 (exit 203) and 9 miles south on Highway 9. For more information call (800) 404–3535.

Copper Mountain Resort offers good skiing stats, with an annual snowfall of 255 inches and 350 acres of "extreme skiing." Copper is a great place for beginners to gain confidence and also offers an outstanding children's ski school. On the other end of the scale, guided extreme-skiing tours are available for dauntless experts. Club Med stationed itself here with its first ski village in North America. Copper is located just off I–70 at exit 195. For information call (970) 968–2882 or (800) 458–8386.

Nighttime-skiing devotees rave about the twilight runs at **Keystone,** billed as the largest night-skiing single-mountain operation in the country. Lift tickets are valid until 9:00 P.M., so you can ski well after the sun sets. Chances of snow here? One hundred percent. Keystone has one of the largest snowmaking operations in North America. As the pacemaker in snow production, Keystone continues to improve on its already successful Mother Nature–enhancing efforts. Accommodations at Keystone are well designed, and the resort commits itself to guest service and fine cuisine. Racing enthusiasts will want to ask about Keystone's Mahre Training Center, which offers coaching, lift tickets, and a session with Phil or Steve Mahre. Phil won a gold medal and Steve a silver at the Sarajevo Olympics in 1984. Keystone is located east of Dillon on Highway 6. For information call (800) 404–3535.

Nonskiers can try ice skating or ice hockey. Keystone Lake in Keystone Village is the largest Zamboni-maintained outdoor ice rink in North America. Rent skates or ice-hockey equipment at the rental shop near the lake.

Skiers at Arapahoe Basin.

To arrange a guided snowshoe tour, plan a fly-fishing trip (year-round), or shop for the latest in outdoor clothing, stop at **Summit Guides** (970–468–8945) located near the lake. Spend time browsing the shops next to Keystone Lake. You'll find everything from gourmet chocolate to T-shirts.

LUNCH: Alpenglow Stube, P.O. Box 38, Keystone, CO 80435; (800) 354–4386. Treat yourself to the Stube Skiers Buffet at North America's highest award-winning gourmet restaurant. The buffet is a feast of freshly smoked meats, homemade soups, and fresh bread. The Stube is located at the top of North Peak in the Outpost Lodge. With lunch or dinner reservations, non-skiers can ride two gondolas to the restaurant. The Alpenglow Stube also serves dinner, with entrees such as wild game grill, pan-seared tuna, and duck breast.

Another lunch option in the warm months is **Pizza on the Plaza** (970–496–3729), located next to the Keystone Activities & Dining Center in Keystone Village. This restaurant has a selection of pasta, pizza, and sandwiches.

Afternoon

Summer visitors will want to cruise the paved bike path in Keystone. Pick up a map at the Keystone Activities & Dining Center, located in Keystone Village, directly behind Keystone Lodge. **Sports Shaq** (970–496–4245), located near Keystone Lake, rents bicycles, paddleboats, canoes, kayaks, and in-line skates.

Set sail on **Lake Dillon.** Take a cruise aboard a 25-foot sailboat with an experienced guide. Your skipper will take you on a ninety-minute tour of the lake. Call Keystone Activity Center at (800) 354–4386.

Keystone Resort offers a weekly cooking class where guests don a chef's hat and apron, participate in hands-on training and preparation of an evening meal, then feast on the five-course dinner. Certified Executive Chef Bob Burden conducts the class. For more extensive culinary training, enroll in the four-day workshop. The resort's award-winning chefs lead the classes. Call (800) 354–4386.

DINNER: Keystone Ranch, 1437 Summit County Road 150, Keystone. Located 3 miles from Keystone Village, this elegant 1930s ranch homestead offers a phenomenal dining experience. It's pricey, but you will be pampered by the professional waitstaff as you savor six courses of gourmet Colorado cuisine. The fixed-price menu offers appetizers such as chilled pheasant and Piney Ridge venison, followed by soup, salad, sorbet, and an entree of elk with wild mushrooms, roast rack of lamb, or tenderloin of beef, among others. Ask your server if you can relocate to the living room for dessert, a grand finale that includes Grand Marnier soufflé or chocolate demitasse. This cozy room, with its roaring fire and comfy couches, is the ideal place to linger over a glass of port, espresso, and after-dinner conversation. An elk-antler chandelier adds to the rustic charm. Dinner reservations are handled through Keystone Activity Center, (800) 354–4386.

LODGING: Keystone Resort, Box 38, Keystone, CO 80435; (800) 404–3535; www.keystoneresort.com. Choose Keystone Lodge in the village or a condominium in a more secluded area. The lodge has a complete workout facility. Luxury home rentals are also available.

Day 2 / Morning

BREAKFAST: **Edgewater,** connected to Keystone Lodge, has a breakfast buffet that includes waffles, egg dishes, and pastries. Outside dining is available in the summer. The restaurant serves breakfast from 6:30 to 10:30 A.M. daily and is open for lunch until 2:00 P.M.

A splendid way to see the countryside in summer is on horseback. **Keystone Stables** (970–496–3550) can arrange a one-hour or a full-day ride. If you prefer to travel by auto, contact **Tiger Run Tours** (970–453–2331) to go exploring in a 4x4 off-road vehicle. During winter, the company offers snowmobile tours.

LUNCH: Hop on the gondola to the top of **Keystone Mountain** to rendezvous with the llamas. The animals carry lunch as you hike with a guide on the intermediate 1-mile path to the picnic site. Lunch includes items such as chicken fajitas, fresh fruit salad, and strawberry shortcake. Minimum age is six. The llama lunch is available July 4 through Labor Day weekend. For reservations call the Keystone Activity Center at (800) 354–4386.

Winter visitors will want to feast on the "Skier's Lunch" at **Ski Tip Lodge** (on Montezuma Road, 1 mile east of Keystone Village; 970–496–4950). The buffet includes soups, salads, and fresh bread, served in the cozy setting of a log lodge. Call for the winter schedule and reservations.

There's More

Dirt Camp. "Take your mountain bike to school." Professional mountain-bike racers teach basic riding techniques to beginners and advanced skills to accomplished riders. Sign up for a two-hour, half-day, or two-day clinic at Keystone. Call (800) 711–DIRT (3478).

Special Events

January. Early every January, spectators swarm to Breckenridge to watch teams from around the world compete in the International Snow Sculpture Championships. Squads sculpt colossal pieces of art—some stunning, others whimsical—from twenty-ton blocks of snow at this crowd-pleasing event. Call (970) 453–6018.

Breckenridge Ullr Fest. Another week with partying on the agenda is this creative celebration, held in late January, which honors the mythical Norse god of winter. The festivities include a parade, ice skating, and a visit by Ullr himself. Call (970) 453–6018.

April. Breckenridge Beach Daze. Spring is welcomed in style beginning April Fools' Day with a parade and crowning of the Town Fool. With snowfall at generally the heaviest of the season, conditions delight skiers. Call (970) 453–6018.

Eenie Weenie Bikini Contest. Men and women ski or snowboard on Copper Mountain's Main Vein ski run for prizes in this zany competition. For information call (970) 968–2882, extension 7885.

May. Annual Taste of Breckenridge. Wine, cuisine, and competition. This town knows how to throw a party, and the Annual Taste is no exception. Chefs gather and rival for the desired Chef's Hat. Call (970) 453–6018.

September. Taste of Keystone and Colorfest Open Golf Tournament. Feast on the best of the best, enjoy fabulous fall colors, and play a few rounds of golf. For dates call the Keystone Activity Center at (800) 354–4386.

Other Recommended Restaurants and Lodgings

Breckenridge

The Allaire Timbers Inn, 9511 Highway 9 South Main, P.O. Box 4653, Breckenridge, CO 80424; (970) 453–7530. This rustic log inn offers ten guest rooms, each with private bath and mountain views. Enjoy views of Ten Mile Range as you relax in the outdoor spa. Full breakfast and happy hour included.

Hearthstone Restaurant, 130 South Ridge Street; (970) 453–1148. Order one of the daily specials, such as smoked trout salad or eggplant primavera. Open for dinner only.

Mi Casa Restaurant, 600 South Park Avenue; (970) 453–2071. This popular après-ski spot serves great margaritas, chunky salsa and chips, and fish tacos. The atmosphere is lively and the bar is packed.

The Village at Breckenridge, 535 South Park Avenue; (970) 453–2000 or (800) 800–7829. This ski-in/ski-out complex has 455 units, ranging from studios to three-bedroom suites. The lobby features an elk-antler chandelier, antique snowshoes on the wall, and an upright piano. Cozy up next to the fireplace in the library just off the lobby. From Denver, take I–70 west to Frisco, turn south on Highway 9, and drive 9 miles to the town of Breckenridge.

Keystone

Ski Tip Lodge, P.O. Box 38, Keystone, CO 80435; (970) 496–4950 or (800) 222–0188. This rustic retreat was once a stagecoach stop. Rooms are small and cozy. You won't be distracted by television or the telephone. The lodge also operates as a restaurant, with four-course dinners, lunch during the winter, and Sunday brunch in the summer. Breakfast is included with lodging. Ski Tip Lodge is on Montezuma Road, 1 mile east of Keystone Village.

Sleigh-ride dinner at Soda Creek Homestead (800–354–4386). Bundle up for the brisk trip via sleigh pulled by Belgian draft horses to this restored 1880s homestead. Guests can choose steak, chicken, or vegetable kabob for dinner. Price is $68 per person, low season.

For More Information

Breckenridge Resort Chamber, 555 South Columbine Street, Box 1909, Breckenridge, CO 80424; (970) 453–2913 or (800) 221–1091; www .breckenridge.com.

Copper Mountain Resort Chamber, P.O. Box 3003, Copper Mountain, CO 80443; (970) 968–6477.

Keystone Resort, Box 38, Keystone, CO 80435; (800) 222–0188; www.keystoneresort.com.

Summit County Chamber of Commerce, P.O. Box 2010, Frisco, CO 80443; (970) 668–5800 or (800) 530–3099; www.summitchamber.org.

Vail and Beaver Creek

Alpine Splendor

2 Nights

Styled after the likes of European resorts, Vail Village feels like a reproduction of a charming ski town in Bavaria. Mountainside chalets, large wooden clock spires, and the occasional *"S'il vous plait"* create an international flavor here more prominent than in any other area of the state.

Vail's little sister, nearby Beaver Creek, has followed the trendsetter's footsteps to become as fashionable an area. Some observers say Beaver Creek has emerged as an equal to the well-to-do Vail. The slopes of Beaver Creek rate the same in panache, and the luxurious accommodations are second to none.

- ☐ Betty Ford Alpine Gardens
- ☐ Music festivals
- ☐ Fine dining
- ☐ High-altitude golf
- ☐ World-class shopping
- ☐ Ski museum
- ☐ High-speed gondola

Hollywood types descend on Aspen rather than Vail, but there is still the occasional report of a glitterati sighting.

In relation to the history of Colorado, Vail is an infant. Just over four decades old, Vail became a ski area before it became a town. Today, first-class restaurants thrive in Vail and Beaver Creek, and you will want to indulge in the superb sustenance. Jagged, snowcapped peaks of the spectacular Gore Range tower above Vail and Beaver Creek, which creates a picture-perfect scene year-round.

Day 1 / Morning

From Denver, travel 100 miles (two hours) west on I–70 to Vail. Take the Vail Village exit (number 176) and follow signs to the public parking just north of the village.

LUNCH: Chap's Grill & Chophouse at Vail Cascade Resort & Spa, 1300 Westhaven Drive, Vail; (970) 479–7014. After checking into the Vail

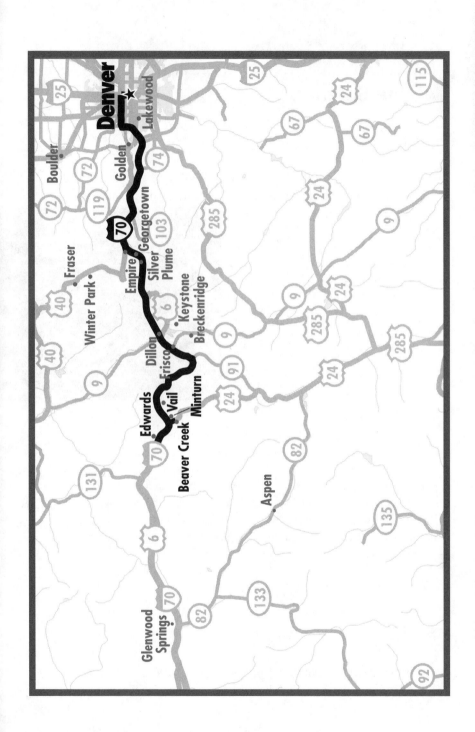

Cascade, sit on the patio outside Chap's (some say this is the best deck in the entire valley) and enjoy a burger, salad, or vegetable wrap. This restaurant is so good, you'll want to eat here more than once during your stay.

Afternoon

After lunch, join the crowd in browsing the upscale boutiques, galleries, and sports shops of **Vail Village.** Take the free shuttle that departs every fifteen minutes in front of the Vail Cascade Resort & Spa. The pedestrian mall, with its geranium-filled planters and stylish bistros, is a destination of its own. You'll no doubt see fur-clad, diamond-covered women and hear not only French but a smattering of Spanish, Japanese, or Swedish as you meander the cobblestone pathway or linger in one of the outdoor cafes.

For a signature baby bear, mama bear, or papa bear necklace, visit **The Golden Bear,** 286 Bridge Street (the intersection of Bridge Street and Gore Creek Drive), Vail Village; (970) 476–4082. This company is practically an institution in Vail. Hours change with the season, but the store is open every day of the year except Christmas and Thanksgiving.

You don't have to be a skier to ride the Eagle Bahn high-speed gondola at Lionshead. This supersophisticated gondola travels at 19.7 feet per second, ascending the mountain in just eight to twelve minutes. Speed is just the beginning. The twelve-passenger cabin comes with heat, so you will commute to the summit in comfort. At the top sits the colossal **Eagle's Nest Adventure Ridge,** which offers both day and night activities. Tube, sled, snow bike, snowmobile, snowshoe, snowboard, ice skate, or watch the action from the **Blue Moon Bar.** You can rent snow bikes, ice skates, snowshoes, thrill-sleds, and even snow boots and snowsuits. For information call (970) 476–9090. During summer, take a mountain bike on the gondola and ride down, or rent a bike at the top.

DINNER: La Tour Restaurant, 122 East Meadow Drive, Vail; (970) 476–4403. La Tour is recognized as one of the best French restaurants in Vail. Chef Paul Ferzacca presides over this contemporary restaurant while Ferzacca's wife, Lourdes, expertly manages the dining room. The steak tartare is perfection, the Dover sole divine, and the service superb. For dessert, indulge in the chocolate truffle terrine with fresh berries. La Tour is open for dinner only, Tuesday through Sunday, at 5:30 P.M.

LODGING: Vail Cascade Resort & Spa, 1300 Westhaven Drive, Vail; (970) 476–7111 or (800) 420–2424; www.vailcascade.com. Location, location, location. Nestled at the base of Vail Mountain, this sophisticated

The clock tower in Vail Village is a familiar landmark.

ski-in/ski-out resort also offers a warm, easy-going charm. Sink into one of the overstuffed chairs in the elegant lobby for an après-ski cabernet and views of Gore Creek that runs right through the resort's backyard. Request a deluxe room with mountainside (rather than courtside) view.

Relax on your private balcony and watch anglers fly-fish in Gore Creek and cyclists travel the bike path. Spa services range from a hot stone massage to an alpine body glow. Squash anyone? The Cascade offers three squash courts; indoor running track; pool; and tennis, racquetball, and basketball courts. The resort also offers a theater with first-run movies. To get there take exit 176 off I–70. At the second roundabout, veer right onto South Frontage Road and follow signs to Lionshead. The resort is located 0.25 mile after Lionshead.

Day 2 / Morning

BREAKFAST: Chap's Grill and Chophouse, at Vail Cascade Resort & Spa, offers a full breakfast buffet (with made-to-order omelets) and a continental buffet. The buffet includes salmon, hot and cold cereals, bagels, and breakfast pastries.

If skiing is an indispensable part of your vacation, you'll love this getaway. Choose the excitement of **Vail Mountain.** Vail Mountain has 5,289 skiable acres, making it the largest single ski mountain in North America. Skiers may also want to try the smooth groomers of **Beaver Creek.**

Summer activities run the gamut from golf to river rafting. With eleven 18-hole courses in the Vail Valley, you'll find plenty of variety.

Beaver Creek Golf Club, at the foot of Beaver Creek Mountain, offers views of the surrounding ranges in the White River National Forest. For information call (970) 845–5775.

The **Lodge and Spa at Cordillera** has three courses, including one mountain course and a valley course that each provide views of the Sawatch and Gore Mountain Ranges. For information call (970) 926–5100.

Eagle-Vail Golf Course, located between Vail and Beaver Creek, has reasonable fees. Contact Eagle-Vail Golf Course, 0431 Eagle Drive, Avon; (970) 949–5267.

River rafters can contact **Timberline Tours** (P.O. Box 131, Vail, CO 81658; 970–476–1414 or 800–831–1414) for a variety of trips on the Colorado, Arkansas, and Eagle Rivers.

LUNCH: Golden Eagle Inn (located on Beaver Creek Plaza, next to the new outdoor ice rink; 970–949–1940) serves Florida blue crab cakes with asparagus and smoked chicken fettuccine, as well as a wide selection of other entrees.

If you are in Vail at lunchtime, try **Garfinkel's** (970–476–3789), located next to the Eagle Bahn Gondola in Lionshead. Its menu says SKI HARD—PARTY HARDER. Here you'll find pool, Foosball, sports on television, beer on tap, and menu choices such as BLT on Texas toast and chicken quesadilla.

Afternoon

At an altitude of 8,200 feet, the **Betty Ford Alpine Gardens,** located in the **Gerald R. Ford Park,** are the highest public alpine gardens in the world. The botanical gardens are named for Mrs. Ford's contributions to the Vail Valley. Nearly 500 varieties of plants and flowers are featured in the gardens, which are open from "dawn to dusk, snowmelt to snowfall." Admission is free. The Betty Ford Alpine Gardens are located at the east end of Vail Village along the Gore Creek walking path. For additional information contact Vail Alpine Garden Foundation, 183 Gore Creek Drive, Vail; (970) 476–0103.

Another excellent outdoor experience is a visit to the **Vail Nature Center** (601 Vail Valley Drive, Vail; 970–479–2291). Walk the quiet trails on seven acres of mountain vegetation with an experienced naturalist. Visit the interpretive center and inquire about special programs that include a Wildflower Walk, a Beaver Pond Tour, and a Morning Bird Walk. Other classes include Flyfishing and Stream Ecology, as well as Nature's Medicine Chest and Pantry, in which participants learn about plants used to create many modern medicines. The center is open late May through early October from 9:00 A.M. to 5:00 P.M. daily. Admission is $1.00 for persons ages seven and older.

To see memorabilia from the famous 10th Mountain Division, visit the **Colorado Ski Museum and Colorado Ski Hall of Fame** (231 South Frontage Road, Vail; 970–476–1876). This is one of several museums in the country dedicated to the history of skiing. The museum is open from 10:00 A.M. to 5:00 P.M. Tuesday through Sunday; closed during May and October.

DINNER: Chap's Grill & Chophouse. The business card for Chap's reads, "Prime perfection," and the comment is entirely accurate. This four-diamond AAA steakhouse serves an excellent selection of regional game, beef, and seafood. No matter what entree you choose, begin with Chap's signature soup, the smoked pheasant soup, served in an individually sized black kettle that looks like it's traveled across the prairie. Everything about this restaurant says Western, from the cowboy photos on the wall to the hefty flatware and cast-iron miniature skillets in which the side dishes are served on a wooden trivet. The bread basket includes parmesan bread sticks, wheat bread, and traditional San Francisco sourdough served with a selection of butter, kalamata olive spread, or a garlic spread. The filet mignon is grilled to perfection, and the oven-roasted Chilean sea bass is divine. Order coffee (and dessert, if you have room) just to appreciate the presentation, which includes crystallized sugar on a stick and hazelnut cookies. Sit outside on the deck when the weather permits. Heat lamps on the patio take the chill off in the fall. Chap's is open seven days a week; reservations are recommended.

LODGING: Vail Cascade Resort & Spa.

Day 3 / Morning

BREAKFAST: Blu's, (193 East Gore Creek Drive; 970–476–3113) offers a great breakfast menu and a fabulous patio next to Gore Creek.

Return to Denver via I–70 east.

There's More

Gerald R. Ford Amphitheater, located next to Gore Creek east of Vail, is an open-air theater that hosts the Vail International Dance Festival, the Bravo! Vail Valley Music Festival, and the Budweiser Hot Summer Nights Free Concert Series. Call (970) 476–2918.

Kayaking. You really don't have to be a daredevil to try this sport. Novices may start with a kayak designed especially for beginners. For a lesson contact ***Alpine Kayak and Canoe,*** 40690 U.S. Highway 6 and 24, Avon; (970) 949–3350. Beginners to advanced, singles to groups welcome.

Minturn. Located 7 miles west of Vail via I–70, this town (population approximately 1,300) retains its down-to-earth atmosphere but is slowly changing its image. Visit the ***Minturn Market*** for everything from fresh produce to hand-knit sweaters. Open weekends summer through early fall.

Special Events

April. Taste of Vail Après-Ski Event is a palate-pleasing list of activities that include port wine seminars, cooking demonstrations, winemaker dinners, and a mountaintop picnic. For additional information call Vail/Beaver

Creek reservations at (800) 622–3131 or Taste of Vail at (303) 479–0220.

Colorado Microbrewery Tasting draws beer lovers from around the state. Held annually at the Hyatt Regency Beaver Creek, this event is informative and entertaining. Call (970) 949–1234.

May. Teva Whitewater Festival. Vail's annual summer kick-off event features amateur and expert kayak and raft team competition on Gore Creek and the Eagle River. Call (800) 525–3875.

July through August. Bravo! Vail Valley Music Festival. Music fills the valley during these well-attended concerts, held at the Ford Amphitheater, at the Vail Interfaith Chapel, and in Beaver Creek. For information call (970) 827–5700.

November. Hyatt Regency Beaver Creek Resort Wine Symposium. A seminar, reception, and four-course dinner highlight this event, held at the Hyatt Regency Beaver Creek. For details call (970) 949–1234.

Other Recommended Restaurants and Lodgings

Beaver Creek

The Charter (P.O. Box 5310, Beaver Creek, CO 81620; 800–525–6660 or 970–949–6660; www.thecharter.com) is recognized in both the *Condé Nast* and *Zagat* surveys. The Charter offers everything from lodge rooms to five-bedroom condominiums with all the facilities of a first-class hotel. Guests may use the indoor/outdoor pool, sauna, fitness facilities, and full-service spa.

The Ritz-Carlton Bachelor Gulch, 0130 Daybreak Ridge, P.O. Box 9190, Avon, CO; (970) 748–6200 or (800) 576–5582; www.ritzcarlton.com. It may come as a surprise that you can stay at this elegant resort—where every flower is fresh, staff are super friendly, and you can borrow the resort's resident Labrador retriever (named Bachelor) to go on hikes with you—for as little as $140/night, during off-peak travel months. (You'll still have to pay the $19/day rate for the valet to park your car.) The luxury year-round resort is situated in a stunning setting on Beaver Creek Mountain. Winter visitors will find superb skiing conditions and summer visitors can golf, fly fish, mountain bike, or go on a field trip with the resort's wildlife concierge and plant a tree.

Edwards

The Lodge and Spa at Cordillera, 2205 Cordillera Way, P.O. Box 1110, Edwards, CO 81632; (970) 926–2200 or (800) 877–3529. Rated in the top fifteen America's Best Spas by *Travel & Leisure* readers, the Lodge and Spa at Cordillera is the place to be pampered. With its European chateau atmosphere, world-class fitness facility, and mountain setting, this lodge has much to offer. Four magnificent golf courses are available. Summer visitors may hike, ride horses, play tennis, or spend time in the indoor and outdoor swimming pools. Winter brings snowshoeing, nearby downhill skiing, or Nordic skiing on 15 miles of trails on the property. Rates vary with the season and can be as low as $150 for a double queen in spring and fall. To get to the Lodge and Spa at Cordillera, take the Edwards exit (number 163) off I–70 and turn south. Turn right onto Route 6 at the one and only stoplight in Edwards, and then left onto Squaw Creek Road. Continue for about 2 miles to the security gate, located across from the Cordillera Equestrian Center.

Vail

Black Bear Inn, 2405 Elliott Road; (970) 476–1304. This log-cabin inn is located along beautiful Gore Creek. A full breakfast and afternoon appetizers are included with stay.

Larkspur Restaurant, 458 Vail Valley Drive; (970) 479–8050. Described as having a "contemporary, California" menu that includes both caviar and asparagus salad, the Larkspur is one of the finest restaurants in the region. Service is superb. Larkspur has seasonal hours, so be sure to call ahead.

Joe's Famous Deli & Homemade Ice Cream, 288 Bridge Street (across from Vendetta's) in Vail Village; (970) 479–7580. Yes, there is a Joe, and his homemade ice cream and gelato are outstanding. This is a great place for a casual breakfast or lunch. They serve breakfast burritos and Joe's famous breakfast sandwiches on focaccia bread in the morning, and grilled sandwiches, including a reuben and hot pastrami, for lunch.

The Lodge at Vail, 174 East Gore Creek Drive; (970) 476–5011 or (800) 231–0136; www.lodgeatvail.com. This luxury resort nestles at the base of Vail Mountain. Walk out the door into the heart of Vail Village. The lodge's superb restaurant, the Wildflower, offers lunch specials at $8.95 and wickedly delicious desserts.

Savory Inn & Cooking School of Vail, 2405 Elliott Ranch Road; (970)

476–1304; www.savoryinn.com. Set among lofty pines and the meandering Gore Creek, this romantic B&B is the ultimate mountain lodge retreat. Join a cooking class where you'll receive hands-on instruction about everything from sushi to barbecued ribs. You can also sign up for the "Evening in Italy" dinner. A local chef teaches you how to prepare veal saltimbocca with asparagus risotto ($85/person).

Sitzmark Lodge, 183 Gore Creek Drive; (970) 476–5001 or (800) 476–5001; www.sitzmarklodge.com. This charming inn offers creekside and mountainview rooms, each with a balcony that overlooks Vail Village.

Sweet Basil, 193 East Gore Creek Drive; (970) 476–0125. Lunch is a better bargain than dinner at this popular restaurant, but you can be assured that whenever you dine here, the food and service will be outstanding. Sweet Basil offers seasonal specials such as mushroom appetizers and chocolate truffles in the autumn, when mushrooms are abundant.

Minturn

Turntable Restaurant, 1160 Main Street, Minturn; (970) 827–4164. Don't let the exterior of this plain-looking structure stop you from trying this outstanding no-frills restaurant. The Turntable is a local favorite on Sundays for great breakfast burritos and the morning newspaper. Check out the "Blue Plate Specials" on the board. The only drawbacks are the line out the door on weekends and the sometimes frazzled servers. Open daily from 6:30 A.M. to 9:30 P.M.

For More Information

Eagle Valley Chamber of Commerce, P.O. Box 964, Eagle, CO 81631; (970) 328–5220.

Vail/Beaver Creek Reservations, P.O. Box 7, Vail, CO 81658; (800) 427–8308 or (970) 845–5990; www.vail.com or www.beavercreek.com.

Vail Valley Tourism and Convention Bureau, 100 East Meadow Drive, Suite 34, Vail, CO 81657; (800) 525–3875 or (970) 476–1000; www.visit vailvalley.com.

Leadville

Historic Mining Town High in the Rockies

1 Night

At an elevation of 10,200 feet, Leadville is the country's highest incorporated city. The "Cloud City" boasts the highest of many things, including the highest church steeple in North America; views of the state's two tallest peaks, Mount Elbert and Mount Massive; and as local judge Neil Reynolds likes to say, "the highest court in the country."

- ☐ Mining museum
- ☐ Burro races
- ☐ Halloween cemetery tour
- ☐ Mineral Belt Trail
- ☐ Victorian B&Bs
- ☐ Lattes

Here the air is thin and the residents hardy. Even when the temperature hovers at freezing, many locals wear shorts and sandals.

This former mining boomtown is one of the state's most historic communities. The "Unsinkable" Molly Brown (of *Titanic* fame) and "Baby Doe" Tabor are legendary past residents. Horace Tabor made his fortune here in the glory days; divorced his wife, Augusta; and married the beautiful, young "Baby Doe." Tabor died penniless but instructed Baby Doe to "hang on to the Matchless." She froze to death thirty-six years later in her cabin next to the Matchless Mine above Leadville.

In its heyday in the late 1800s, Leadville was one of the country's biggest silver-mining areas, with a rough-and-rowdy reputation. Saloons, brothels, and gambling halls lined the streets and public hangings were frequent.

Today, lattes have arrived, and Leadville is enjoying another boom. Refurbished bed-and-breakfast inns, coffeehouses, and Victorian homes painted in soft pastels greet visitors. Nearby Ski Cooper, Vail, and Copper Mountain offer an abundance of ski runs.

The National Mining Hall of Fame and Museum showcases past and present mining methods through dioramas; replicas of an underground hardrock mine; prospector's cave; and displays of gold, silver, and other minerals.

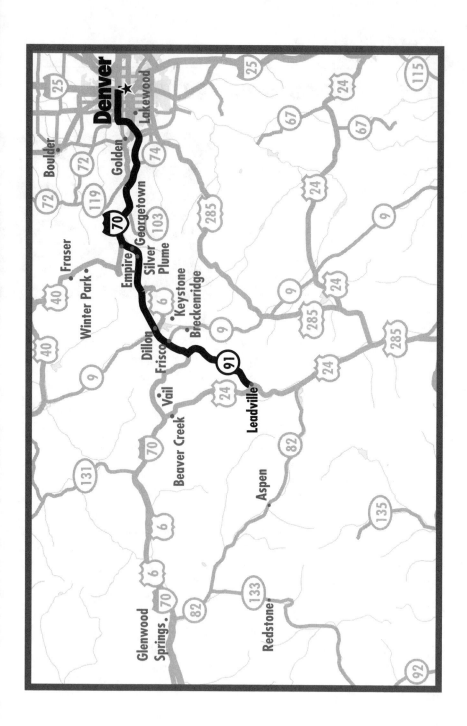

Even though the town has a relatively small population (2,800), it supports two weekly newspapers. The *Leadville Chronicle* and the *Herald Democrat* hit the stands every Thursday with announcements of council meetings, local news, the occasional ice-fishing derby, and what's happening around town.

Visitors will enjoy this friendly mountain community, where the town has two stoplights and residents park snowmobiles in their front yards.

Day 1 / Morning

Leadville is 103 miles southwest of Denver. Take I–70 west to the Copper Mountain exit (exit 195). Turn south onto Colorado Highway 91 and continue 24 miles to Leadville.

LUNCH: Columbine Café, 612 Harrison Avenue; (719) 486–3599. The Columbine serves breakfast (great breakfast burritos) and lunch (try the black-bean burger) daily from 6:00 A.M. to 3:00 P.M.

Afternoon

Be sure to make a stop at the Chamber of Commerce Visitor Center (809 Harrison Avenue, P.O. Box 861, Leadville, CO 80461; 800–933–3900; www.leadvilleusa.com). Here you can pick up maps, brochures, and weather reports, as well as a copy of the *Leadville Magazine,* which has a good map of town. Directions to each site seem to begin "From the stoplight." The light (one of two in town) at Sixth and Harrison is a handy landmark. The visitor center is open 9:00 A.M. to 5:00 P.M. daily.

The **National Mining Hall of Fame and Museum** (120 West Ninth Street; 719–486–1229) is housed in a 70,000-square-foot Victorian school building and has countless exhibits, displays, murals, historic photographs, and mining memorabilia. Don't miss the twenty-three-ounce specimen of gold retrieved from the Little Jonny Mine, the mine that helped make Molly Brown a wealthy woman.

Jewelry, mining-related books, and mineral specimens are for sale at the gift shop on-site. Summer hours for the museum (May through October) are 9:00 A.M. to 5:00 P.M. daily. Winter hours (November through April) are 10:00 A.M. to 2:00 P.M. Monday through Saturday. Admission is $6.00 for adults, $5.00 for seniors, and $3.00 for children six to eleven. Kids under six are admitted free.

Stop in at the **Silver Dollar Saloon** (315 Harrison Avenue; 719–486–9914), which locals have dubbed "The Dollar." Food is limited to

The National Mining Hall of Fame and Museum in Leadville is housed in a former Victorian school building.

popcorn, beef jerky, pistachios, and cashews, so it's not a dinner option; however, as one of Leadville's oldest establishments, the Silver Dollar is well worth a visit. The bar opened in 1879 and today shows off its original handsome oak back bar with inlaid diamond-dust mirror. The McMahon family purchased the bar in 1942, which explains the photos of Ireland, Guinness on the list of available beers, and its reputation as an Irish pub. In true pub style, sit at the bar and make yourself at home.

DINNER: For more substantial fare, visit **Quincy's Steak & Spirits** (416 Harrison Avenue; 719–486–9765). This fine restaurant offers a one-item menu, but it's a dandy. Prime rib (choice of eight, twelve, sixteen, or twenty ounces) is the selection on Friday and Saturday, and filet mignon is on the menu Sunday through Thursday. New York cheesecake and chocolate mousse are dessert options. A full-service bar is available. Don't fret about a reservation unless your party numbers eight or more. Quincy's is open year-round from 5:00 to 9:30 P.M. daily, except Christmas, Thanksgiving, and "when the Denver Broncos play in the Super Bowl."

LODGING: The **Leadville Country Inn,** 127 East Eighth Street; (719) 486–2354 or (800) 748–2354; www.leadvillebednbreakfast.com. As one of Leadville's premier Victorian B&Bs, the Leadville Country Inn has nine rooms, each uniquely decorated with period furniture. You'll find four-poster beds, an antique copper tub, and a carriage house at this restored Queen Anne Victorian. Prices range from $68 to $158.

Day 2 / Morning

BREAKFAST: The Leadville Country Inn serves a full breakfast, which may include an egg casserole, quiche, or German puff pancakes with banana-orange sauce.

If you didn't get enough Victoriana at the Leadville Country Inn, the **Healy House** (912 Harrison Avenue, Leadville; 719–486–0487) is a good stop. Take a self-guided tour through this 1878 two-story, Victorian home. The smoking room has a beautiful mahogany desk once owned by Colorado governor Jesse McDonald. Each bedroom upstairs had its own heating stove. Healy House is open Memorial Day through Labor Day from 10:00 A.M. to 4:30 P.M., or by appointment.

In the summer, visitors may attend a one-woman performance depicting the life of Baby Doe Tabor. Shows begin at 7:00 P.M. Tuesday and Friday at the Healy House. Adult ticket price is $14.00; children twelve and under, $6.00. Call (719) 486–0487 for information.

There's More

Colorado Trail. Access the Lake County portion of this 471-mile hiking trail, which stretches across the state, at Tennessee Pass off U.S. Highway 24 north of Leadville.

Mineral Belt Trail. This 12-mile paved path loops around town. Rent bikes at Bill's Sport Shop, 225 Harrison Avenue; (719) 486–0739.

Ski Cooper, 9 miles north of Leadville on Highway 24, offers $33 lift tickets. This was the original training site for the 10th Mountain Division. Chicago Ridge Sno-Cat Tours are available for backcountry adventures. Snowboarders are welcome at Ski Cooper. Open late November through the end of March. Rentals and lessons also available. Call (719) 486–3684 or (719) 486–2277 or (800) 707–6114.

Tabor Opera House, 315 Harrison Avenue, Leadville; (719) 486–3900. Horace (H. A. W.) Tabor built the opera house in 1879, and opening night was November 20 of that year. In those days, the opera house was said by many to be the finest theater between St. Louis and San Francisco. Self-guided, tape-narrated tours are available in the summer from 10:00 A.M. to 5:00 P.M.

Special Events

August. International Pack Burro Race. This 21-mile race is a favorite with spectators every summer and is the highlight of Boom Days. Gentlemen and ladies lead their burros to the top of Mosquito Pass, at an elevation of 13,183 feet above sea level. Burros carry a thirty-five-pound pack and are led rather than ridden to the summit and back to Leadville. Call (719) 486–3900 or (800) 933–3901.

October. Downtown Murder and Mayhem Tour or Cemetery Tour. (These tours rotate: one year is the downtown tour and the next is the cemetery tour.) The weather is perfectly spooky for a guided tour of twenty-one murder sites or the cemetery. City Judge Neil Reynolds, a fifth-generation Leadville resident, entertains with endless ghost stories. He casts an elegant figure with his handlebar mustache, walking stick, and pipe. In addition to serving as Municipal Court Judge, Reynolds is a faculty member at Colorado Mountain College and is chairman of the Lake County Historical Preservation Advisory Board. For details call the chamber at (719) 486–3900 or (800) 933–3901.

Other Recommended Restaurants and Lodgings

Cloud City Coffee House, 711 Harrison Avenue, Leadville; (719) 486–1317. Lattes, espressos, and conversation abound here. Sandwiches, soups, salads, and quiche are also available. Open Monday through Saturday from 6:00 A.M. to 7:00 P.M., and Sunday from 6:00 A.M. to 6:00 P.M.

Delaware Hotel, 700 Harrison Avenue, Leadville; (719) 486–1418 or (800) 748–2004; www.delawarehotel.com. This Victorian hotel is listed on the National Register of Historic Places and is conveniently located in the middle of town.

Ice Palace Inn Bed and Breakfast, 813 Spruce, Leadville; (719) 486–8272 or (800) 754–2840. This charmer has a parlor where guests may enjoy hot chocolate in front of a roaring fire.

Tennessee Pass Cookhouse, located 1 mile from the base of Ski Cooper; (719) 486–8114 or (719) 486–1750; www.skicooper.com/cookhouse .html. In the winter, guests arrive via snowmobile, snowshoes, or cross-country skis, and in the summer, visitors may hike, mountain bike, or ride in a back-country vehicle. The four-course dinner includes your choice of elk, trout, or lamb. Fifty dollars per person includes equipment, guides, and dinner, but no tax, gratuity, or alcohol. Lunch is available on weekends and holidays. Tour meets at Piney Creek Nordic Center at Ski Cooper at 6:00 P.M. Call ahead for reservations.

For More Information

Chamber of Commerce, 809 Harrison Avenue, Leadville, CO 80461; (719) 486–3900 or (800) 933–3901; www.leadvilleusa.com.

Glenwood Springs

Take a Soak

1 Night

Located at the foot of spectacular Glenwood Canyon and next door to the Colorado River, Glenwood Springs boasts the world's largest natural outdoor hot-springs pool. And what a lagoon it is! Relax in the steamy, soothing waters as you gaze out onto the mountainous backdrop.

- ☐ Hot springs
- ☐ Historic hotels
- ☐ Glenwood Caverns
- ☐ Vapor Caves
- ☐ Firefighter memorials

Before it became known for its resort atmosphere, this area was the meeting place for the Utes, who called the region *Yampah,* which means "big medicine." Today you can indulge in a massage or herbal Jacuzzi at the Yampah Spa and Vapor Caves.

The town's Hotel Colorado is known for its historic stateliness. When Theodore Roosevelt stayed here in 1905 after hunting bear in the area, the grand lodge came to be called the Summer White House of the West. One story says that hotel maids fashioned a bear from fabric after Roosevelt's unsuccessful hunt, hence the origination of the teddy bear. The Hotel Denver, located across from the train station, began as a boardinghouse. Today, the renovated lodge has its own brewpub.

The region offers a wealth of sports activities that include golf, rafting, and fishing during summer, and skiing, snowmobiling, and ice fishing during winter. A nighttime visit to the hot springs is a good end to any day.

Day 1 / Morning

From Denver, head west on I–70 for 158 miles to Glenwood Springs. You'll travel the four-lane interstate through Glenwood Canyon. This 18-mile stretch is billed as one of the most remarkable and beautiful roadways ever built.

LUNCH: Hot Springs Pool Deli, 401 North River Street, Glenwood Springs; (970) 945–7131. This casual restaurant has daily specials that

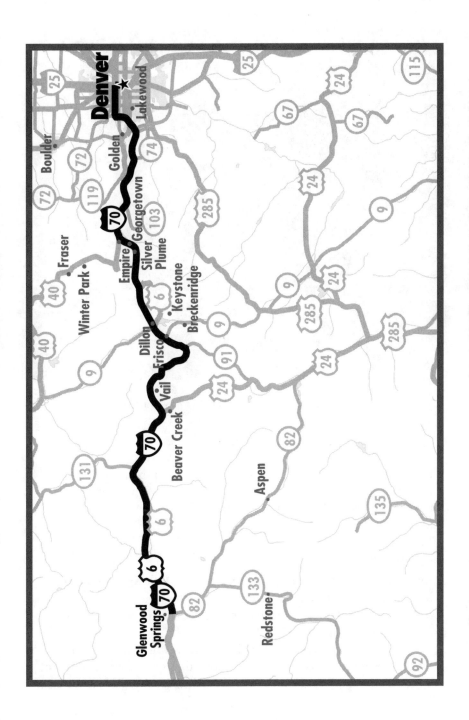

Glenwood Springs boasts the largest natural outdoor hot-springs pool.

change, but you might find grilled cheese with seven-bean soup or cream of potato soup. Other choices include roast beef dinner, stuffed baked potatoes, and cheeseburgers. The restaurant is open from 7:30 A.M. to 8:00 P.M. daily.

Afternoon

After lunch, sunbathe in the grassy area near the **Hot Springs Pool,** or, if it's winter, soak in one of the two steamy pools and watch snowflakes fall. The larger pool is maintained at 90 degrees Fahrenheit and the smaller pool at 104 degrees.

Every six hours some three-and-a-half million gallons of water from the springs refill the large pool. Kids love the water slide. At the Hot Springs Athletic Club, guests can use the indoor Jacuzzi, play racquetball, or lift weights for an additional fee.

The pools are open every day of the year (except when they are being cleaned) and have been since 1888. Hours are 9:00 A.M. to 10:00 P.M. during the winter and 7:30 A.M. to 10:00 P.M. during summer. A daily pass is $11.00 for adults and $7.00 for children ages three to twelve. For more information call (970) 945–7131 or (800) 537–7946.

Across from the Hot Springs Pool is the **Glenwood Springs Center for the Arts** (970–945–2414), which exhibits work by local artists. Hours are Monday through Friday from 10:00 A.M. to 4:00 P.M. and Saturday and Sunday from noon to 4:00 P.M.

Visit the two **Storm King Mountain Memorials,** which honor the fourteen firefighters who lost their lives while battling a fire in nearby South Canyon on July 6, 1994. A sculpture of three firefighters is located at Two Rivers Park in Glenwood Springs; take Sixth Street west to Devereaux Road and turn left to Two Rivers Park. The other memorial is a trail located 2 miles outside the city, at the scene of the blaze. To reach the trail, take I–70 west from Glenwood Springs to the Canyon Creek exit (number 109); drive east for 0.5 mile, park, and hike the 1.5-mile trail at the base of Storm King Mountain.

DINNER: **Glenwood Canyon Brewing Company,** located in the Hotel Denver, 402 Seventh Street; (970) 945–1276. This restaurant and pub are housed on the site of a turn-of-the-twentieth-century bottling plant. Exposed brick and large windows create a pleasant atmosphere in both the bar and the restaurant. Handcrafted beers on tap include Hanging Lake Honey Ale (made with local honey) and Vapor Cave India Pale Ale. For starters, try the Canyon Quesadilla or the Macho Nachos. In brewery tradition, brewpub bread bowls include soup or stew served in hollowed-out loaves of round bread. The Wisconsin Cheddar cheese beer soup is delectable. Other choices include grilled salmon fillet, baked baby back ribs, and Maine lobster soft tacos. Authentic old-fashioned root beer made with local honey is available. The brewery opens at 11:00 A.M. daily.

LODGING: **Hotel Colorado,** 526 Pine Street; (800) 544–3998 or (970) 945–6511; www.hotelcolorado.com. This dignified lodging, with its 128 rooms, counts among its visitors American presidents William Howard Taft and Theodore Roosevelt. The hotel is ideally located, adjacent to the Hot Springs Pool. Many rooms are decorated with period antiques. Ask to see the penthouse suites on the fifth floor—you'll have to climb the stairs to see the two bell-tower suites, but doing so is worth the effort.

Day 2 / Morning

BREAKFAST: The **Grand Lobby** in the Hotel Colorado has traditional breakfast fare as well as nontraditional items, including a breakfast quesadilla, and smoked trout and a bagel. The restaurant serves breakfast from 7:00 to 11:00 A.M. daily.

Walk the short distance from Hotel Colorado to the **Yampah Spa and Vapor Caves** and sweat out your cares in the 115-degree steam caves. Pamper yourself with a European body wrap, a mud bath, an herbal facial, or a rose-petal masque. Rest in the solarium after your massage. The Vapor Caves are open from 9:00 A.M. to 9:00 P.M. daily. To make an appointment for a massage, contact Yampah Spa and Vapor Caves, 709 East Sixth Street, Glenwood Springs; (970) 945–0667.

Stories say that famous gunman Doc Holliday came west to Glenwood Springs in 1887 in search of a cure for his tuberculosis, but the disease was already in an advanced stage. Holliday died at age thirty-five, supposedly in bed with his boots on at the Glenwood Hotel. Today you can visit the grave of the legendary gunslinger. The trail to Holliday's grave begins at Twelfth Street and Bennett Avenue. From there it's a moderate 0.5-mile hike to the historic Linwood Cemetery. Look for the signs that lead to Holliday's grave. Anonymous donors often leave a deck of cards or a whiskey bottle on the site.

LUNCH: Daily Bread Cafe and Bakery, 729 Grand Avenue; (970) 945–6253. Breads and pastries baked from scratch highlight the menu at this restaurant. The spinach salad satisfies even the grandest appetite. Other options include taco salad, tuna grill, and a bacon, mushroom, and onion burger. Save room for a piece of peach or chocolate Kahlúa pecan pie. The cafe is open from 7:00 A.M. to 2:00 P.M. Monday through Friday, from 8:00 A.M. to 2:00 P.M. Saturday, and for breakfast only from 8:00 A.M. to noon Sunday.

Afternoon

Glenwood Caverns Adventure Park, 51000 Two Rivers Plaza Road; (970) 945–4228 or (800) 530–1635; www.glenwoodcaverns.com. Located 1.2 miles north of Glenwood Springs, this family entertainment and education destination offers a Panorama Nature Trail, Discovery Rock (where kids can pan for jewels), and Iron Mountain Saloon. Tours of Historic Fairy Caves are also available. The Iron Mountain Tramway carries visitors 4,300 feet up the side of the mountain in a gondola cabin. Ticket prices for the

Tramway are $15 for adults, $10 for children ages 3 to 12. Glenwood Caverns Adventure Park is open year-round.

There's More

Amtrak. Take the train from Denver's Union Station to Glenwood Springs. The five-and-a-half-hour trip takes passengers through fabulous scenery and more than thirty-five tunnels. For a schedule call Amtrak at (800) 872–7245.

Frontier Historical Museum, 1001 Colorado Avenue, Glenwood Springs; (970) 945–4448. The museum holds the bedroom furnishings from Colorado's legendary couple Horace and Baby Doe Tabor. From May through September the museum's hours are 11:00 A.M. to 4:00 P.M. Monday through Saturday. From October through April its hours are 1:00 to 4:00 P.M. Monday, Thursday, Friday, and Saturday.

River rafting. Spend a half-day or an entire day in a raft on the Colorado or Roaring Fork Rivers. Contact Rock Gardens Rafting, Inc., 1308 County Road 129, Glenwood Springs; (970) 945–6737.

Snowmobiling. The Sunlight to Powderhorn Trail, a recreational trail, runs from Sunlight Mountain Resort all the way to Powderhorn near Grand Junction. The trail is well groomed and well marked. For rentals and information call Rocky Mountain Sports, 2177 Forest Service Road 30, Glenwood Springs; (970) 945–8885.

Sunlight Mountain Resort. This small resort, 10 miles southwest of Glenwood Springs off Highway 82, offers friendly service and affordable rates. You can rent downhill or cross-country gear, take lessons, and enjoy a day on the slopes for much less than it would cost at many other resorts. Many lodges offer a "ski, swim, and stay" package deal with lift ticket and pool pass included. Take Highway 82 south (also known as Grand Avenue) from Glenwood Springs to Four Mile Road (County Road 117). Signs will direct you to the ski area. Additionally, shuttles run regularly from town to the resort. For information call Sunlight Mountain Resort at (800) 445–7931 or (970) 945–7491.

Special Events

Third full weekend in June. Glenwood Springs's Strawberry Days began in 1897. It's the city's biggest and most popular happening, and you won't want to miss the free strawberries and ice cream.

June–August. Summer of Jazz. On Wednesday evenings musicians gather to put on a free show of blues, Dixieland, and jazz. The show starts at 6:30 at Two Rivers Park, Highway 6 and Two Rivers Park Road. For information call (970) 945–6589.

Other Recommended Restaurants and Lodgings

Glenwood Springs

Hotel Denver, 402 Seventh Street, Glenwood Springs; (970) 945–6565 or (800) 826–8820. Built in 1906, this lodge is located directly across from the train station and offers special weekend package deals.

Ingrid's Cup and Saucer (310 Seventh Street, across from the train depot; 970–928–8973) offers fresh bread, pastries, quiche, coffee, and tea.

Italian Underground, 715 Grand Avenue; (970) 945–6422. This classic Italian restaurant offers red-checked tablecloths, excellent food, historic photos of Glenwood Springs on the walls, and a cozy, downstairs location. You'll find classic favorites such as linguine with pesto sauce and fettuccine Alfredo. You may also discover a long wait for a table, so try to arrive early. (No reservations accepted.) The atmosphere is lively and the entrees are less than $10. The Italian Underground is open daily from 5:00 to 10:00 P.M.

Nineteenth Street Diner, 1908 Grand Avenue; (970) 945–9133. Order a Philly cheese steak, then adjourn to the bar to watch some sports on the television at this casual restaurant.

Sacred Grounds Coffee House and Delicatessen, 725 Grand Avenue; (970) 928–8804. Locals gather here for java.

Sopris Restaurant and Lounge, located 5 miles south of Glenwood Springs on Highway 82; (970) 945–7771. This restaurant has an extensive wine list and fresh seafood, steak, and veal. Open from 5:00 P.M. daily.

Redstone

To get to Redstone, drive 12 miles south on Highway 82 to Carbondale and continue west on Highway 133 another 24 miles to Redstone.

Redstone Inn (82 Redstone Boulevard; 970–963–2526 or 800–748–2524) offers lodging and a restaurant. Prices are affordable (from $40 to $195), and guests can choose a room with shower down the hall, a cozy room in the clock tower with great views, or a suite with private veranda. Enjoy Brie-stuffed mushrooms and Colorado prime rib on the patio overlooking the pool, or dine in the formal restaurant.

For More Information

Central Reservations, (888) 445–3696.

Glenwood Springs Chamber Resort Association, 1102 Grand Avenue, Glenwood Springs, CO 81602; (970) 945–6589; www.visitglenwood.com.

Aspen

One of the World's Most Beautiful Settings

2 Nights

Aspen is indeed the place to schmooze, schuss, and cruise the après-ski hot spots, but this famous town is also a cultural mecca and recreational paradise. Visit during the summer months, when the Aspen Music Festival and

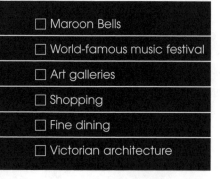

☐ Maroon Bells

☐ World-famous music festival

☐ Art galleries

☐ Shopping

☐ Fine dining

☐ Victorian architecture

School is in full swing, and you'll get a taste of everything from classical to opera as melodies permeate idyllic afternoons. Raft the rivers, climb the mountains, or uncover that elusive bargain in one of the trendy boutiques. Snowcapped peaks, Victorian homes, and tree-lined streets welcome you to this region, which combines jet-setters, celebrities, longtime residents, and tourists.

On the slopes, Aspen's runs rate as world-class. Off the slopes, Aspen is a bona fide community with year-round residents, town festivals, and Friday-night little-league games.

Day 1 / Morning

In the winter drive west on I–70 to Glenwood Springs and then southeast on Colorado Highway 82 to Aspen (a total of 220 miles from Denver). During the summer months, take the scenic route (160 miles from Denver). Follow I–70 west to Copper Mountain, take Highway 91 south through Leadville to the junction with Highway 82, and travel over Independence Pass into Aspen.

When you arrive in Aspen, stop at the **Aspen Chamber Resort Association** (425 Rio Grande Place; 970–925–1940). From Main Street, turn north onto Mill Street. Turn right onto Rio Grande Place and immediately turn right into the parking circle. The center is open from 8:00

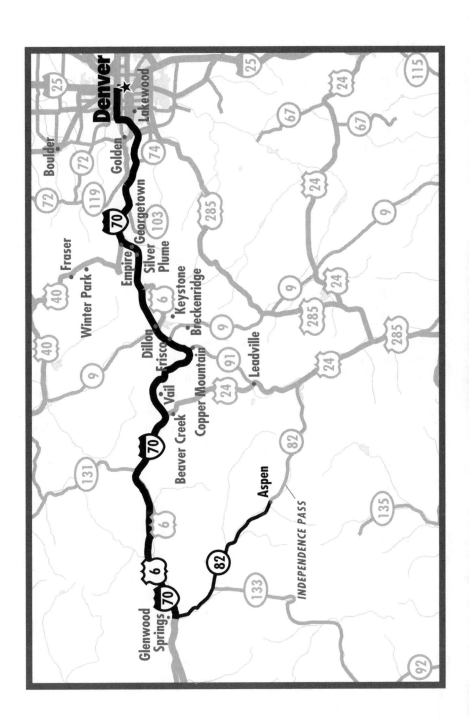

A.M. to 5:00 P.M. Monday through Friday; closed weekends and holidays. Visit www.aspenchamber.org.

LUNCH: Boogie's Diner (534 East Cooper Avenue; 970–925–6610) has appetizers such as Chubby Checker Chicken Fingers and Boogie's Baltimore Chicken Wings. Entrees include the Monster Mash Meat Loaf Dinner; Elvis's favorite, "The Hound Dog"; and macaroni and cheese. Indulge in Ben & Jerry's ice cream for dessert.

Afternoon

Art lovers can explore to their heart's content in Aspen's more than forty galleries. Pick up the complimentary copy of *Aspen Magazine*'s Gallery Guide, which has a map and listings. You'll find a superior selection of photography, paintings, sculpture, jewelry, weavings, and more. **Footloose and Fancy Things** (240 South Mill Street; 970–925–9155) has a selection of handmade moccasins, jewelry, belts, and a large collection of original E. S. Curtis photogravures.

To see exhibits from local and nationally acclaimed artists, visit the **Aspen Art Museum** (590 North Mill Street; 970–925–8050). The museum is housed in a former hydroelectric plant on the banks of the Roaring Fork River. The museum is open from 10:00 A.M. to 6:00 P.M. Tuesday, Wednesday, Friday, and Saturday; from 10:00 A.M. to 7:00 P.M. Thursday; and from noon to 6:00 P.M. Sunday. Admission is $5.00.

"Power shop" the exquisite boutiques, recreational stores, and bookshops that Aspen offers. **Aspen Sports** (408 East Cooper Avenue; 970–925–6331) has an extensive selection of outdoor clothing.

DINNER: Lucci's, 508 East Cooper Avenue; (970) 925–8866. Visit this cozy downstairs restaurant for affordable Italian dining. Entrees run from $5.00 to $20.00. In addition to the usual spaghetti and meatballs and lasagna, the menu also offers grilled lamb chops and veal piccata. The chicken marsala is superb. Open for dinner from 5:30 to 9:00 P.M. nightly.

LODGING: The **St. Regis Aspen,** 315 East Dean Street; (970) 920–3300 or (888) 454–9005; www.stregis.com. Nestled at the foot of Aspen Mountain and only steps away from the boutiques and bistros downtown, the St. Regis offers a choice address. A sophisticated ambience, international clientele, and one of the best sun-bathing pools in Aspen are among the first things guests will notice about this tasteful hotel. An extremely courteous staff and small luxuries, such as the "tomorrow's weather forecast" card placed in your room each night, create its congenial atmosphere. Guest rooms are decorated in soft florals; larger-than-life marble bathrooms come complete with scales and terry robes. Rates vary with type of room and time of year. A standard room begins at $240 in the off-season and climbs from there. Be prepared to pay an extra $26 per day for parking.

Day 2 / *Morning*

BREAKFAST: **Poppycock's** (665 East Cooper Avenue; 970–925–1245) specializes in affordable breakfasts and terrific smoothies.

Ski & Snowboard School of Aspen offers a program for skiers called Beginner's Magic. Participants get three days (Friday to Sunday) of lift tickets, lessons, and equipment rentals for $219. A one-day class is available for $99. First-time snowboarders may try First Time Riders. Prices are the same. Call (970) 925–1220 or (800) 525–6200.

If skiing is not on your agenda, there are numerous other options.

Take a walking tour of Aspen and learn about the historic past of this community. Originally, the area was hunting land for the Ute Indians and later prospered with silver mining in the late 1800s. Call **Heritage Aspen,** formerly **Aspen Historical Society,** at (970) 925–3721 for information.

The **Silver Queen Gondola,** at the base of the ski area, lifts riders to the 11,212-foot summit of Aspen Mountain in twenty minutes. At the top are views of Elk Mountain Range. The gondola is open 10:00 A.M. to 4:00 P.M. daily, mid-June through August, and weekends the first half of June and the month of September. Ask about free concerts, nature walks, and high-altitude Frisbee golf at the summit.

LUNCH: In winter, skiers and nonskiers alike can ride the Silver Queen Gondola to have lunch at **Sundeck Restaurant** (970–920–6335), located at the top of Aspen Mountain. Relax on the outdoor deck as you enjoy the views and lunch items such as elk chili or pizza. The Sundeck serves lunch from 11:00 A.M. to 3:30 P.M. daily.

Afternoon

Among the most photographed peaks in North America, **Maroon Bells** is located just outside Aspen. With nearly 100 miles of trails, you can spend hours taking pictures and hiking this scenic area. Cars are not allowed on Maroon Creek Road between 8:00 A.M. and 5:00 P.M. June through Labor Day and weekends in September. If you are visiting at that time, plan to take the Roaring Fork Transit Authority shuttle to the base of the mountains. The driver gives an interesting history of the area and points out places where avalanches have occurred. If you drive your car to Maroon Bells, take Highway 82 from Aspen for 1 mile west and exit the roundabout at Maroon Creek Road.

As home to Aspen's art community, the **Wheeler Opera House** (320 East Hyman Avenue; 970–920–5770) has been restored to its original Victorian splendor. The three-story building is both a museum and a state-of-the-art performance center. This showpiece structure features velvet stage curtains, a red carpet, and lavish period furnishings. Take a tour or, better yet, attend a ballet, opera (during the Aspen Music Festival), or theater performance. The Wheeler Opera House is located on the corner of Mill Street and Hyman Avenue Mall. For more information visit www.wheeleroperahouse.com.

DINNER: Su Casa, 315 East Hyman Avenue; (970) 920–1488. If you like green chili, this is the place for dinner. Chips and chunky salsa, delicious (and potent!) margaritas, and fajitas served with pico de gallo and jicama salad help make Su Casa a favorite. Su Casa serves dinner from 5:00 to 10:00 P.M. nightly.

LODGING: The St. Regis Aspen.

Day 3 / Morning

BREAKFAST: Paradise Bakery, 320 South Galena Street; (970) 925–7585. Follow your nose to this local favorite, established in 1976. Cinnamon rolls baked on-site, cappuccino, and a copy of the *Aspen Times* begin your day. Paradise Bakery opens at 7:00 A.M.

Return to Denver via Highway 82 west to Glenwood Springs and I–70 east.

There's More

Ashcroft mining town. Located 13 miles from Aspen in the Castle Creek Valley, Ashcroft once boasted 2,500 residents in its heyday as a mining camp in the late 1800s. Today you can tour the old buildings and hike the nearby trails. To get to Ashcroft from Aspen, follow Highway 82 west to Castle Creek Road. Turn left and travel on Castle Creek Road for 12 miles. For information call Heritage Aspen, formerly the Aspen Historical Society, at (970) 925–3721.

River rafting. For a trip down the Roaring Fork, contact **Colorado Riff Raft** (555 East Durant Avenue, P.O. Box 4949, Aspen, CO 81612; 800–759–3939 or 970–925–5405). Cruise the Pinball Rapids and the Raft Ripper Rapids on the Arkansas River. Another rafting company is **Blazing Adventures** (P.O. Box 5068, Snowmass Village, CO 81615; 800–282–7238 or 970–925–5651).

Rocky Mountain Institute, 2317 Snowmass Creek Road, Old Snowmass; (970) 927–3851. This world-famous think tank was created with research in mind. Free guided tours are conducted Friday at 2:00 P.M.; visitors can take a self-guided tour anytime from 9:00 A.M. to 4:30 P.M. Monday through Friday. To get to the institute from Aspen, drive north on Highway 82 for 14 miles to Old Snowmass and go left. Follow Snowmass Creek Road for 1.7 miles.

Special Events

June. The *Food & Wine Magazine* Classic at Aspen is one of the largest and most prestigious events of its kind. The world's leading chefs and wine experts gather to participate in cooking demonstrations, wine and food tastings, and seminars. Call (970) 925–9000.

June–August. Aspen Music Festival and School. An impressive roster of visiting conductors and guest artists highlight this renowned event, which attracts musicians, students, and audiences. For a complete calendar call (970) 925–3254 or the concert hot line at (970) 925–3172.

July. The annual Independence Day Parade brings out the entire community for a parade and old-fashioned fun. Wave the American flag and watch veterans in uniform, kids on bikes, men and women on Harleys, and fire trucks parade by. The town hosts a community barbecue after the parade and a display of spectacular fireworks launched high above town from the slopes of Aspen Mountain. For information call (970) 925–1940.

July–August. Aspen Theater in the Park. Experience contemporary theater in an intimate theater tent. For tickets call (970) 920–5070.

Other Recommended Restaurants and Lodgings

Jimmy's: An American Restaurant and Bar, 205 South Mill Street, Aspen; (970) 925–6020. Enjoy a cocktail on the outdoor deck. The menu includes chops, steaks, and ribs. Open daily from 5:30 P.M. to 2:00 A.M.

The Little Nell, 675 East Durant Avenue, Aspen; (970) 920–4600; www
.littlenell@relaischateaux.com. This Relais & Chateaux property, located
in the heart of Aspen, exudes graciousness. Impeccable service and elegant
rooms help make the Little Nell a magnificent mountain retreat.

St. Moritz Lodge & Condominiums, 334 West Hyman Avenue, Aspen;
(970) 925–3220 or (800) 817–2069; www.stmoritzlodge.com. Rooms are
basic but affordable. A continental breakfast is included, and in the summer
the pool is pleasant. In true European style, shared hostel rooms are available, as well as condominiums.

Sardy House, 128 East Main, Aspen; (970) 920–2525 or (800) 321–3457;
www.sardyhouse.com. The parlor of this B&B summons guests to relax in
the inviting velvet-covered sofas and chairs. Furnishings are classy and
comfortable, and you'll find his-and-her terry robes in your room as well
as a towel warmer, feather comforter, and cherry-wood armoire. Breakfast
is served on the patio outside next to the pool or in the antiques-filled
dining room.

T-Lazy-7-Ranch, 3129 Maroon Creek Road, Aspen; (970) 925–4614.
Located in a beautiful area on the road to Maroon Bells, the T-Lazy-7 is a
great place to get away from it all. Enjoy snowmobiling in winter and
horseback riding in summer.

Wienerstube Restaurant, 633 East Hyman Avenue; (970) 925–3357. A
longtime locals' favorite, the Wienerstube specializes in eggs Benedict,
Austrian sausages, and homemade Viennese pastries. The community table
is popular with single diners. Open for breakfast and lunch only, 7:00 A.M.
to 2:30 P.M.

For More Information

Aspen Chamber Resort Association, 425 Rio Grande Place, Aspen, CO
81611; (970) 925–1940 or (800) 262–7736; www.aspenchamber.org.

Aspen Skiing Company, P.O. Box 1248, Aspen, CO 81612; (970)
925–1220 or (800) 525–6200.

Grand Junction and the Grand Valley

Peaches and Wine— How Sweet They Are

2 Nights

Emerging from its reputation as primarily an agricultural and industrial area, Grand Junction is also recognized for its commitment to the arts. Add to this the glorious red canyons of Colorado National Monument and an area so rich in fossils that it delights dino lovers of all ages and you have a treasure trove of an excursion.

- [ ] Winery tours
- [ ] Dino-digging
- [ ] Colorado National Monument
- [ ] Art on the Corner
- [ ] Outdoor recreation

Stroll the tree-lined sidewalks of Main Street Mall and you'll see how Grand Junction is cultivating its image. Enjoy shaded streets, galleries, water fountains, historic structures, boutiques, and free parking. The only "skyscraper" in town has ten stories. The Art on the Corner outdoor exhibit features more than ninety impressive sculptures.

Winemakers have taken a liking to the region's fertile, fruit-producing land and have successfully established 13 wineries in the valley. Drive from vineyard to vineyard and sample a chardonnay, cabernet, Riesling, or fruit wine.

Best of all may be the dinosaur bones and tracks that survived in the Grand Valley. The fossils fascinate any adult or child in a T-Rex tizzy. Wanna-be paleontologists can explore to their heart's content.

Grand Junction makes the perfect jumping-off spot for any number of outdoor adventures. Set up base camp for a few days in this area and you'll have an almost infinite list of sites to uncover.

Day 1 / Morning

Travel west on I–70 to Grand Junction, located 258 miles from Denver.

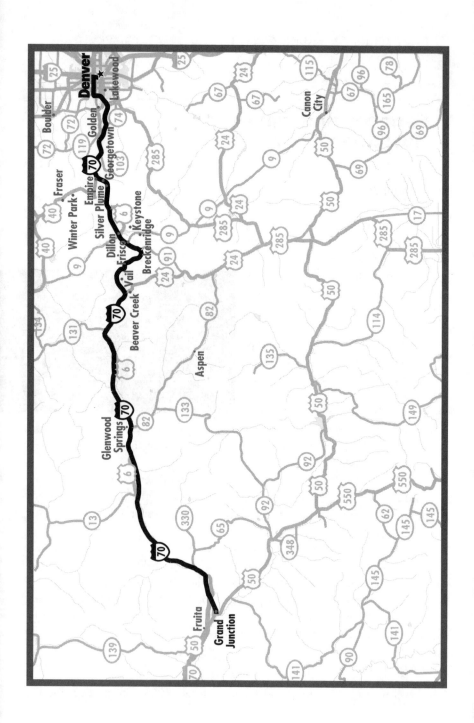

Plan on four-and-a-half hours for the trip, including breakfast.

BREAKFAST: For a midmorning break, stop at the **Eagle Vail Cafe** (41310 Highways 6 and 24, Eagle Vail; 970–949–6393). The cafe serves breakfast (try the *huevos rancheros*) from 8:00 to 11:00 A.M. Monday through Saturday; closed Sunday. To get there from I–70, take the Minturn exit (after West Vail) and travel west on Highway 6. The restaurant is located on the left side of the road. Look for the red canopy near the entrance.

When you arrive in Grand Junction, stop at the visitor center (740 Horizon Drive; 970–256–4060) to stock up on maps and information. This facility has an exceptional display of photographs of the area. The staff here is eager to welcome visitors and answer questions. Be sure to pick up a map of the local wineries.

Take a jaunt downtown to admire the **Art on the Corner** outdoor sculptures, located on Main from First to Seventh Streets. Many of the works are available to purchase. The community votes every year for one sculpture, which becomes part of the permanent display.

LUNCH: **Crystal Cafe,** 314 Main Street, Grand Junction; (970) 242–8843. This family-run restaurant has been a success since the day it opened. Ceiling-size skylights create a light, airy setting, and cuisine here is second to none. Anyone who seeks incredible desserts has come to the right place. Other guaranteed items include quiche of the day served with salad garnish, homemade soup of the day, and the grilled eggplant sandwich. For dessert choose Lila's fresh lemon tart with whipped cream or Marsha's double chocolate cake a la mode with hot fudge. Open Monday through Saturday, from 7:00 A.M. to 2:00 P.M., and also Thursday through Saturday from 5:00 to 9:00 P.M. Closed Sunday.

Afternoon

Visit the **Western Colorado Center for the Arts** (1803 North Seventh Street; 970–243–7337). The gallery has a collection of Native American tapestries, as well as contemporary art. The museum is open daily from 9:00 A.M. to 5:00 P.M. Admission is $2.00 for adults; free for those under twelve.

When you're ready for a break, stop at **Enstrom's** (200 South Seventh Street; 970–242–1655 or 800–367–8766) for a sample truffle or one of many luscious confections. This successful candy store, in the Enstrom family for three generations, receives orders from all over the world for its

World Famous Almond Toffee. Made fresh on-site, it gets rave reviews.

The **Museum of Western Colorado** (462 Ute Avenue; 970–242–0971) chronicles the geologic and cultural history of western Colorado. Pottery, Ute baskets, and artifacts are displayed. The museum is open Monday through Saturday from 9:00 A.M. to 5:00 P.M., Sunday, noon to 4:00 P.M., Memorial Day through Labor Day; Tuesday through Saturday from 10:00 A.M. to 4:00 P.M. the remainder of the year. Admission is $5.00 for adults and $3.00 for ages two to seventeen.

To see lifelike dinosaur replicas that rumble and move, visit **Dinosaur Journey** (550 Jurassic Court, Fruita, 8 miles west of Grand Junction; 970–858–7282 or 888–488–DINO). Visitors are visually transported to the Jurassic period with the help of robotic, snarling creatures that will have your skin crawling and the kids running for cover. The believable Utah Raptor sends tremors through the crowd as it attacks another robotic reproduction. Stand on the earthquake simulator and feel the plate tectonics tremble as you begin to comprehend how the earth has transformed through time. Hands-on exhibits are outstanding.

Dinosaur Journey is open daily year-round. Hours are 9:00 A.M. to 5:00 P.M. Monday through Saturday and 10:00 A.M. to 5:00 P.M. Sunday. Admission is $6.00 for adults and $3.50 for kids and seniors.

Let the kids tag along with paleontologists as they conduct their on-site research. **Dinosaur Expeditions** offers several-day sessions in the summer months that include meals, transportation, equipment, and instruction about excavation. Inquire by calling (888) 488–DINO.

DINNER: Dolce Vita, 336 Main Street, Grand Junction; (970) 242–8482. This stylish eatery offers an urban atmosphere and creative cuisine. You could make a meal from the appetizers alone, but you won't want to miss out on the incredible entrees. Begin with nachos Italian-style or the *bruschetta,* which is grilled bread with garlic, roma tomatoes, basil, and olive oil topped with goat cheese. Next feast on Linguine Dolce Vita, a wonderful combination of shrimp, mushrooms, garlic, pine nuts, spinach, and pasta, or choose grilled marinated chicken breast, served with garlic mashed potatoes and vegetables. Walk the couple of blocks from your lodging at Hawthorn Suites. Dolce Vita is open from 11:00 A.M. to 10:00 P.M. Monday through Friday and from 11:30 A.M. to 10:00 P.M. Saturday; closed Sunday.

LODGING: Hawthorn Suites, 225 Main Street, Grand Junction; (970) 242–2525 or (800) 527–1133; www.hawthorn.com. The beauty of this

Local wineries grow their own grapes.

facility is its convenient location. Park the car and walk to the galleries, restaurants, and shops on Main Street. City Market is 1 block away, so you can stock up on a deli sandwich before taking off for Colorado National Monument or the Grand Mesa. Hawthorn Suites offers an indoor swimming pool, outdoor hot tub, complimentary parking, complimentary hot breakfast buffet, and a coffee pot in each room. Prices begin at $99 for two persons and go up to $119 summer and fall.

Day 2 / Morning

BREAKFAST: Full breakfast is included at Hawthorn Suites. Cereal, quiche, hash browns, breakfast pastries, coffee, juice, and milk are available on the breakfast buffet.

Morning is a glorious time to be at **Colorado National Monument,** when the pastel orange of the sky is at its most radiant. Millions of years of weather have created a theatrical exhibition of the forces of nature here. Sheer ridges, muted hues, and rugged textures characterize the maze of ravines and majestic landscape.

Golden eagles, bighorn sheep, mountain lions, chipmunks, and squirrels reside here. Encompassing 32 square miles, Colorado National Monument offers short walks and day trips or longer backcountry junkets. Hike the easy 1-mile-round-trip **Canyon Rim Trail,** which parallels a cliff edge, to enjoy a view of **Wedding Canyon.**

Monoliths, rock spires, and desolate mesas provide the backdrop for not only hikers but Nordic skiers and horseback riders. For a trail ride check with **Rimrock Adventures** (970–858–9555). It offers hour-long or half-day rides into Devil's Canyon. Ask about the evening saddle-horse and pack-mule rides and scrumptious cookouts.

Drive the 23-mile **Rim Rock Drive,** which serves as the main road through the park and provides access to the visitor center and picnic area. From the road you can see much of the monument, but it would be a shame not to get out of the car and enjoy the breathtaking scenery. Stop at the visitor center, located 4 miles from the west entrance, for information about the geology and history of the monument, along with maps and a slide show. Rangers are on hand to suggest trails. Summer campfire programs are available. To get to the west entrance, take I–70 west to Fruita and follow the signs. To reach the east entrance, follow Monument Road west from downtown Grand Junction. Admission is $5.00 per vehicle for a seven-day pass. For more information contact Colorado National Monument Headquarters at (970) 858–3617.

LUNCH: Picnic at one of several areas in Colorado National Monument.

Afternoon

Visiting the local wineries is an excellent choice for the afternoon. Travel east from Grand Junction on U.S. 6 about 12 miles to the small farming town of Palisade. Stop at the Palisade Chamber of Commerce (309 Main Street; 970–464–7458) for information and a map. **Jurassic Tours** (P.O. Box 626, Fruita, CO 81521; 970–256–0884; www.jurassictours.com) offers guided winery tours, visits to geological sites, and customized tours of just about anywhere you might want to visit. One of the best deals is the winery tour. For $25 per person, a guide will pick you up at your lodge and escort you on a four-hour circuit of several of the area's excellent wineries.

GISDHO Shuttle also offers tours. Contact them at (970) 523–7662 or (888) 226–5031; www.gisdho.com.

Begin at **Carlson Vineyards** (461 35 Road, Palisade; 970–464–5554). This mom-and-pop operation distinguishes itself with not only its excellent peach, plum, and cherry wines but also its wit. Ask for a sample of the Tyrannosaurus Red, made with Colorado grapes. The winery offers tours and samples year-round every day from 11:00 A.M. to 6:00 P.M.

The oldest winery in the state is **Colorado Cellars Winery** (3553 East Road, Palisade; 800–848–2812). This winery produces about 15,000 cases of wine a year. The tasting room is open from 9:00 A.M. to 4:00 P.M. Monday through Friday and from noon to 4:00 P.M. Saturday.

Plum Creek Cellars (3708 G Road; 970–464–7586), located just outside Palisade, is open daily from 10:00 A.M. to 5:00 P.M. for samplings. Taste the 100 percent Colorado-grown wines, including pinot noir, merlot, sauvignon blanc, and Riesling.

Rocky Mountain Meadery/Rocky Mountain Cidery (3701 G Road, Palisade; 970–464–7899) produces honey wine—also known as mead—and has a well-stocked gift store. The winery offers tours and tastings daily from 10:00 A.M. to 5:00 P.M.

Grande River Vineyards (787 Elberta Avenue, Palisade; 970–464–5867) specializes in chardonnay and red and white Bordeaux-style blends. Tasting-room hours vary.

St. Kathryn Cellars (785 Elberta Avenue; 970–464–9288) is Colorado's newest winery, located down the street from Grande River Vineyards. In addition to a tasting room and gift shop, this winery has a nice picnic area.

Canyon Wind Cellars (3907 Highways 6 and 24, Palisade; 970–464–0888) has a beautiful setting, especially during the fall harvest, when the grapes are ready to be picked. Tours and tastings are available by appointment.

Corley Vineyards (3820 G 25 Road; 970–464–5314). Tasting-room hours are by appointment only.

DeBeque Canyon Winery (3943 G Road; 970–464–0550). This winery produces pinot noir, cabernet sauvignon, syrah, and merlot. Tasting-room hours are 10:00 A.M. to 5:00 P.M. Friday through Sunday, or by appointment.

Two Rivers Winery (2087 Broadway; 970–255–1471). Tasting-room hours are Monday through Saturday 10:30 A.M. to 6:00 P.M. and Sunday from noon to 5:00 P.M. Two Rivers produces cabernet sauvignon, chardonnay, merlot, and Riesling.

DINNER: Bistro Italiano, 400 Main Street, Grand Junction; (970) 243–8622. The menu includes traditional or seafood lasagna, homemade pasta, several veal dishes, pizza, and more. There's also a pledge on the menu from Brunella, the owner, to "bring a piece of Italy to Grand Junction." *Buon appetito!* Call to make sure the restaurant is open, because hours change with the seasons. Reservations accepted for parties of six or more.

LODGING: Hawthorn Suites.

Day 3 / Morning

BREAKFAST: Hawthorn Suites.

There's More

Adobe Creek Golf Course, 876 18½ Road, Fruita; (970) 858–0521. This 18-hole course offers affordable greens fees and a country club atmosphere.

Cross Orchards Historic Farm (3073 Patterson/F Road; 970–434–9814) gives a sense of early farm life. In the late 1800s this apple orchard ranked as one of the largest and most productive in the United States. Wander the grounds and view exhibits that include plows, wagons, and old farming tools. The gift shop sells novelties and food items. Cross Orchards is open daily May through October from 9:00 A.M. to 3:00 P.M., as well as for special events throughout the year. Admission is $3.00 for adults, $2.50 for seniors, $2.00 for children. Family groups, $8.00.

Grand Junction Symphony. Enjoy outstanding classical performances with talented musicians and guest artists. For a schedule call the symphony at (970) 243–6787.

Grand Mesa. The 63-mile Grand Mesa and Scenic Historic Byway, just east of Grand Junction, bisects the magnificent Grand Mesa, the world's largest flat-top mountain. This site should be high on your list to explore. To reach the Grand Mesa and Scenic Historic Byway from Grand Junction, travel east on I–70 for 30 miles to exit 49. The route follows Highway 65 through Plateau Canyon to the Grand Mesa summit. This trip is splendid in September when the aspen leaves are golden. Spend the night in a rustic cabin at *Alexander Lake Lodge* (866–525–2539). The lodge also has a restaurant. Other options are *Spruce Lodge Cabins* (800–850–7221) or *Mesa Lakes Resort* (888–420–6372).

Powderhorn Resort. Located 35 miles east of Grand Junction; (970) 268–5700. Small, friendly, and accommodating, this ski resort offers two restaurants, a lodge, ski rentals, and a lounge. Snowmobilers can undertake the 120-mile recreational trail that connects Powderhorn Resort to Sunlight Mountain Resort in Glenwood Springs. The well-maintained track crosses White River and Grand Mesa National Forests.

Rock climbing. For personalized instruction with a qualified guide, contact Desert Crags and Cracks, P.O. Box 2803, Grand Junction, CO 81502; (970) 245–8513. Owner-director Kris Hjelle has been climbing for twenty-five years.

Special Events

Late April. Fruita Fat Tire Festival. Join bicyclists for excursions along Kokopelli's Trail, which runs all the way to Moab, Utah. There's also plenty of carbo-laden food.

May. Spring Barrel Tasting. This two-day event features Colorado's premier wine-producing vineyards, with wine tastings, tours, and more.

July. Dinosaur Days. This weeklong festivity celebrates the mammoth creatures in a creative way, with dinosaur parades, concerts, and some silliness, too.

Late August. Palisade Peach Festival. Celebrate the peach season at this several-day event, held late in the month when the famous western-slope peaches are ripe and juicy.

Late September. Colorado Mountain Winefest. Grand Junction and Palisade host this three-day event dominated by wine tastings, celebrations of the grape, and gorgeous fall colors.

Other Recommended Restaurants and Lodgings

Adam's Mark Hotel, 743 Horizon Drive, Grand Junction; (970) 241–8888 or (800) 444–2326. This property has 264 rooms, tennis courts, a pool, and a fitness room.

Chef's New World Cuisine, 936 North Avenue, Grand Junction; (970) 243–9673. This fine restaurant was recognized by *Wine Spectator* magazine for its pairing of food and wine. The *Wine Spectator's* Award of Excellence is well deserved by Chef's, which offers some 170 wine selections. Open for dinner only Tuesday through Sunday, from 5:00 to 10:00 P.M.

Los Altos, 375 Hillview Drive, Grand Junction; (970) 256–0964 or (888) 774–0982; www.colorado-bnb.com/losaltos. This exceptional B&B pampers guests in luxurious decor and comfort. Each of its six rooms has a private bath and view of the spectacular Grand Valley. The romantic Vista Suite features a gas fireplace, king-size bed, reading room, and two outdoor decks. For breakfast, innkeepers Lee and Young-Ja Garrett go out of their way to ensure that guests don't leave with an empty stomach. Breakfast may include pancakes or an egg casserole with homemade muffins, fresh fruit, and coffee or tea. Ask for directions when making a reservation.

Rockslide Brewery, 401 Main Street, Grand Junction; (970) 245–2111. Here you'll find Big Bear Stout, Rabbit Ears Amber Ale, and a menu that includes buffalo wings, a Philly steak sandwich, burgers, and pizza.

The Winery, 642 Main Street, Grand Junction; (970) 242–4100. This restaurant is an excellent choice for a romantic dinner. The specialty here is steak, but choices also include orange-marinated swordfish, king crab, and salmon. Open 5:00 to 10:00 P.M. daily.

For More Information

Colorado National Monument, Fruita, CO 81521; (970) 858–3617.

Grand Junction Visitor & Convention Bureau, 740 Horizon Drive, Grand Junction, CO 81506; (970) 244–1480 or (800) 962–2547; www.visit grandjunction.com.

Museum of Western Colorado, 462 Ute Street, Box 20000-5020, Grand Junction, CO 81502; (970) 242–0971.

Palisade Chamber of Commerce, 309 South Main Street, Palisade, CO 81526; (970) 464–7458.

SOUTHERN
ESCAPES

Colorado Springs

Pikes Peak Grandeur

2 Nights

Tourists flock to Colorado Springs in numbers reaching up to six million annually, and it's no secret why: The area offers a mild, dry climate and a magnificent landscape, along with countless attractions.

☐ Historic luxury resort

☐ U.S. Air Force Academy

☐ Manitou Springs

☐ Garden of the Gods

☐ Hiking

☐ Horseback riding

☐ Pikes Peak and the world's highest cog railway

☐ Mountain zoo

The elegant Broadmoor, with its breathtaking location, superb service, three championship golf courses, world-class spa, and fine restaurants, is reason enough to visit. Add to this Pikes Peak, Cheyenne Mountain Zoo, and Garden of the Gods, and you'll find more than enough to explore.

Nature provides many of the enticements that lured explorers long ago and captivate visitors today. One look at the 14,110-foot summit of Pikes Peak on a cloudless Colorado day leaves visitors in awe. More than a century ago, Katharine Lee Bates was so inspired by the magnificent view that she wrote the celebrated words to "America the Beautiful."

The glorious Pikes Peak region indeed brings to mind the phrases "spacious skies" and "purple mountain majesties."

Day 1 / Morning

Take I–25 south from Denver for 70 miles of incredible views. You'll pass pine forests, and you may even catch a glimpse of Pikes Peak. Hold off for breakfast until you arrive at The Broadmoor. Exit at Circle Drive (number 138). Circle Drive turns into Lake Avenue, and The Broadmoor is located at the end of the road. Signs will direct you to the hotel.

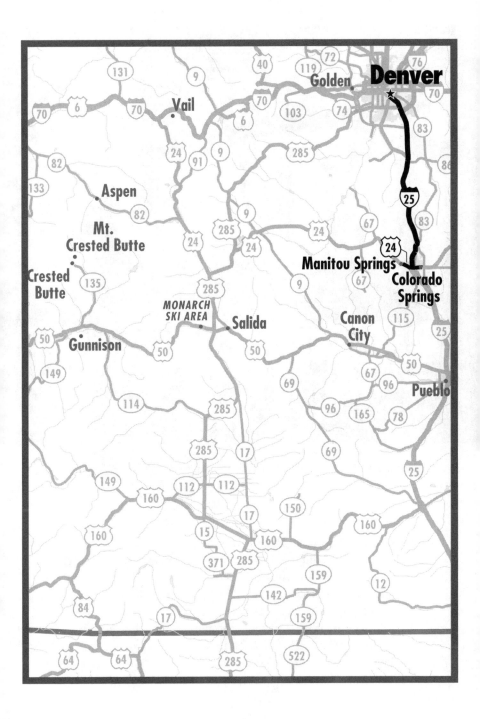

The Broadmoor sets the standard for luxury and service in the West.

BREAKFAST: Espresso Broadmoor is a favorite with guests for its relaxed setting and shining brass espresso machine. Try the vegetable quiche or a fresh-baked ham-and-cheese croissant. The cafe is located around the corner from the main lobby of The Broadmoor and is open from 6:30 A.M. to 11:00 P.M. daily.

Next, check with the concierge about a tour of The Broadmoor. As one of the country's most elegant resorts, this 3,000-acre property, which sits at the foot of Cheyenne Mountain, features everything from tennis courts to its own lake, as well as a state-of-the-art spa and fitness center.

After your tour, head to what is billed as the most visited attraction in the area, **Garden of the Gods** (1805 North Thirtieth Street; 719–634–6666). To get there, take U.S. Highway 24, turn north on Ridge Road, and follow the signs. Garden of the Gods is open year-round, and admission is free.

The unusual red sandstone formations, which were molded by wind and water over millions of years, were declared sacred grounds to the Ute, Arapaho, and Cheyenne Indians. The area provides a dramatic backdrop for a late-morning hike, bicycle tour, or horseback ride. **Academy Riding Stables** has a horse suited to each rider's abilities and will give guided tours of the park. Rides are available throughout the summer months. Call Academy Riding Stables at (719) 633–5667 for information.

For details on hiking or biking, check with Garden of the Gods Visitor Center. The center is open from 8:00 A.M. to 8:30 P.M. during summer and from 8:30 A.M. to 5:30 P.M. in winter. At the center you can also learn more about the geology, vegetation, and history of the area. Naturalists are available during the summer months to conduct walks around the park.

Learning the names of the unique formations is as much fun as admiring the boulders themselves. Look for Balanced Rock, the Kissing Camels, and Toothsome Rocks. The region is recognized worldwide for its challenging climbs, and you may see technical rock climbers inching up the sandstone walls.

LUNCH: Marigold Cafe and Bakery (4605 Centennial Boulevard; 719–599–4776) has a menu that changes daily, but you'll find fresh-baked pastries and items such as cream of chicken soup, Greek salad, delicious scalloped potatoes, and beef stew. The restaurant serves breakfast, lunch, and dinner. Marigold Cafe is closed Sunday.

Afternoon

Glen Eyrie Castle (3820 North Thirtieth Street, Colorado Springs; 719–594–2477 or 800–944–4536; www.gleneyrie.org) is a huge estate that was built by the founding father of Colorado Springs, Gen. William Palmer, for his wife. The property includes riding stables and nine reservoirs in addition to the castle. The mansion boasts twenty-four fireplaces and is listed on the National Register of Historic Places.

Visitors can indulge in the Formal Victorian Tea (Sunday only; $11.50 for tea; $3.00 for tour) or the Cream Tea, served Monday through Saturday ($8.00 for tea; $3.00 for tour). Afternoon tea, scones with Devonshire cream, a truffle, fresh fruit, and a slice of pound cake are served in the Music Room. Tours begin at 1:00 P.M. Glen Eyrie is located just north of Garden of the Gods. Reservations are essential for tours or tea.

Visit the **Colorado Springs Fine Arts Center** (30 West Dale Street; 719–634–5581). This fine gallery and museum houses a world-class collection of art, including works by Charles Russell, Georgia O'Keeffe, and John James Audubon. International touring exhibits are also showcased in this art deco building. Adult ticket price is $5.00; seniors and students six to sixteen, $3.00; children five and under, free.

DINNER: Phantom Canyon Brewing Company, 2 East Pikes Peak Avenue, Colorado Springs; (719) 635–2800. Traditional pub grub of the best kind is served here, and you can wash down those beer-battered fish-and-chips with an excellent ale or stout. Feast on London broil or flank steak with roasted-garlic mashed potatoes and creamed spinach and leeks, or beer-braised pot roast with mashed potatoes and gravy. Try a Queen's Blonde Ale, Phantom India Pale Ale, or Zebulon's Peated Porter, all of which are brewed on-site. Billiards are available upstairs, and you're likely to meet a local or two who frequent this preferred place to quaff a cold one. The microbrewery is open 11:00 A.M. to midnight on weekdays and 11:00 to 1:30 A.M. Saturday and Sunday.

LODGING: The Broadmoor, 1 Lake Avenue, Colorado Springs; (800) 634–7711; www.broadmoor.com. This famous resort is a tourist attraction in itself. Service is impeccable, and the amenities at The Broadmoor are nothing less than first-class. Rooms are luxurious, and many offer splendid views of Cheyenne Mountain and the resort's Cheyenne Lake.

Spencer Penrose opened the pink-stucco, elaborately decorated hotel in the early 1800s to become none other than a world-class resort. The intricate chandeliers, marble fountain, and curved staircase helped to create an Italian Renaissance style. The Broadmoor soon secured a reputation as one of the most superb hotels of its day, appealing to VIPs of all types. Since its grand opening in June 1918, this showpiece of the Rockies has hosted numerous presidents, dignitaries, and movie stars. Former guests include U.S. Presidents Hoover, Eisenhower, Nixon, Reagan, and the senior Bush; foreign notables Margaret Thatcher and the King of Siam; and celebrities Bob Hope, Bing Crosby, John Wayne, and Jimmy Stewart.

During the winter season, from November to April, rates run from $130 for a double to $335. May through October the rates start at $295 for a double and go up to $450.

Day 2 / Morning

BREAKFAST: Feast on pan-seared fillet of mountain trout or on eggs and a cheese buttermilk biscuit at the **Lake Terrace Dining Room,** located on the mezzanine level of The Broadmoor.

Today's agenda begins with a sojourn to the awe-inspiring and majestic backdrop to Colorado Springs, **Pikes Peak.** If you're feeling energetic and fit, you can arrange to hike to the summit, but you'll want to schedule two days to finish the 26-mile round-trip. For information on hiking visit the office of Pike National Forest (601 South Weber Street; 719–636–1602).

There are easier ways to reach the summit, mainly in the comfort of your car or via **Pikes Peak Cog Railway.** Either way, you'll want to have a jacket. At 14,100 feet, the air is thin and chilly and has half the oxygen found at sea level.

The 9-mile route takes a little more than three hours round-trip, including a forty-minute stopover at the top. On the trip up you may spot deer or other animals, and there will be several photo stops. Little can compare to the panoramic vista from the summit. You can view Denver to the north, the Sangre de Cristo Mountains to the south, and the Great Plains to the east.

LUNCH: The appropriately named **Summit House** offers a snack bar and shopping, or you may wish to wait and have lunch in Manitou Springs.

To reach the depot take I–25, then exit 141 west on U.S. 24 for 4 miles; turn onto Manitou Avenue West and proceed 1.5 miles to Ruxton Avenue; turn left and drive about 0.5 mile to 515 Ruxton Avenue, Manitou Springs. Train fare from April through June is $24.50 for adults, $13.00 for children ages three through eleven, and free for children under age three who are held on an adult's lap. Prices increase slightly for the months of July and August. For additional information write Pikes Peak Railway, Box 351, Manitou Springs, CO 80829, or call (719) 685–5401. Reservations are essential.

For a breezier trip down, try a bicycle descent. **Challenge Unlimited** drives clients (kids, Grandma, Mom, and Dad) by van to the summit and escorts them down as they ride bikes on the 20-mile ride. Say "Wheeeee!" Twenty-one-speed mountain bikes, helmets, cold-weather gear, and all other necessary equipment are provided. The ride up in the van takes an hour, and the descent on bikes takes about two and a half hours. Contact Challenge Unlimited, 204 South Twenty-fourth Street, Colorado Springs; (800) 798–5954.

Spend some time in **Manitou Springs,** a small artists' community with attractive Victorian homes, gift shops, and galleries. Health-seekers arrived in this town in the late 1800s to "take the cure" by drinking water from the mineral springs. Home to Manitou Springs Mineral Water, this National Historic District is a good place to spend the afternoon exploring on your own or taking the free walking tour offered by the local Chamber of Commerce (354 Manitou Avenue, Manitou Springs; 719–685–5089).

Named for the clamor the wind makes as it blows through the tunnels, **Cave of the Winds** is both impressive and touristy. Still, if you are fascinated by stalagmites, stalactites, subterranean chambers, and narrow passageways, you've come to the right place. Cave of the Winds (719–685–5444) is located off Highway 24, north of Manitou Springs on Serpentine Drive.

The **Discovery Tour** is the shortest and easiest. The tour is a guided walking tour, 0.5 mile in length, and lasts forty-five minutes. There are some stairs, a cement trail, handrails, and good lighting. Cost is $15.00 for adults, $8.00 for children ages six through fifteen, and free for children under six. The **Lantern Tour** is a reenactment of tours in the 1800s. Guides are dressed in authentic 1800s attire and each participant carries a candle lantern. The tour is 2 miles long and lasts ninety minutes. Participants should be in above-average physical condition. There are no lights other than the candle lantern. $18 for adults. The **Explorer Trip** is the most strenuous and difficult. Children under thirteen are not permitted on this three- to four-hour exploration. Cost is $80 per adult, with a $20 deposit when you make a reservation. Cave of the Winds is open daily. Hours are 9:00 A.M. to 10:00 P.M. from May 1 through Labor Day weekend. Hours are 10:00 A.M. to 5:00 P.M. from Labor Day to May 1.

DINNER: The **Penrose Room at The Broadmoor.** This luxurious restaurant specializes in gourmet cuisine in an elegant, romantic setting. A three-piece orchestra serenades as you choose from the elaborate menu selection of pan-seared foie gras, chateaubriand (carved tableside), roasted rack of Colorado lamb, Maine lobster, and dessert soufflé.

Evening

Top off the evening with a visit to **The Broadmoor's Golden Bee.** Located on the lower level of the International Center at The Broadmoor, this authentic nineteenth-century English pub is ideal for sipping a yard-long schooner of beer and singing old-time favorites with the ragtime pianist. The crowd is merry, the honky-tonk is loud, and the mood is festive. Patrons are often given a stick-on "bee" to wear. Don't miss this distinguished-by-day, boisterous-by-night pub.

LODGING: The Broadmoor.

Day 3 / Morning

LATE BRUNCH: If it's Sunday, you'll want to enjoy the incredible brunch in **The Broadmoor's Lake Terrace Dining Room.** Live classical piano music filters throughout the dining area, and artistic ice sculptures decorate the tables. You'll find a buffet-style extravaganza that features cold poached salmon, fresh fruit, a carving station with a variety of meats, and a large dessert selection. The Broadmoor's acclaimed bananas Foster is a treat.

After breakfast, stroll around the peaceful lake or strike up a game of tennis. **The Broadmoor's Spa and Fitness Center** staff will arrange for a multitreatment program to fit your needs, whether you're in the mood for maximum relaxation or maximum workout.

Cheyenne Mountain Zoo (4250 Cheyenne Mountain Zoo Road; 719–633–9925; www.cmzoo.org) is poised on the slopes just above The Broadmoor. This unique mountain zoo, which focuses on the plights of many endangered species, is regarded as one of the most superior in the country and is home to more than 800 animals, such as Siberian tigers, black leopards, hippos, and Mexican gray wolves. At 6,800 feet above sea level, the zoo provides sensational views of Colorado Springs and the surrounding area. The zoo is open every day of the year. Hours are 9:00 A.M. to 6:00 P.M. Memorial Day weekend through Labor Day weekend and 9:00 A.M. to 5:00 P.M. the remainder of the year.

LUNCH: Picnic at the zoo or take advantage of the snack bar.

Afternoon

On your way back to Denver via I–25 north, visit the **U.S. Air Force Academy.** Take exit 156B off I–25. Shortly after entering the grounds, you'll see an imposing B-52 bomber on display. Stop at the **Barry Goldwater Air Force Academy Visitor Center** (719) 333–2025, open daily in summer from 9:00 A.M. to 6:00 P.M. and in winter from 9:00 A.M. to 5:00 P.M. The gift shop has displays and films about the history of the academy.

You can walk to the **Cadet Chapel** from the visitor center. The chapel, which is an architectural marvel, has seventeen spires that rise 150 feet into the sky. The public is welcome to visit Monday through Saturday from 9:00 A.M. to 5:00 P.M. and Sunday from 1:00 to 5:00 P.M. Sunday services are held at 9:00 and 11:00 A.M., and the public is welcome to attend. For information call (719) 333–4515.

There's More

Holidays at The Broadmoor. Spending the Fourth of July or Thanksgiving Day at The Broadmoor is a luxurious, relaxing way to celebrate with your family, and it may be less expensive than you think. Enjoy traditional roasted Colorado Tom Turkey on Thanksgiving Day in the elegant Penrose Room for $34 per person. A basic double room Thanksgiving night begins at $130. Enjoy culinary and ice sculpting demonstrations by The Broadmoor's culinary team. Observe as the team constructs a gingerbread village.

ProRodeo Hall of Fame and American Cowboy Museum, 101 ProRodeo Drive, Colorado Springs; (719) 528–4764. Cowboys and cowgirls alike will get a kick out of this museum, which contains an excellent exhibit of Western art, photographs, and displays of cowboy and rodeo gear. Admission is $6.00 for adults, $5.00 for seniors, and $3.00 for children ages six through twelve; children under six are admitted free.

U.S. Olympic Complex, 1 Olympic Plaza, Colorado Springs; (719) 578–4618. Stop at the visitor center and the U.S. Olympic Hall of Fame for a guided tour of this thirty-six-acre complex, the elaborate training center for more than half of the U.S. Olympic sports. You'll see five sophisticated gymnasiums and a weight-training room on the tour, as well as the Indoor Shooting Center, which has two 50-meter ranges. Proceeds from merchandise sold at the visitor center help support the athletic programs. Summer hours at the complex are Monday through Saturday from 9:00 A.M. to 5:00 P.M. and Sunday from 10:00 A.M. to 5:00 P.M. Winter hours are Monday through Saturday from 9:00 A.M. to 4:00 P.M. and Sunday from noon to 4:00 P.M.

Special Events

March/April. Easter Sunrise Services at Garden of the Gods. This spring tradition is an impressive sight as worshippers gather in the dramatic setting of these awesome formations. The inspirational service is well worth requesting that 5:00 A.M. wake-up call. For information call (719) 572–1348.

July. Pikes Peak Hill Climb. Held on the Fourth of July. The annual "Race to the Clouds" is the second oldest auto race in America, right behind the Indianapolis 500. Former winners of the rigorous event are Bobby Unser (he has won the Hill Climb thirteen times), Al Unser, Mario Andretti, Rick Mears, and Roger Mears. Contact Pikes Peak Hill Climb Association, 135 Manitou Avenue, Manitou Springs; (719) 685–4400.

August. Pikes Peak or Bust Rodeo. Billed as Colorado's largest outdoor rodeo, this event, held early in the month, draws big names in the pro-rodeo circle. The city decks out in Western wear and welcomes cowboys and cowgirls with foot-stompin' enthusiasm. For information call (719) 635–3548 or (719) 520–6711.

Pikes Peak Marathon is considered to be one of the world's most demanding. The race is a great spectator sport—unless, that is, you're into grueling runs. If that's the case, you'll want to compete. For information call (719) 473–2625.

Other Recommended Restaurants and Lodgings

Antlers Adam's Mark Hotel, 4 South Cascade Avenue, Colorado Springs; (719) 473–5600 or (800) 528–0444. This comfortable hotel offers a complete range of services and a microbrewery. Judge Baldwin's Brewing Company, Colorado Springs's first microbrewery, serves not only a specialty ale brewed on-site but burgers, pastas, and soups. Atmosphere is casual. Lunch and dinner are served here daily, and breakfast is available Sunday morning.

The Hearthstone Inn, 506 North Cascade Avenue, Colorado Springs; (719) 473–4413 or (800) 521–1885; www.hearthstoneinn.com. This nonsmoking B&B is elegantly furnished with antiques, overstuffed chairs, and a wood-burning fireplace in the parlor. Some rooms have a view of Pikes

Peak, while others feature a private porch. There are no TVs or phones in the rooms. A full gourmet breakfast is included.

MacKenzie's Chop House, 1280 Tejon Street, Colorado Springs; (719) 635–3536 or www.mackenzieschophouse.com. Located in a historic building, this cozy restaurant exudes sophistication and charm. A highly professional staff, superb menu, and the best outdoor patio in town make MacKenzie's an excellent choice. Try the artichoke dip or New Zealand mussels for an appetizer and the peppered pork loin or tuna chop for an entree. Call for reservations.

Primitivo Wine Bar, 28 South Tejon, Colorado Springs; (719) 473–4900. This restaurant serves contemporary cuisine and was named in *Wine Spectator* for their excellent selection of wines.

Walter's Bistro, 1606 South Eighth, Colorado Springs; (719) 630–0201. Walter's offers intimate dining, contemporary cuisine, and a fine selection of wines. Open Monday through Friday from 11:30 A.M. to 2:00 P.M. and 6:00 to 9:30 P.M. and Saturday (dinner only) from 6:00 to 9:30 P.M.

For More Information

Colorado Springs Chamber of Commerce, 2 North Cascade Avenue, Suite 110, Colorado Springs, CO 80903; (719) 635–1551.

Colorado Springs Convention & Visitor Bureau, 104 South Cascade, Suite 104, Colorado Springs, CO 80903; (719) 635–7506 or (800) 888–4748; www.coloradosprings-travel.com.

Manitou Springs Chamber of Commerce, 354 Manitou Avenue, Manitou Springs, CO 80829; (719) 685–5089.

Salida and the Upper Arkansas Valley

Rediscover Southern Colorado

1 Night

With more 14,000-foot mountains than any other location in Colorado, the Sawatch Mountain Range is one step short of heaven for climbers. Rafters and kayakers love to shoot the Class-III rapids of the Arkansas River. Golf enthusiasts will appreciate Salida's 9-hole course, with views of the Collegiate Peaks.

Salida is reinventing itself as an art community. The town counts twenty-five galleries, including Mountain Spirit Winery and Gallery, where you can sample a glass of blackberry cabernet or raspberry merlot as you view the watercolors, pastels, and ceramics.

One of the best things about the Upper Arkansas Valley is its spectacular landscape. Salida is surrounded by the Pike and San Isabel National Forests, which offer abundant backcountry areas to explore. One thing is certain: There is something to suit every outdoor lover.

- ☐ Rafting
- ☐ Skiing
- ☐ Snowboarding
- ☐ Sno-Cat tours
- ☐ Rockhounding
- ☐ Fishing, golf, horseback riding
- ☐ Galleries
- ☐ Christmas Mountain USA
- ☐ Wine tasting

Day 1 / Morning

Salida is located 157 miles southwest of Denver. Follow U.S. Highway 285 south to Highway 291 and then turn left (southeast). This takes you directly into the heart of the downtown historic district of Salida. Monarch Ski & Snowboard Area is located 18 miles west of Salida on U.S. Highway 50.

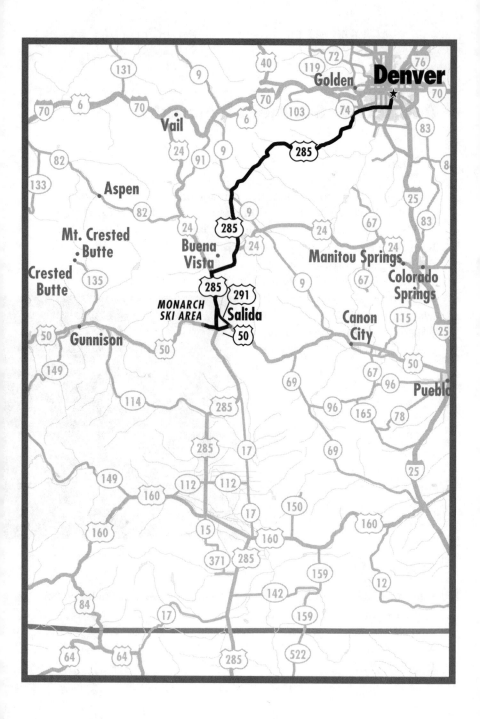

LUNCH: For a no-nonsense meal and a bit of local gossip on the side, eat at **Country Bounty** (413 West Rainbow Boulevard on Highway 50, Salida; 719–539–3546). Chicken-fried steak and mashed potatoes, a hot roast beef sandwich, fried chicken, and Rocky Road Pie are specialities of the house. Open daily from 6:30 A.M. to 9:00 P.M.

Afternoon

Monarch Ski & Snowboard Area recognizes the increasing interest in winter's fastest-growing sport, snowboarding. "Shredders" are welcomed and indulged at **Meadows Terrain Park**. Monarch Ski & Snowboard Area holds several snowboarding competitions throughout the season, including the Big Air and Boardercross events.

Monarch is an ideal family ski area for all levels. The natural bowl area is a challenge for experts with its legendary powder. Annual snowfall is 350-plus inches, and the ski area boasts about its absence of snow-making equipment. The resort has a special "snowline," which gives callers the latest snowpack report: (800) 228–7943.

Adventurers interested in a day in the backcountry with a guide can take advantage of **Monarch Sno-Cat Tours.** For $200 per day guests travel by Sno-Cat to Monarch's 900 acres of above-timberline terrain to ski or snowboard on the Continental Divide. Participants learn about backcountry safety before they head out on their adventure into untamed territory. For more information call (888) 996–7669.

Summer activities include a ride on the **Monarch Scenic Tram** to the 12,012-foot summit for incredible views from the observation tower. Telescopes are available, and maps identify the peaks. The tram operates daily mid-May through late September from 9:00 A.M. to 4:00 P.M. For more information call (719) 539–4789.

Other summer pastimes include an afternoon at **Salida Golf Club** (404 Grant Street, Salida; 719–539–1060). This 9-hole course has views of the Collegiate Peaks as well as some challenging holes that wreak havoc upon even the best golfers. The club has an excellent restaurant and serves reasonably priced breakfast, lunch, and dinner.

Rafters can float through **Brown's Canyon** with **Noah's Ark** (P.O. Box 850, Buena Vista, CO 81211; 719–395–2158). The company is located 6 miles south of Buena Vista on Highway 285. A half-day trip covers 10 miles on the Arkansas River, and you'll bounce through eight moderate rapids. A full-day trip consists of lunch and a few more rapids than the half-day outing, including Seidell's Suckhole, a Class IV. Multiday excursions are another option. The company can accommodate all levels of rafting experience. Rafting season is from mid-May to the end of August.

Rafting is a major tourist attraction in this area. Twenty companies are located in the Salida area to provide guided trips. Call (877) 772–5432 for a list.

Many consider the **Arkansas River** to be one of the finest fishing rivers in the state. Without a doubt, this area is a natural destination for anglers. Rewards are not only drop-dead-gorgeous scenery but the prospect of landing a sizable rainbow trout. **Ark Anglers** (7500 Highway 50, Salida, next to the Holiday Inn; 719–539–4223; www.arkanglers.com) will arrange a guided fly-fishing trip that includes either walk-and-wade fishing or float fishing. For additional information contact the Division of Wildlife Office (7405 Highway 50, Salida; 719–539–3529).

Visitors are welcome to observe daily activities that might include feeding, sorting, or moving fish at **Mount Shavano Trout Hatchery and Rearing Unit** (7725 County Road 154, Salida; 719–539–6877). Four million fish, including brown, rainbow, and cutthroat trout, as well as kokanee salmon, are hatched annually at this location. Guided tours are available during summer. The facility is located 0.5 mile northwest of Salida on Highway 291 and is open from 8:00 A.M. to 4:30 P.M. every day of the year. Admission is free.

Take a trail ride into the backcountry of Sawatch Range. **Mount Princeton Riding Stables** (15870 County Road 162, Nathrop; 719–395–6498) provides a horse suited to every rider's ability.

Rock hounds will find Colorado's richest mineral and gem locations in the upper Arkansas River Valley, west of Salida. For information pick up a brochure at the Chamber of Commerce (406 West Rainbow Boulevard, Salida; 719–539–2068).

Mountain biking is a major activity from late spring through fall. Bikes and trail maps can be obtained at **Absolute Bikes**, 330 West Sackett Avenue (888–539–9295) or **Otero Cyclery**, 108 F Street (719–539–6704). Shuttle service is available through **High Valley Center** (800–871–5145).

DINNER: Amicas, 136 East Second Street, Salida; (719) 539-5219. Amicas took over the space formerly occupied by the popular restaurant Il Vicino. Thankfully, you'll still find delicious gourmet pizza, award-winning beer, and a casual atmosphere. Study the menu on the wall, place your order at the counter, and sit back with a mug of Loyal Duke Scotch

Ale as you wait for your wood-fired pizza to be served. Try the Michaelangelo's Pizza (Italian sausage, caramelized onions, goat cheese, and pesto). Amicas is open for lunch and dinner daily.

LODGING: Tudor Rose Bed & Breakfast, 6720 County Road 104, P.O. Box 89, Salida, CO 81201; (719) 539–2002 or (800) 379–0889; www .thetudorrose.com. Spacious, elegant, and tranquil describe the Tudor Rose. Surrounded by thirty-seven acres, this secluded B&B offers six comfortable rooms that range in price from $65 to $120. The Henry Tudor Suite, with a king-size feather bed and Jacuzzi for two, is the most requested by honeymooners. Although it's just on the edge of town, be sure to ask for directions when you make a reservation.

Day 2 / Morning

BREAKFAST: Tudor Rose Bed & Breakfast, 6720 Country Road 104, Salida; (719) 539–2002. Full breakfast is included with your stay at Tudor Rose. Two seatings are offered. During winter months, times are 8:00 and 9:00 A.M. Beginning Memorial Day, seatings are 7:30 and 8:30 A.M. Enjoy items such as eggs Benedict, stuffed french toast, or breakfast burritos.

Return to Denver via Highway 285.

There's More

Llama trekking. Full-day and multiday hikes are offered by Spruce Ridge Llama Treks (4141 County Road 210, Salida; 719–539–4182). Travel through national forests as llamas haul the gear. All equipment is provided.

Mount Princeton Hot Springs. Two outdoor swimming pools, two indoor hot tubs, and natural rock pools attract crowds to this location. Overnight accommodations and dining are also available. For more information contact Mount Princeton Hot Springs, 15870 County Road 162, Nathrop; (719) 395–2447.

Mountain Spirit Winery, 15750 County Road 220, located 12 miles west of Salida; (719) 539–1175. This family-run winery is located on a five-acre farm in apple-orchard country. Stop for a tour and a sample of the award-winning blackberry cabernet. For more information visit www.mountain spiritwinery.com.

Mountain Spirit Winery and Gallery, 201 F Street, Salida; (719) 539–7848. The gallery serves samples of the wines produced at the winery. They do not sell wine by the glass, but they will sell you a bottle. Sample the merlot as you view the watercolors, pastels, crystal, photography, ceramics, pottery, and jewelry. Open 10:00 A.M. to 5:00 P.M. Monday through Saturday.

Salida Hot Springs Pool. Soak in the hot mineral springs or swim in the 25-meter lap pool. Summer hours are from 1:00 to 9:00 P.M. daily. Winter hours are from 4:00 to 9:00 P.M. Tuesday through Thursday and from 1:00 to 9:00 P.M. Friday through Sunday. Located at Centennial Park, 410 West Rainbow Boulevard, Salida; (719) 539–6738.

Visit the **Salida Museum,** located next to the Chamber of Commerce, at 406 West Rainbow Boulevard. This museum displays mining, railroad, and early settler memorabilia. Open Memorial Day through Labor Day from 10:00 A.M. to 4:00 P.M.

Special Events

June (Father's Day Weekend). FibArk (First in Boating on the Arkansas). This international raft and kayak race attracts kayakers, spectators, and the entire Salida community for a long weekend of music, a parade, and the highlight: a 26-mile kayak race from Salida to Cotopaxi. For details call (719) 539–7254.

Artwalk. The last weekend in June. Celebrate the arts and stroll the many galleries of historic downtown Salida.

July. The town sponsors an old-fashioned Fourth of July celebration, complete with street dancing, a chili cook-off, fireworks, and music.

The Aspen-Salida Music Festival held early in July features a series of concerts that include performances from the Aspen concert series.

November. Christmas Mountain USA. The holiday season begins the Friday after Thanksgiving with the annual lighting of Salida's Tenderfoot Mountain by Santa. Thousands of bulbs outline a 500-foot Christmas tree. Holiday Park adds to the festive season with more than one hundred decorated trees lining a path along the Arkansas River.

December. On New Year's Eve skiers and snowboarders at Monarch Ski Area carry lighted torches as they weave their way down the mountain in a celebration that begins at 4:00 P.M. Fireworks follow. For details call (719) 539–3573.

Other Recommended Restaurants and Lodgings

Salida

Dakota's Bistro, 122 North F Street; (719) 530–9909. This restaurant serves regional, international, and bistro fare. Dakota's has seasonal hours, so call ahead.

Fiesta Mexicana, 1220 East Highway 50; (719) 539–5203. Fiesta Mexicana serves authentic Mexican cuisine.

Laughing Ladies, 128 West First Street; (719) 539–6209. This fun restaurant serves a variety of food, including Mexican and American. They are known for their daily specials and fresh fish. Open for lunch and dinner; closed Tuesday and Wednesday.

The River Suites at Monarch Shadows, 16724 Highway 50 West; (719) 539–6953. Situated 10 miles from Monarch Ski & Snowboard Area and 9 miles from Salida, this first-class accommodation offers cabins with a wood-burning stove, a private hot tub, a television, and a complete kitchen. The two-bedroom cabin can accommodate six adults. Rates range from $125 to $175 and change with the seasons.

For More Information

Salida Chamber of Commerce, 406 West Rainbow Boulevard, Salida, CO 81201; (719) 539–2068 or (877) 772–5432; www.salidachamber.org.

For information on camping, hiking, and other national forest activities, contact the Salida Ranger District Office, 325 West Rainbow Boulevard, Salida, CO 81201; (719) 539–3591; www.salidacolorado.com.

Gunnison

Hospitality on the Western Slope

2 Nights

Gunnison offers a welcome contrast to fast-paced resorts. Here the daily whistle blows at noon in small-town tradition, streets are wide, and folks say "Howdy." In this neck of the woods, Cattlemen's Days is the social highlight of the summer.

☐ Old mining towns

☐ Cumberland Pass

☐ Pristine backcountry

☐ Blue Mesa Reservoir

☐ Pioneer Museum

As the gateway to Gunnison National Forest, the town of Gunnison sits in the heart of some of the state's most dramatic wilderness. Unspoiled, vast, and ideal for outdoor recreation, the Gunnison Valley begs to be hiked, biked, four-wheeled, fished, and explored.

Gunnison is the perfect place to set up base camp. The town offers good shopping, superior restaurants, and a sunny disposition. You're as likely to see a rancher driving a truck filled with bales of hay as you are a college student with tattoos and a pierced nose.

You'll encounter an interesting history here and virtually unlimited access to pristine wilderness. And you will be welcomed with genuine hospitality.

Day 1 / Morning

Gunnison is located about 200 miles southwest of Denver. Take U.S. Highway 285, traveling southwest from Denver, to Poncha Springs. Continue west on U.S. Highway 50 into Gunnison. Plan on a three-and-a-half- to four-hour drive from Denver.

Your first stop in Gunnison is the Visitor Center (also the **Gunnison Country Chamber of Commerce)** (500 East Tomichi Avenue; 970–641–1501 or 800–274–7580), to stock up on maps and brochures. The office is open daily from 8:00 A.M. to 6:00 P.M. Memorial Day through Labor Day, and Monday through Friday from 8:00 A.M. to 5:00 P.M. the

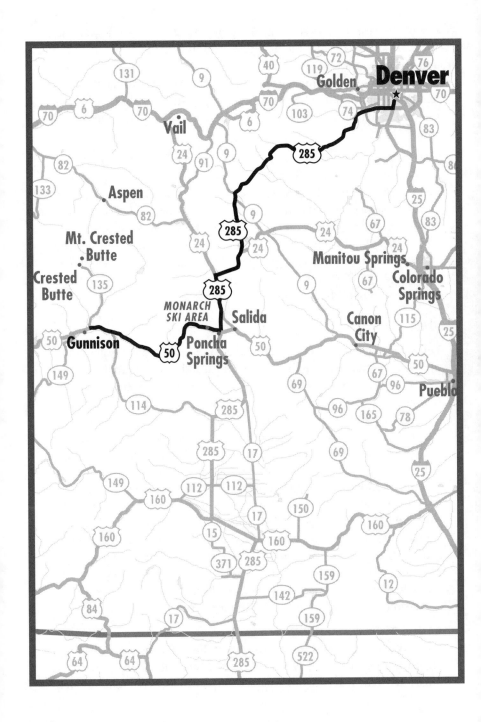

rest of the year. It is located on the right side of the street as you enter town. Be sure to pick up the brochure "Ghosts of a Town: 20 Circle Tour Trips of the Gunnison Country."

Across the street is **Jorgensen Park,** where you can in-line skate during the summer and play ice hockey when the weather turns cold. Equipment rentals are available at the city's warming hut, located at the park.

LUNCH: Stuff yourself for next to nothing at the **Blue Iguana** (303 East Tomichi Avenue, Gunnison; 970–641–3403), where the most expensive item on the menu is about $8.00. Decor consists of red vinyl tablecloths, a giant chile pepper in the dining room, and a menu painted on the wall. Choices include a build-your-own burrito for less than $4.00 and combination plates for a couple of dollars more. A popular hangout for students attending Western State College, the Blue Iguana has picnic tables both inside and out. The restaurant is open from 11:00 A.M. to 10:00 P.M. Monday through Saturday and is closed Sunday.

Afternoon

For an introduction to town, take the 2.5-mile, self-guided walking tour of historic Gunnison with the help of a map and brochure available at the Visitor Center. On the route you'll see Gothic Revival architecture, the first stone house in Gunnison, and the oldest existing church in town.

To shop at a unique store that sells designer Western-style furniture, you'll need to drive to the edge of town. **Back at the Ranch** (100 Spencer Avenue, Gunnison; 970–641–0727) is worth the mileage. This fashionable store is packed with cowboy art and distinctive home furnishings. Open Monday through Saturday, 9:30 A.M. to 5:30 P.M.

You'll find an exceptional display of area memorabilia at **Pioneer Museum** (East Highway 50, Gunnison; 970–641–4530). In addition to antique cars and wagons, you'll see old saddles, an arrowhead collection, and ranch machinery that dates to the early days. The museum is open Memorial Day through Labor Day from 9:00 A.M. to 5:00 P.M. Monday through Saturday; the museum is closed the remainder of the year. Admission is $8.00 for adults and $1.00 for children ages six to twelve.

DINNER: The aroma of roasted garlic tantalizes your senses when you walk in the door at **Garlic Mike's Italian Cuisine** (2674 North Highway 135, Gunnison; 970–641–2493), 2 miles north of Gunnison on Highway 135. Italian dining doesn't get much better. From the red-checked tablecloths to the immense stone fireplace and bustling open kitchen, this cafe exudes charm. Some of the choices from the menu are Filetto di Salmon al Forno con Formaggio, Sirloin Steak Gorgonzola, and Lasagne da Campania. Desserts include Chocolate Truffle Cake, chocolate mousse, and Tiramisù Cake, among others. Weather permitting, dine outside on the pleasant riverfront patio. The hours change with the season, so call ahead.

LODGING: The **Mary Lawrence Inn** (601 North Taylor, Gunnison; 970–641–3343), built in 1885 and renovated in 1989, offers guests a homey atmosphere amid antiques, handmade quilts, and Victorian decor. In the early 1900s, Mary Lawrence, a teacher and school administrator, operated the building as a boardinghouse. Today you'll find homemade goodies in the cookie jar, a large deck where guests gather in the late afternoon, and an inviting sun porch filled with comfy chairs and magazines. Each of the eight guest rooms has a private bath. This inn is particularly kid-friendly and offers two-room suites. Rates range from $69 to $129 depending on the room and season.

Day 2 / Morning

BREAKFAST: Mary Lawrence Inn. Join other guests in the sunny dining room at the fourteen-person oval table for a full breakfast that may include Asparagus Eggs Benedict or Gingerbread Pancakes with Nectarine Cream Sauce.

Plan ahead for a picnic lunch and stop at **Farrell's Restaurant** (310 North Main Street; 970–641–2655) to pick up a sandwich, coleslaw, and a giant chocolate chip cookie or two. Food here is prepared from scratch, and you'll find a selection of fresh breads and pastries. Closed Saturday and Sunday. **City Market Deli,** 880 North Main Street, is another option for a picnic lunch.

Take Colorado 135 north out of Gunnison to Almont to begin a loop tour of old mining towns. The brochure "Ghosts of a Town: 20 Circle Tour Trips of the Gunnison Country," from the Visitor Center, guides you on a trip through towns that thrived during the gold rush of the late 1800s. Roads are narrow and often have only one lane, but you won't need a four-wheel-drive vehicle. Much of this route is closed in winter, so ask about road conditions before you depart.

After you pass through Almont, follow the signs to **Tincup,** a sleepy little town that has one cafe, one general store, one *Denver Post* stand, and a handful of residents. **Frenchy's Cafe** doesn't have an exact address, but you won't have trouble finding it. Pies here are especially good, and menu items are named after mining terms and local places. You'll find Miner's Muck (biscuits with sausage gravy) and Minnie Hall (a burger with cheese and bacon).

Stories vary about the source of Tincup's name, but some say that a local entrepreneur sold whiskey by the tin cup to miners in the late 1800s. Another version states that early settlers searched the streams for gold with tin cups.

On the edge of town is the **Tincup Cemetery,** which may be unlike any graveyard you have ever seen. For starters, *cemetery* is misspelled *cemetary,* which makes the location all the more endearing. If you look closely, you'll see that someone has carved an "e" into the wooden sign. Graves are separated by religion, and you'll see signs that say JEWISH KNOLL, CATHOLIC KNOLL, PROTESTANT KNOLL, and BOOT HILL for those who may not have religious faith.

As you proceed up Cumberland Pass Road, you'll climb above treeline to the 12,015-foot summit of **Cumberland Pass.** The road is narrow and the air thin, but the rewards are awesome views, glorious wildflowers, and, on most days, blue skies. As you descend, keep your eyes peeled for deer and elk along the road.

LUNCH: Your next stop is **Pitkin,** where there's a picnic site with several tables located just behind the Pitkin Historical Society Museum on Main Street. Pitkin is twice the size of Tincup. Ask a local what the population is, and you may get a one-minute narration about how much the town has grown. The answer? "About eighty-five persons, give or take a baby or two."

Afternoon

Tour the small but interesting **Pitkin Historical Society Museum**— sorry, no phone—and visit with local volunteers. The museum is open from 11:00 A.M. to 3:00 P.M. daily during summer. Donations are welcome. For more information write Pitkin Historical Society, P.O. Box 218, Pitkin, CO 81241.

For a fishing license, gas, snacks, nightcrawlers, or an I LOVE PITKIN bumper sticker, stop at **Silver Plume General Store** (204 Ninth Street, Pitkin; 970–641–3866).

On the north edge of Pitkin is the **Kid's Fishing Pond.** This crystal-

A sign welcomes visitors to Tincup (also spelled Tin Cup), an old mining town near Gunnison.

clear lagoon is reserved for youngsters. The nearby sign says NO ADULTS, PLEASE.

An optional side trip, in which getting there is truly half the fun, is a visit to the **Alpine Tunnel,** constructed by the Denver South Park and Pacific Railroad in 1882. An engineering feat, the tunnel cut through the Continental Divide and, at an elevation of 11,523 feet, was the highest railroad station in the United States. The tunnel was abandoned in 1910, but today you'll see remains of original buildings. A knowledgeable volunteer is on-site to answer questions and give a history lesson for as long as you're willing to listen. Admission is free. Follow the marked road 3 miles beyond Pitkin and continue on a narrow dirt path for 10 miles to the tunnel. Once you're on the dirt road, there's virtually no place to turn around. It takes about thirty minutes to motor the 10 miles of rough road, but the scenery is fantastic and the drive will keep you on the edge of your seat.

Continue on the circle trip through **Ohio City,** which is not a city but a small burg, until the road intersects with Highway 50 west into Gunnison.

DINNER: As the name implies, the **Trough** (located a mile west of Gunnison on Highway 50; 970–641–3724) emphasizes hearty portions. The Trough is a longtime favorite in these parts, and the bounteous meals include blackened prime rib, pork chops, and fresh seafood. The selection varies, and on occasion there are some exotic additions, such as ostrich, kangaroo, and caribou. The menu lightheartedly lists prices for knives, forks, spoons, salt and pepper shakers, and mugs, and the dessert selection reads, "Sorry, cow pie is only available during stock drives!" Open for dinner only at 5:30 P.M. nightly.

LODGING: Mary Lawrence Inn.

Day 3 / Morning

BREAKFAST: Mary Lawrence Inn.
Return to Denver via U.S. Highways 50 and 285.

LUNCH: Go a few miles out of your way after you reach Bailey to **Buck Snort Saloon** (15921 Elk Creek Road; 303–838–0284). This legendary mountain bar-restaurant has a reputation for Buckburgers, renegade regulars, and a great deck that overlooks the river. The Buck Snort is open from noon until midnight on weekends; it opens at 4:00 P.M. Wednesday through Friday and closes Monday and Tuesday. Travel south at Pine Junction (Route 126) for 6 miles to Pine. Signs will direct you to the Buck Snort.

There's More

Blue Mesa Reservoir. This lake in Curecanti National Recreation Area is the largest body of water in Colorado. Because of its easy access, the lake is popular with sailboarders, boaters, and anglers. Blue Mesa Reservoir is

15 scenic miles west of Gunnison on Highway 50.

Four-wheel-drive tours. Alpine Express (970–641–5074) will take you on a guided tour of the considerable four-wheel-drive trails in the area.

Morrow Point boat tour. You'll see towering canyon walls and possibly an eagle or two as you travel for ninety minutes in a forty-two-seat covered pontoon boat through **Morrow Point Reservoir.** To get to the departure point, there is a 232-step hike down (and back up after the boat trip) and 0.25 mile of flat walking. During summer, trips depart twice a day, at 10:30 A.M. and 12:30 P.M. Contact Elk Creek Marina (970–641–0707) for reservations and information.

Special Events

May. Blue Mesa Fishing Tournament awards cash prizes for the biggest fish caught in this annual competition.

June. Rage in the Sage Race is a mountain-bike race event that takes place on the sagebrush plains near Gunnison.

July. Cattlemen's Days is a several-day festival that includes a parade, a carnival, barbecues, a rodeo, a dance, and more. The celebration was initiated by a group of ranchers and businessmen in the 1930s and has been an annual happening since then. For more information call the Chamber of Commerce at (970) 641–1501.

August. The Classic Car Show is a weekend event in which owners gather with their vintage automobiles at Jorgensen Park.

Other Recommended Restaurants and Lodgings

Almont

Harmel's Ranch Resort (P.O. Box 399, Almont, CO 81210; 970–641–1740) offers vacation packages that include lodging, meals, and activities such as horseback riding, river rafting, fishing, square dancing, and trapshooting. This family mountain guest ranch sits at the confluence of Spring Creek and the Taylor River and is surrounded by the Gunnison National Forest. Open May through September. Visit www.harmels.com for more information.

Gunnison

Columbine Victorian Hotel (134 West Tomichi Avenue; 970–641–6834 or 888–970–1880) began operation as a hotel in 1880 and, with its recent restoration, has become a popular accommodation. Rooms have high ceilings, clawfoot tubs, down comforters, and Victorian furnishings.

Mario's Pizza (213 West Tomichi Avenue; 970–641–1374) serves munchies such as oven-baked chicken wings and Italian focaccia bread. Entrees include vegetarian lasagna, ravioli, and barbecue pizza.

Mochas! (901 North Main Street; 970–641–2006) is a drive-through coffeehouse where you can get your daily shot of espresso in a hurry.

For More Information

Curecanti National Recreation Area, National Park Service, 102 Elk Creek, Gunnison, CO 81230; (970) 641–2337.

Gunnison Country Chamber of Commerce, 500 East Tomichi Avenue, P.O. Box 36, Gunnison, CO 81230; (970) 641–1501 or (800) 274–7580; www.gunnisonchamber.com.

Crested Butte and Mount Crested Butte

Wildflower Capital of Colorado

2 Nights

Referred to by locals as "the last great Colorado ski town," Crested Butte greets visitors with glorious alpine basins, dynamic terrain, and down-home friendliness.

Crested Butte Mountain Resort and the town of Crested Butte are located a comfortable 3 miles apart. The two areas blend trendiness with a sense of community. Bronzed cyclists cruise through town on mountain bikes as horses graze non-chalantly in the pasture across from the town hall.

- ☐ Walking tour of historic town
- ☐ Mountain golf course
- ☐ Wildflower Festival
- ☐ Mountain-biking mecca
- ☐ Extreme skiing

Crested Butte traces its roots to the 1800s mining boom and is listed as a National Historic District. Today you'll find art galleries, shops, and restaurants that serve cuisine ranging from sushi to fried chicken.

When someone says, "Meet me at Paradise," the person is speaking of Paradise Warming House, midway up Crested Butte Mountain. In winter the mountain has gentle slopes for beginners and enough extreme terrain to thrill the gnarliest of dudes.

As a summer destination, Crested Butte's attractions are unequaled. Wildflowers flourish in lush meadows, the countryside basks in mild mountain weather, bicycling is bliss, and the living is easy.

Day 1 / Morning

Crested Butte is 230 miles from Denver. To get there, take U.S. 285 south-west from Denver to Poncha Springs. Continue west on U.S. 50 to Gunnison and travel north on Highway 135 for 30 miles to Crested Butte.

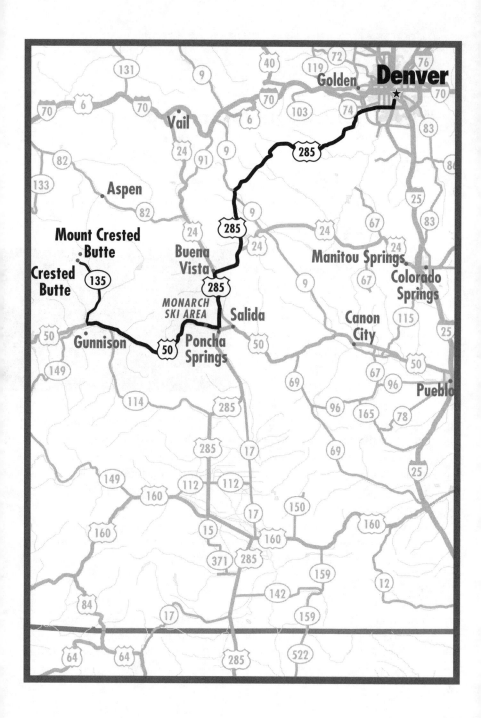

LUNCH: After three and a half hours on the road, you'll be ready for lunch about the time you arrive in Gunnison. For traditional favorites such as steak, sandwiches, and seafood, eat at **Palisades Restaurant & Saloon** (820 North Main Street, Gunnison; 970–641–9223). Open daily 11:00 A.M. to 9:00 P.M. Sunday hours are 7:00 A.M. to 9:00 P.M.

Afternoon

Your first stop in Crested Butte is the Chamber of Commerce and Visitor Center (601 Elk Avenue—the town's main street—at the four-way stop; 970–349–6438). It has a wealth of valuable information. Familiarize yourself with Crested Butte on a self-guided walking tour; a map is available at the visitor center. Be sure to check out the defunct two-story outhouse, located in the alley behind the Company Store, at Elk Avenue and Third Street. One explanation for the two levels is that during winter, the first level became inaccessible because of snow.

For up-to-date news on area fly fishing, stop at **Dragonfly Anglers** (307 Elk Avenue; 970–349–1228 or 800–491–3079), where the latest fishing information is written on a chalkboard. The staff will arrange guided overnight or day trips to the Gold Medal Black Canyon of the Gunnison River or custom trips to a remote Gunnison County lodge. You can also buy a rod, flies, and a fishing license.

Rendezvous Gallery & Framing (418 Elk Avenue; 970–349–6804) has a selection of work by local artist Sean Guerrierio. Notice his characteristic benches along Elk Avenue.

DINNER: **Soupçon Restaurant** is a real find, literally. Located in the alley behind the Forest Queen Hotel and Restaurant (129 Elk Avenue), Soupçon serves phenomenal French food in an intimate European atmosphere. The cafe is housed in a modest log cabin, and the small dining area makes for a romantic dinner. Tables are close together but not disturbingly so. Start with baked polenta or escargot, then move on to an entree such as roast duck or elk tenderloin. For reservations call Soupçon Restaurant at (970) 349–5448.

LODGING: **Sheraton Crested Butte Resort,** 6 Emmons Road, Mount Crested Butte; (970) 349–8000 or (800) 325–3535. Located in the heart of the mountain village, this amenity-conscious lodge offers 252 rooms that range in price from $65 to $213. A pool with a mountain view, workout facility, cozy lobby, and a daily newspaper delivered to your door are included. It's a short walk to the lifts from the Sheraton.

Day 2 / *Morning*

BREAKFAST: The **Woodstone Grille** at the Sheraton. The restaurant is open from 7:00 to 10:30 A.M. A full breakfast buffet is available for $9.50. Continental breakfast buffet is also available. This restaurant is also open for dinner, serving excellent oven-roasted entrees. The warm atmosphere is perfect after a day on the slopes. Try the **Woodstone Deli** (located next to the Grille, 970–349–8030), serving "to go" sandwiches, for lunch.

The **Silver Queen Quad Lift** offers a breathtaking ride to the top of Crested Butte Mountain. You'll get glorious views of the town of Crested Butte below and the surrounding snow-covered peaks. During summer, hike the trails. As the sign at the top of the mountain says, GET ACQUAINTED WITH THE LOCALS, which include yellow-bellied marmots, blue grouse, and red-tailed hawks. If you have energy to burn, walk back down to the base of the ski area.

During winter, skiers will want to be on the slopes the moment the lifts open. Beware the double-black-diamond runs with names like Total Recall, Rambo, and Toilet Bowl. Beginners will want to learn on wide, gentle slopes such as Little Lizzie and Houston.

LATE BRUNCH OR LUNCH: The food at the **Idle Spur,** home of the Crested Butte Brewery & Pub (226 Elk Avenue, Crested Butte; 970–349–5026), is exactly what one would imagine from a brewpub—and much more. Appetizers include Cajun-style popcorn shrimp and game sausage. For an entree, select from items such as elk steak, filet mignon, and jumbo Gulf prawns. The Rodeo Stout and India Pale Ale are two of the excellent beers brewed on-site. Brewery tours are available. Brunch begins at 10:00 A.M. on weekends. Actor Tom Skerritt and his son-in-law own this restaurant that's a favorite with locals.

Afternoon

During summer you can enjoy a leisurely lunch and still make it for a 1:00 P.M. tee time at the **Club at Crested Butte** (385 Country Club Drive, Crested Butte; 970–349–6127). At 9,000 feet above sea level, this mountain course, designed by Robert Trent Jones II, is one of the most beautiful in the state. The course is open to the public, and reservations are recommended. During winter the course is transformed into a superb **cross-country ski track.** Ask about the Club's sleigh-ride dinners.

DINNER: Sometimes you just want to overdo it with skillet-fried chicken, mashed potatoes and gravy, powder biscuits with homemade preserves, and sweet corn in cream sauce. Luckily, **Slogar Bar & Restaurant** (Second Street and Whiterock Avenue, Crested Butte; 970–349–5765) will satisfy the craving. Meals are served family-style in the Victorian setting of this antiques-filled restaurant. Steak dinners are also available. Reservations are recommended.

LODGING: Sheraton Crested Butte Resort.

Day 3 / Morning

BREAKFAST: Coffee is the first order of the day. For a variety of caffeine-laden drinks, try **Camp 4 Coffee** (Fourth Street and Elk Avenue, 970–349–5148) or **Paradise Cafe** (Third and Elk; 970–349–6233). Look for the painted parrot in the window at Paradise.

If weather permits, drive to Gunnison via **Ohio Pass.** You'll travel on a gravel road that twists and turns through lush forests, wild meadows, and spectacular mountain scenery. During summer, you'll see brilliant wildflowers, and in fall, golden aspen. The elevation is about 10,000 feet above sea level. Follow County Road 12 from the west end of Crested Butte. Driving time to Gunnison is about one hour.

At Gunnison, take U.S. Highway 50 east to Poncha Springs and then U.S. Highway 285 to Denver.

There's More

Dinner at 10,000 feet. Technically, guests arrive via a Sno-Cat–pulled sleigh at Bubba's on the Mountain, a restaurant located at Paradise Warming House, halfway up Crested Butte Mountain. Entree choices include prime rib, shrimp scampi, and Colorado lamb. Enjoy incredible views of the Elk Mountain Range. For details call (970) 349–2211.

Last Tracks Fondue is another option. Ride the Keystone Lift to Twister Warming House at 4:30 P.M. daily for a spectacular three-course fondue dinner. After dinner, you have the option of skiing or snowshoeing back to the base area. You may also ride the lift down. Call (970) 349–2211.

Mountain biking. As a mountain-biking haven, Crested Butte has an abundance of backcountry trails, single-track paths, and four-wheel-drive roads.

Rocky Mountain Biological Laboratory (P.O. Box 519, Crested Butte, CO 81224; 970–394–7231) is a nonprofit corporation that facilitates research for scientists and promotes environmental education. Wildflower tours are available Wednesday afternoons the months of June, July, and August.

Ski mountaineering. For guided expeditions of the backcountry, contact Adventures to the Edge, Ltd. (P.O. Box 91, Crested Butte, CO 81224; 800–349–5219). The company offers several options, including a hut-to-hut ski trek, as well as classes in avalanche awareness, winter mountaineering, and ice climbing. For the less daring there's snowshoeing.

Special Events

March and April. With its radical terrain, Mount Crested Butte is ideal for daredevils. Skiers and snowboarders gather here for the U.S. Extreme Freeskiing Championships and the U.S. Extreme Boarderfest. Spectators are welcome.

June. Fat Tire Bike Festival, Crested Butte, attracts mountain-bike zealots from around the world for a week of clinics, rides, races, and more.

July. Wildflower Festival. Alpine hikes, garden tours, and butterfly walks are a few of the events that happen during this celebration of summer, when the area becomes a dazzling display of bluebells, columbines, and a host of other flowers.

August. Crested Butte Chamber Music Festival. Concerts that feature renowned musicians are performed in informal settings.

December. Rocky Mountain Holidays. Celebrate the holidays mountain-style in the historic town of Crested Butte. Enter one of several contests that include gingerbread-house making, wreath decorating, and snowman building.

Other Recommended Restaurants and Lodgings

Crested Butte

Cristiana Guesthaus Bed and Breakfast, 621 Maroon Avenue, P.O. Box 427, Crested Butte, CO 81224; (800) 824–7899. This European-style lodge is ideally located several blocks from the shops and restaurants on Elk Avenue and near the free shuttle to the ski area. Each of the twenty-one rooms has a private bath. After a day of skiing or exploring, you'll appreciate the outdoor hot tub and the warm lobby with its stone fireplace. Breakfast includes homemade muesli, granola, and pastries. Hosts Martin and Rosemary Catmur are avid outdoorspeople and can suggest a hiking or cross-country ski trail.

Mount Crested Butte

The Avalanche, a popular bar-restaurant located at the base of the ski area across from Club Med (970–349–7195), serves breakfast, lunch, and dinner. This is a locals' favorite. The Avalanche serves great pizza, fish-and-chips, and mahimahi fish tacos.

Crested Butte International Hostel, 615 Teocalli Avenue, Crested Butte; mailing address: P.O. Box 1332, Crested Butte, CO 81224; (970) 349–0588; www.crestedbuttehostel.com. Forget any preconceived ideas you might have when you hear the word *hostel*. (You *don't* have to scrub the common area before checking out.) This accommodation offers cozy, convenient, and low-cost lodging.

For More Information

Crested Butte/Mount Crested Butte Chamber of Commerce, 601 Elk Avenue, P.O. Box 1288, Crested Butte, CO 81224; (970) 349–6438 or (800) 545–4505.

Crested Butte Vacations, 600 Gothic Road, P.O. Box 5700, Dept. 81, Mount Crested Butte, CO 81225; (800) 544–8448; www.crestedbutteresort.com.

Durango

One of America's Best Small Towns

3 Nights

Durango may push the envelope for a *quick* getaway, but this escape is well worth the 333-mile drive. Tucked between the spectacular San Juan Mountains and the Animas River Valley, this scenic town captures the hearts of visitors.

☐ San Juan Skyway

☐ Hot springs

☐ Durango & Silverton Narrow Gauge Railroad

Named by *Outside* magazine as one of the most desirable small cities in the country, Durango is a mecca for sports enthusiasts. Durango is also the home station for the popular Durango & Silverton Narrow Gauge Railroad. You'll hear the whistle blast and see the yellow cars behind the steam locomotive as it arrives and departs on daily runs. The town also boasts several delightful B&Bs, a couple of microbreweries, and a string of shops and art galleries.

The San Juan Skyway, a 236-mile route designated as one of six "All American" roads by the U.S. Department of Transportation, loops through alpine forests, rolling hills, and towering mountains. The skyway connects several towns, including Durango, Telluride, Ridgway, Ouray, and Silverton. You can drive the entire route in six hours or take days to soak in the incredible scenery and recreation the area offers.

Spend some time in Ridgway, population 820, located at the northern entrance to the San Juan Skyway, 81 miles north of Durango. Nearby Ridgway State Park has more than 1,000 acres of water for boating, fishing, and swimming. There are easy trails that can be hiked even in winter. You'll have plenty of elbow room here.

Day 1 / Morning

Plan on seven hours (longer with a lunch stop) to drive the 333 miles to Durango. From Denver, take U.S. Highway 285 southwest to Monte Vista and continue west on Highway 160 to Durango.

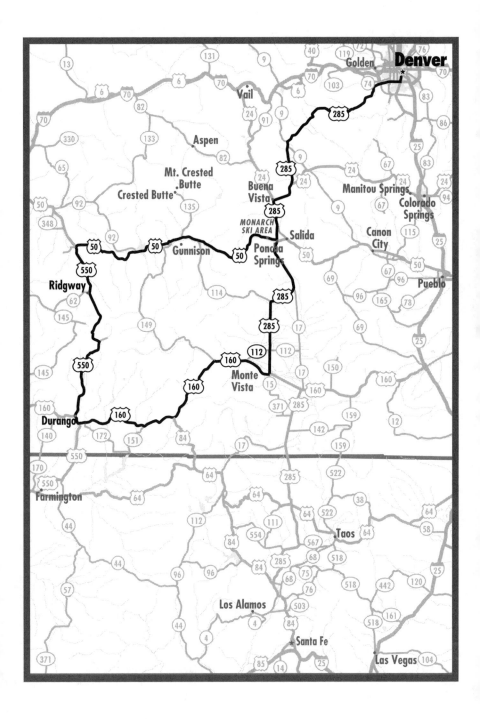

COFFEE BREAK OR LUNCH: Bongo Billy's, 713 South Highway 24, Buena Vista; (719) 395–2634. Bongo Billy's roasts its own beans for its delicious coffee. The lunch menu consists mostly of soup and sandwiches, including a vegetarian hummus sandwich. The restaurant is open from 7:00 A.M. to 9:00 P.M. during the summer (on Sunday it closes at 7:00 P.M.) and from 7:00 A.M. to 6:00 P.M. during the winter. To get to Bongo Billy's, turn north onto Highway 24 and head into Buena Vista. The restaurant is on the right side of the highway.

Afternoon

Downtown Durango is a National Historic District. Main Avenue dates back to the late 1800s, and the Durango & Silverton Narrow Gauge Railroad goes back to the days when the town served as a transportation center for the region's booming silver and gold mines. Today you'll find a mix of galleries, tourist shops, museums, and restaurants. The Visitor Center, at 111 South Camino del Rio (970–247–0312), has a comprehensive guide to the town's galleries, as well as other valuable information on the area. The Visitor Center is open Monday through Saturday from 8:00 A.M. to 5:00 P.M. and Sunday, 10:00 A.M. to 4:00 P.M.

DINNER: Steamworks Brewing Company (801 East Second Avenue, Durango; 970–259–9200) is such a good restaurant that you'll want to dine here more than once. Hardwood floors, exposed brick, an ebullient staff, and superb food and beer provide an unbeatable combination. Try the Lizard Head Red, an excellent amber ale; or the Steam-Engine Steam. The Southwest Chicken Pizza is a savory selection from the wood-fired pizza choices. Other menu items include Jamaican Style Buffalo Wings and Colorado Trail Steak, a charbroiled, eighteen-ounce ribeye bone-in cut served with sautéed mushrooms, au gratin potatoes, and vegetables. Brewery tours are available. Steamworks Brewing Company is open daily from 11:00 A.M. until last call.

LODGING: Rochester Hotel, 721 East Second Avenue, Durango; (970) 385–1920 or (800) 664–1920. Each of the fifteen guest rooms in this hotel is decorated in a Western-film motif. High-ceilinged rooms with names such as City Slickers, How the West Was Won, and Butch Cassidy and the Sundance Kid are furnished in "cowboy Victoriana." A neon sign in front, framed movie posters on the walls, freshly baked chocolate chip cookies in the lobby, and classic Westerns playing on the big-screen TV make this B&B a fun place to hang your cowboy hat. For more information visit www.rochesterhotel.com.

Day 2 / Morning

BREAKFAST: Rochester Hotel serves a different entree each day, such as *huevos rancheros* or multigrain waffles. Guests may also enjoy fresh cranberry-and-oatmeal scones or lemon-ginger muffins.

This morning, ride on Colorado's most famous train, the **Durango & Silverton Narrow Gauge.** You'll travel through the San Juan National Forest wilderness on the coal-fired steam locomotive to the old mining town of Silverton.

A round-trip ride takes eight and a half hours: three and a quarter hours each way and a two-hour stop in Silverton. The Durango & Silverton Narrow Gauge runs from early May through the last Sunday in October. July through mid-August, trains depart weekdays at 7:30, 8:15, and 9:00 A.M. The Winter Holiday Train runs from late November through the first of April and travels to Cascade Canyon. Refreshments and snacks are available on the train. Reservations are recommended. Contact Durango & Silverton Narrow Gauge, 479 Main Avenue, Durango; (970) 247–2733 or (800) 872–4607; www.durangotrain.com.

LUNCH: The **Pickle Barrel,** 1304 Greene Street, Silverton; (970) 387–5713. House specials change daily, but you might find selections such as a green chile Cheddar burger or fillet of chicken sandwich. Regular menu items include a hot pastrami sandwich, burgers, and soup. The Pickle Barrel is located in a historic brick building and is open for lunch daily from 11:30 A.M. to 3:00 P.M. Also open for dinner from 5:00 to 9:00 P.M. Memorial Day through September.

Afternoon

At an altitude of 9,318 feet above sea level, the old mining town of **Silverton** was home to gambling halls and saloons in the late 1800s, when miners removed "silver by the ton" from the region. Today you'll find tourist shops, restaurants, and Victorian architecture here. The **San Juan County Historical Museum** (1567 Greene Street; 970–387–5838), located in the old San Juan County Jail, displays mining artifacts. The museum is open daily from 9:00 A.M. to 5:00 P.M. June 1 to mid-September and then from 10:00 A.M. to 3:00 P.M. until mid-October.

DINNER: Cyprus Cafe, 725 East Second Avenue (across the street from the Rochester Hotel), Durango; (970) 385–6884. The Cyprus specializes in Mediterranean cuisine within a sleek urban setting. The menu offers appetizers such as *spanakopita* (a spinach and feta cheese mixture in phyllo dough) and *baba ganoush*. Lunch entrees include *souvlakia,* the Cyprus burger, and *falafel.* The dinner menu features Tunisian prawns, rainbow springs trout, and Cyprus pasta.

LODGING: Rochester Hotel.

Day 3 / Morning

BREAKFAST: Le Rendezvous Swiss Bakery (750 Main Avenue, Durango; 970–385–5685) is more than a bakery. The cafe serves a Swiss breakfast that consists of cheese, a roll, and an apple and also offers stuffed croissants, breakfast burritos, and *huevos rancheros*. Open 7:00 A.M. to 3:00 P.M. daily.

Drive a portion of the spectacular **San Juan Skyway** on Highway 550 from Durango to Ridgway. You'll parallel the Durango & Silverton Narrow Gauge Railroad for several miles as you pass through the Animas Valley and then climb to 10,000 feet over Coal Bank and Molas Passes. Shortly after crossing Red Mountain Pass at the impressive elevation of 11,075 feet above sea level, you'll reach the pretty little Victorian town of **Ouray,** which calls itself the Little Switzerland of America. From Ouray, continue north on Highway 550 to Ridgway.

LUNCH: San Juan Mountain Bakery and Cafe, 520 Sherman, Ridgway; (970) 626–5803. Offers outdoor dining, views of the San Juans, and a variety of sandwiches.

Afternoon

Ridgway State Park and Reservoir, located 3.5 miles north of Ridgway on Highway 550, offers fishing, swimming, boating, hiking, and camping. With views of the San Juan Mountains and Sneffels Range, this 1,000-acre reservoir is one of the area's main attractions. Stop at the visitor center, located just past the entrance, for maps and information. Contact Ridgway State Park, 28555 Highway 550, Ridgway, CO 81432; (970) 626–5822.

DINNER: The **Adobe Inn and Restaurant,** P.O. Box 470, Ridgway, CO 81432; (970) 626–5939. This restaurant alone is worth your drive across the state. Begin with homemade chips and the best salsa this side of the border. Move on to a house specialty such as Chimichanga de Carne or the Burrito Grande. Owners Joyce and Terre Bucknam use the freshest ingredients available and original recipes. Enjoy your drink on the courtyard patio before dinner. The bar opens at 5:00 P.M., and dinner is served from 5:30 to 9:30 P.M. daily, year-round. To get there, turn south from Sherman Street, which is Highway 62, onto Liddell Drive for 1 block.

LODGING: Chipeta Sun Lodge & Spa, 304 South Lena, P.O. Box 2013, Ridgway, CO 81432; (970) 626–3737 or (800) 633–5868; www.chipeta.com. This solar adobe, Santa Fe–style inn is peaceful and quiet and offers dramatic views of the San Juan Mountain peaks. The stone fireplace dominates the "great room," where guests visit, read, or listen to music. Guest rooms have rustic log furniture, goose-down comforters, and Mexican tile in the private bath. The Sneffels Room has its own spa tub. A favorite with guests is the hot tub in the third floor turret, with views of Sneffels Range. If you prefer, ask for a suite, complete with a gas-log fireplace and two-person hot tub. Rates (beginning at $95 in the off-season) include use of the spa facilities.

Day 4 / Morning

BREAKFAST: Chipeta Sun Lodge & Spa. Help yourself to homemade granola, yogurt, and an entree such as banana pancakes, French toast, or Southwestern eggs, with tea or coffee from the Steaming Bean Coffee Company in Telluride. Visit with other guests in the airy, sun-drenched, two-story solarium.

There's More

Mesa Verde National Park. Cliff dwellings fascinate visitors at this incredible site. The park is located an hour from Durango on Highway 160 west. The park is open 365 days a year. Admission is $10 per vehicle. For more information contact Mesa Verde National Park, P.O. Box 8, Mesa Verde National Park, CO 81330; (970) 529–4465 or (970) 529–4461.

Mild to Wild Rafting, 1111 Camino del Rio, Durango; (970) 247–4789 or (800) 567–6745. True to its name, this company offers everything from two-hour trips (calm enough for "ages three to ninety-three") on the Lower Animas to exciting three- to four-day trips in Class-V white water.

San Juan Skyway. You could spend a day or a week on this 236-mile drive through valleys, canyons, historic mining towns, and incredible mountain terrain. For more information on the Inns of the San Juan Skyway, call (970) 247–0312 or (800) 962–2493.

Ski Purgatory at Durango Mountain Resort. Located 26 miles north of Durango on Highway 550, Purgatory offers an average annual snowfall of 300 inches for some excellent downhill skiing. During summer, rent a mountain bicycle at the base of the ski area, take it on the chairlift, then ride down one of the well-marked trails. For information contact Durango Mountain Resort, 1 Skier Place, Durango, CO 81302; (970) 247–9000; www.durangomountain.com.

Trimble Hot Springs, 6475 County Road 203, Durango; (970) 247–0111. Take a soak in the Olympic-size natural hot-springs pool or schedule a massage. The facility is open daily during summer from 8:00 A.M. to 11:00 P.M. and during winter from 9:00 A.M. to 10:00 P.M. Admission is $8.50 for adults and $6 for children twelve and under. Trimble Hot Springs is located 6 miles north of Durango on U.S. Highway 550.

Special Events

May. On Memorial Day weekend the Iron Horse Bicycle Classic pits elite cyclists in a punishing road race against the Durango & Silverton Narrow Gauge train. For information call (970) 259–4621; www.ironhorsebicycle classic.com.

June. Animas River Days, Durango. Billed as Colorado's premier white-water festival, this event attracts white-water fanatics from around the United States. Spectators watch as contestants guide their crafts through the white-water course. For details contact Animas River Race Association, P.O. Box 3626, Durango, CO 81302; (970) 259–3893.

Mid-September to mid-October. Colorfest. When spectacular fall colors arrive, the entire area celebrates. Days are usually sunny and warm and nights crisp for the events, which include a vintage car show, fishing contests, art shows, and more. For information call (970) 247–0312.

Other Recommended Restaurants and Lodgings

Durango

General Palmer Hotel, 567 Main Avenue; (970) 247–4747 or (800) 523–3358; www.generalpalmerhotel.com. Named for the gentleman who brought the Denver & Rio Grande Western Railroad to Durango, this lovely Victorian hotel offers an elegant lobby, fresh cookies in the afternoon, and a location in the heart of downtown Durango.

Lady Falconburgh's, 640 Main Avenue; (970) 382–9664. Located downstairs in the Century Mall, this busy restaurant is named for Lady Falconburgh, who was born in England in 1637 and was reportedly "flirtatious and fond of ale." Falconburgh's offers many choices of stouts (ask to see the four-page bar menu) as well as burgers, smoked trout, quesadillas, and chicken Caesar salad. Open daily from 11:30 A.M. to 10:30 P.M.

The Leland House, 721 East Second Avenue; (970) 385–1920 or (800) 664–1920. Well-appointed suites are available at this lovely inn, located across the street from the Rochester Hotel. The Leland House and the Rochester Hotel are run by the same management.

The Ore House, 147 East College Drive; (970) 247–5707. Steak lovers will be satisfied at this restaurant, which serves beef aged on the premises. Seafood is also available. The Ore House is open from 5:30 to 11:00 P.M. daily.

The Strater Hotel, 699 Main Avenue; (970) 247–4431 or (800) 247–4431. This more-than-a-century-old redbrick hotel is located in the middle of the Main Avenue Historical District, 2 blocks from the Durango & Silverton Narrow Gauge Train Depot. For more information visit www.strater.com.

Tall Timber Resort, 1 Silverton Star; (970) 259-4813; www.talltimber resort.com. This secluded resort, near Durango, boasts pure air, sumptuous cuisine, and a serene setting. What you won't find here are radios, phones, fax machines, or CNN. No roads spoil the vast wilderness. Guests arrive via the Silverton, the last scheduled narrow gauge train in the United States, or by helicopter, soaring over the canyon walls high above the Animas River. Before it was a resort, the meadow was the set for Hollywood favorites, including Robert Redford and Paul Newman's *Butch Cassidy and the Sundance Kid*. White-water rafting, fishing, and hiking are available. You'll have plenty of elbow room and personalized service here: The resort allows a maximum of thirty guests.

Telluride

Wyndham Peaks Resort and Golden Door Spa, 136 Country Club Drive, P.O. Box 2702, Telluride, CO 81435; (970) 728–6800 or (800) 789–2220; www.thepeaksresort.com. It's a little out of the way from Durango (two hours north on Highway 145) and from Ridgway (37 miles south on Highway 145), and it's pricey, but for a special occasion, the Peaks Resort is worth the drive. Luxury accommodations, terraces on more than half of the 174 guest rooms, and a fabulous 42,000-square-foot spa spread over four levels complete this resort. The spa offers an indoor lap pool, oxygen bar, indoor climbing wall (Tom Cruise trained here for his role in *MI2*), and an array of facial and body treatments. The women's spa even has a basin filled with ice water and cucumber slices for weary eyes. This exclusive resort is located at the ski area high above the town, but it's an easy commute to the Victorian charm of Telluride. Park the car for your entire stay and take the free twelve-minute gondola into Telluride. The gondola is smooth and scenic, and you don't have to worry about those pesky parking meters. After you exit the gondola, walk 1 block straight ahead to Smuggler's Brewpub and Grille, at the corner of San Juan Avenue and Pine Street; (970) 728–0919. This is where locals gather to watch sports and quaff a Knuckledragger Extra Pale Ale. The burgers are excellent. Hours are 11:00 A.M. to 11:00 P.M. daily. Coffee aficionados will appreciate the Steaming Bean, 221 West Colorado Avenue, Telluride; (970) 728–0793.

For More Information

Durango Area Chamber Resort Association, P.O. Box 287, 111 South Camino del Rio, Durango, CO 81302; (970) 247–0312 or (800) 525–8855; www.durango.org.

Durango Central Reservations, 945 Main Avenue, Durango, CO 81301; (800) 525–0892.

Inns of the San Juan Skyway, P.O. Box 307, Ridgway, CO 81432; (800) 962–2493.

Taos and Santa Fe, New Mexico

The Southwest Experience

3 Nights

Taos houses more artists and galleries per capita than Paris. This cultural mecca, located just 40 miles south of the Colorado border, continues traditions that began when the Spanish first visited the area.

In the early 1800s Taos was the headquarters for fur trappers who traded pelts for supplies and services. Kit Carson, the legendary figure of the Old West, made his home here from 1826 to 1868. Today you'll discover a town rich in history and an area abundant with recreational possibilities. Explore the museums, old pueblos, and more than eighty art galleries. Dine on traditional northern New Mexico cuisine, which can include red or green chile, posole, tamales, and bread baked in an outside adobe oven.

- ☐ Fine dining
- ☐ Downhill skiing
- ☐ Green Chile Beer
- ☐ Yuletide festival
- ☐ Summer hiking
- ☐ Outdoor opera
- ☐ Galleries

Venture into the rugged backcountry adjacent to millions of acres of pristine wilderness on a summer day-hike or a winter cross-country ski outing and enjoy the extensive trails, fabulous sunsets, and powerful panoramas.

Seventy scenic miles south of Taos lies the town of Santa Fe, one of the oldest cities in the United States. The allure of this picturesque city lies in its gallery-lined streets, superb restaurants, and gorgeous setting. Visit the museums, browse the boutiques, and attend the renowned Santa Fe Opera. You'll delight in the authentic Southwestern ambience of this gracious town.

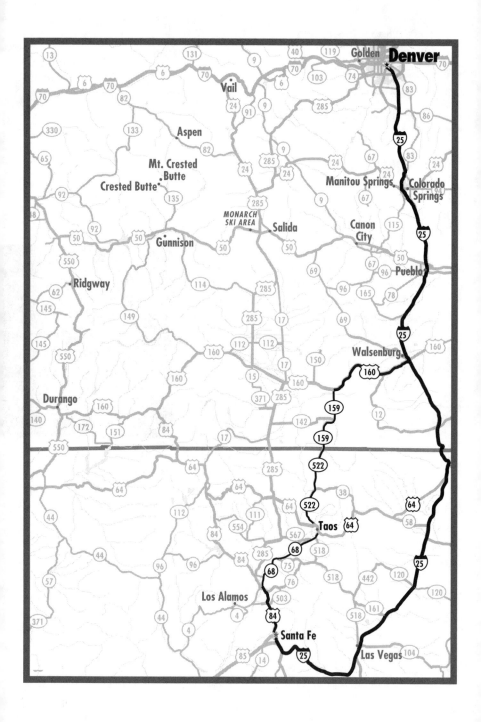

Day 1 / *Morning*

To get to Taos (300 miles from Denver, about five hours) travel south on I–25. At Walsenburg, follow U.S. Highway 160 to Fort Garland, and turn south on Highway 159 through San Luis to Taos.

LUNCH: Plan to have lunch in Walsenburg at **Alys' Fireside Cafe,** 606 Main Street; (719) 738–3993. Alys' has a statewide reputation for its excellent offerings. Lunch may be Baja-style *huevos rancheros* or Southwest corn chowder. The dinner menu offers rack of lamb, prime rib, or grilled quail. For dessert, try chocolate whiskey pudding. Alys' is open for lunch Monday through Friday from 11:30 A.M. to 2:30 P.M., and for dinner Wednesday through Saturday from 6:00 to 9:00 P.M.

From Walsenburg, follow U.S. Highway 160 to Fort Garland and turn south on Highway 159 through San Luis to Taos.

Afternoon

Get a feel for the town at **Taos Plaza,** located in the center of the city. Browse the many galleries and shops for Southwestern souvenirs and art, or sit a spell on one of the decorative benches under the shade of a tree in the historic Plaza.

DINNER: Eske's Brew Pub (106 Des Georges Lane, located half a block east of Taos Plaza; 505–758–1517) serves fresh beer on tap and great pub grub. Try the Taos Green Chile Beer, or order a taster tray for a sampling of the brewed-on-site beers. Bangers and mash, also known as bratwurst cooked in beer served with mashed potatoes, is an excellent selection. The pub has daily specials, including sushi on Tuesday night. Weather permitting, you'll want to sit outside at the picnic tables or on the back patio.

LODGING: San Geronimo Lodge, 1101 Witt Road, Taos; (800) 894–4119 or www.sangeronimolodge.com. Innkeeper Pat Hoffman and her friendly "Taos mutts," Bonita and Bear, give guests a warm New Mexico welcome. The lodge, with hardwood floors and high ceilings, has fireplaces throughout. December is a delightful time to visit because the entire town of Taos is decked out for the season. *Farolitos* (little lanterns), also called luminaria in the southern part of the state, twinkle festively on the rooftops of homes and businesses and the pathway of LeDoux Street, where many galleries are located. Pat is the ideal hostess, making sure guests have gloves, hats, and coats if they arrive unprepared for the winter temperatures. San Geronimo Lodge is built in native adobe and is tucked away on two and a half acres. The lodge has an outdoor hot tub (steaming year-round) and an outdoor chile-shaped swimming pool for use in the summer. Each of the eighteen guestrooms has a television, phone, and private bath decorated with Mexican ceramic tile. Many rooms offer a fireplace and verandah. A licensed massage therapist is available.

Day 2 / Morning

BREAKFAST: San Geronimo Lodge. A full, gourmet breakfast is served in the airy, art-filled dining room at cozy tables for two or four persons. Breakfast includes an entree such as artichoke mushroom baked omelet or apple-stuffed French toast, homemade pastries, and freshly brewed piñon coffee.

There are seven museums in the area, and if you plan to visit several or all, purchase a museum combination ticket for $20. The ticket is honored for up to a year from date of purchase, is transferable, and can be purchased at any of the seven museums.

The **Kit Carson Home and Museum** (on Kit Carson Road, east of the Plaza; 505–758–4741) illustrates the life of Kit Carson, one of the Old West's most famous figures. Here you'll learn about Carson's remarkable life as a fur trapper, mountain man, explorer, and military officer. Exhibits portray the various phases of Carson's life, and several rooms are furnished as they would have been in the Carson era. The Kit Carson Home and Museum is open daily from 9:00 A.M. to 5:00 P.M. in winter and from 8:00 A.M. to 6:00 P.M. in summer.

The combination ticket also includes the **Ernest L. Blumenschein Home and Museum** (222 Ledoux Street; 505–758–0505), filled with European antiques; the **Harwood Museum** (238 Ledoux Street; 505–758–9826), which features nineteenth-century art; and **Hacienda Martinez** (2 miles south of the Plaza; 505–758–0505), a Spanish Colonial hacienda. You can also visit the **Fechin Institute** (227 Paseo del Pueblo Norte; 505–758–1710), former home of Russian artist Nicolai Fechin; the **Millicent Rogers Museum** (on Museum Road, 4 miles north of the Plaza; 505–758–2462), which exhibits northern New Mexico art; and the **Van Vechten Lineberry Museum** (501 Paseo del Pueblo Norte; 505–578–2690), which showcases the work of local artists.

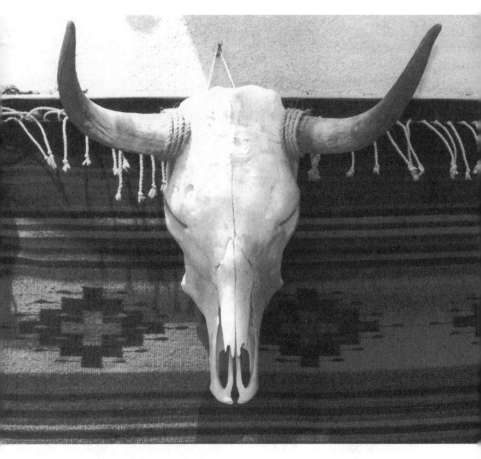

A familiar scene in the Southwest.

LUNCH: Doc Martin's Restaurant, 125 Paseo del Pueblo Norte; (505) 758–1977. Located at the Historic Taos Inn, Doc Martin's has nothing to do with the popular shoe of the same name. Dr. Thomas Paul Martin, also known as "Doc," arrived in Taos in the 1890s and purchased the house where the restaurant is now located. "Doc's daily specials" include items such as chilled cantaloupe soup, Colorado rack of lamb, or grilled tuna, and, for dessert, raspberry soufflé. Open daily for lunch and dinner.

Afternoon

Taos Pueblo, located approximately 3 miles northeast of the town of Taos, is a community inhabited by members of the Taos Pueblo Tribe. The pueblo is made up of ancient adobe structures, many of which are built one on top of another, connected by ladders. Visitors are welcome in designated areas, and many of the private homes are open as small curio or art shops. Tribe members sell homemade fry bread. Taos Pueblo is open to the public except during certain religious ceremonies; the pueblo closes late February through early April. Remember to always ask permission before taking someone's photograph.

DINNER: Apple Tree Restaurant (123 Bent Street; 505–758–1900) serves gourmet meals in its Southwestern-style-decorated adobe rooms. Dine indoors by candlelight or outside on the patio beneath the apple tree. Choose fresh rainbow trout served with a different sauce each night—for example, lemon-basil nut. Other choices include mango carnitas enchiladas and filet mignon with shiitake mushroom–brandy sauce. Reservations are recommended. The restaurant serves lunch Monday through Saturday from 11:30 A.M. to 3:00 P.M., dinner daily from 5:30 to 9:00 P.M., and brunch Sunday from 10:00 A.M. to 3:00 P.M.

LODGING: San Geronimo Lodge.

Day 3 / Morning

BREAKFAST: San Geronimo Lodge.

Drive to **Santa Fe** (about 70 miles south of Taos) and take in the art museums, fine restaurants, and charisma of this cultivated city.

Sign up for a walking tour of downtown and Canyon Road at the **Palace of the Governors** (505–827–6483), North Plaza, or browse the area on your own. You could spend days exploring the several blocks around the Plaza in the center of town. You will see Native American artists, some in colorful dress, sitting in front of the Palace of the Governors, who display and sell jewelry, pottery, and handcrafts.

LUNCH: Blue Corn Cafe (133 Water Street; 505–984–1800) advertises "Tortillas y Tequila" on its business card, and the restaurant delivers. The menu has a seemingly endless list of tequilas and margaritas, including Herradura Gold Tequila and a Tequila Diablo Margarita, but you can't go wrong if you order the house margarita. The cafe's signature red, green, yellow, and blue stripes are sure to catch your attention. Salsa and chips are superb, and the enchilada plate is a winner. The restaurant is open from 11:00 A.M. to 11:00 P.M. daily and has live entertainment on weekends.

Afternoon

Visit the **New Mexico Museum of Fine Arts** (107 East Palace Avenue; 505–827–4455), which features art by Georgia O'Keeffe, John Sloan, and Gerald Cassidy, as well as a permanent collection of work by other artists. Admission is $7.00 for adults and $5.00 for residents; free to persons age sixteen and under. The museum is open from 10:00 A.M. to 5:00 P.M. daily and closed Mondays.

Ask about the four-day pass to four museums. The $15.00 pass includes entrance to the New Mexico Museum of Fine Arts; the Palace of the Governors; the **Museum of Indian Arts and Culture** (710 Camino Lejo; 505–827–6344); and the **Museum of International Folk Art** (706 Camino Lejo; 505–827–6350).

DINNER: **The Restaurant at Inn at Loretto** (211 Old Santa Fe Trail; 505–988–5531 or 800–727–5531) is the ideal place to dine on the pleasant patio adjacent to the Loretto Chapel. The Saint Francis Cathedral bells ring on the hour, adding to the ambience. A starter might include gazpacho, which is so good you'll want to ask the chef for his recipe, or Caesar salad with lime-garlic dressing. A good entree choice is the ginger-crusted salmon or grilled lamb chops.

LODGING: **Inn at Loretto** (211 Old Santa Fe Trail; 505–988–5531 or 800–727–5531), offers Southwestern warmth and hospitality. Located 1 block from the Santa Fe Plaza, this fine hotel offers convenience and charm. The lobby bar has a gas fireplace that burns year-round (with a bighorn sheep's skull above it), leather couches and chairs, Indian drum coffee tables, and Hopi wood carvings on the ceiling. Prices vary with the season. January through April and November through early December offer the best rates, which start at $189 and climb to $500 for a suite. The room rate increases from May through October and during the holiday season.

Day 4 / Morning

BREAKFAST: The **Burrito Co.** (111 Washington Avenue; 505–98– CHILE) is listed by the *Los Angeles Times* as "*the* place in Santa Fe for a breakfast burrito." Two dollars and fifty cents buys two scrambled eggs, cheddar cheese, salsa, and homestyle potatoes, all wrapped in a flour tortilla. Relax on the patio and watch locals and tourists stroll by.

Return to Denver via I–25 north.

There's More

Lumina North Fine Art and Sculpture Gardens (11 Des Montes Road, Taos Ski Valley Road and State Road 230, Taos, NM, 87571; 505–776–3957 or toll-free 877–5–LUMINA; www.luminagallery.com) offers contemporary fine art, photography, and sculpture. This exceptional gallery is well worth the ten-minute drive from Taos. Take Ski Valley Road, also known as State Road 150 (toward Arroyo Seco) for 2.5 miles, turn left onto State Road 230, and take the first right. Lumina is open weekends and by appointment.

Santa Fe Opera. Noted for its classic performances and spectacular setting, the open-air opera is a must if you're in Santa Fe during opera season, which runs from late June through late August. Contact the Santa Fe Opera, P.O. Box 2408, Santa Fe, NM 87504; (505) 986–5900 or (800) 280–4654; www.santafeopera.org.

Taos Ski Valley. Ski light, dry powder during the winter months and hike the rolling, forested trails when summer arrives. Taos Ski Valley has more than a dozen lodges and condominium complexes for overnight accommodations, as well as stays in private homes. To make a reservation, call Taos Valley Resort Association at (800) 776–1111. For information about skiing or hiking, call Taos Ski Valley at (505) 776–2291. To get to Taos Ski Valley, take Highway 150 east from Taos for about 15 miles; Highway 150 dead-ends at the ski area.

Special Events

Mid-June–Labor Day. The Downs at Santa Fe features thoroughbred horse racing. For more information about the races, call (505) 471–3311.

Early July–late August. The Santa Fe Chamber Music Festival features chamber music, jazz, and preconcert lectures in the beautiful setting of the St. Francis Auditorium. Call the box office at (505) 983–2075 for information and tickets. Visit www.sfcmf.org.

Mid-September–early October. Taos Arts Festival features art exhibits, crafts fairs, and receptions at local galleries. In addition, you'll see the brilliant colors of autumn. The festival is sponsored by Taos County Chamber of Commerce; (800) 732–8267.

Late October. Taos Mountain Balloon Rally is a hot-air balloon lover's paradise. Observers can sign up to take a balloon ride or to work with a chase crew. Taste of Taos takes place the same weekend, so you can sample cuisine from some of Taos's finest restaurants.

December. Yuletide in Taos. From the day after Thanksgiving through the entire month of December, farolitos (little lanterns) twinkle along Le Doux Street, where many of the galleries are located. The aroma of piñon burning in the fireplace, a light dusting of snow, and holiday decor will put you in the spirit of the season.

Fifth Annual Brewmasters' Festival. More than ten breweries show off their prizewinning beers, accompanied by traditional Southwestern cuisine.

Other Recommended Restaurants and Lodgings

La Veta

Inn at the Spanish Peaks B&B, 310 East Francisco Street; (719) 742–5313 or www.innatthespanishpeaks.com. This cozy B&B in the town of La Veta (population 1,000) offers the St. Andrews Suite, Costa Rica Suite, and Colorado Suite, each with private bath and deck. The St. Andrews Suite has a four-poster bed so lofty, it comes with a footstool. Husband-and-wife team Bill Stark and Tracy Webb prepare a scrumptious breakfast and welcome guests as if they were family. Before leaving this friendly burg, visit the town's library, where you can check out a bike on the honor system for four hours. La Veta is a twenty-minute drive from Walsenburg. Take Highway 16 west from Walsenburg; turn south on Colorado Highway 12. For more information about La Veta, visit www.lavetacucharachamber.com.

Mid-point between Santa Fe and Taos

Rancho de San Juan, P.O. Box 4140, Española, NM 87533; (505) 753–6818 or (800) 726–7121; www.ranchodesanjuan.com. Staying at Rancho de San Juan is like walking through a Georgia O'Keeffe painting. This luxury Relais & Chateaux property, located midway between Taos and Santa Fe, overlooks the Ojo Caliente River Valley. Stay in a private *casita* and soak in the peace and solitude of the New Mexico desert. Dinner at the on-site restaurant is a superb experience not to be missed. Room rates are $175 to $250, suites are $300 to $400.

Santa Fe

Inn of the Anasazi (113 Washington Avenue; 505–988–3030 or 800–688–8100) is located minutes from the Plaza. Prices range from $199 to $395, depending on the size of the room and the season.

Taos

Taos is considered the B&B capital of the Southwest, counting nearly thirty bed & breakfast inns. Call (800) 939–2215 or visit www.taos-bandb inns.com for information on the many selections, which range from a cozy one-suite accommodation to a room near the Plaza to a more secluded B&B on the mesa.

Casa de las Chimeneas, 405 Cordoba Road; (505) 758–4777 or (877) 758–4777; www.visittaos.com. Translated "House of Chimneys," this B&B offers a convenient location blocks from Taos Plaza. Because it's built on nearly an acre of ground surrounded by large trees, the location feels quiet and secluded. The inn offers an outdoor hot tub, a fireplace in each room, a complimentary evening buffet supper, and a fitness facility. Excellent choice.

Historic Taos Inn (125 Paseo del Pueblo Norte; 505–758–2233 or 800–826–7466) is listed on both the State and the National Register of Historic Places. The two-story lobby of this inn is decorated with Southwestern art and handwoven rugs. Rooms, depending on size and the season, begin at $85 and go up to $225 for a suite.

Bravo!, B53-A Paseo del Pueblo Sur; (505) 758–8100. This casual restaurant serves a bit of everything, from sushi or caviar as an appetizer to pasta primavera, roast duck, Louisiana crawfish, or pizza for the main course. All categories are excellent. Encore!

Lambert's of Taos (309 Paseo del Pueblo Sur; 505–758–1009) serves contemporary American cuisine. The menu changes daily, but you'll find grilled yellowfin tuna, roast duck, pepper-crusted lamb, and more. Open nightly for dinner only.

For More Information

Santa Fe Visitor and Convention Bureau, 201 March Street, P.O. Box 909, Santa Fe, NM 87504; (505) 984–6760 or (800) 777–CITY; www.santafe.org.

Taos County Chamber of Commerce, P.O. Drawer I, 1139 Paseo del Sur, Taos, NM 87571; (800) 732–8267 or (505) 758–3873; www.taoschamber.com.

INDEX

A

Absolute Bikes, 180
Academy Riding Stables, 169
Adam's Mark Hotel, Denver, 78
Adam's Mark Hotel, Grand
    Junction, 163
Adobe Creek Golf Course, 162
Adobe Inn and Restaurant,
    The, 204
Alexander Lake Lodge, 162
Allair Timbers Inn, the, 121
Alpenglow Stube, 118
Alpine Hideaway, 110
Alpine Kayak and Canoe, 129
Alpine Tunnel, 189
Alys' Fireside Cafe, 211
Amicas, 180
Anheuser-Busch Brewery, 36
Antares, 53
Apple Tree Restaurant, 214
Arapahoe Basin, 115
Ark Anglers, 180
Arkansas River, 180
Art on the Corner, 157
Ashcroft, 152
Aspen, 148–54
Aspen Art Museum, 150
Aspen Chamber Resort
    Association, 148
Aspen Historical Society, 151, 152
Aspen Skiing Company, 154
Aspen Sports, 150
Assignments, 78
Augusta Restaurant at the
    Westin, 70

Austin's American Grill, 36
Avalanche, the, 199
Avery House, 39

B

Back at the Ranch, 186
Barry Goldwater Air Force
    Academy Visitor Center, 173
Bear Lake, 15
Beaver Creek, 123–32
Beaver Creek Golf Club, 127
Betty Ford Alpine Gardens, 128
Bikesmith, the, 7
Bisetti's Italian Restaurant, 37
Bistro Italiano, 162
Black American West Museum and
    Heritage Center, 77
Black Bear Inn, 131
Black Forest Restaurant, 29
Black Hawk, 27–33
Blazing Adventures, 153
Blu's, 129
Blue Corn Cafe, 214
Blue Iguana, 186
Blue Mesa Reservoir, 190
Blue Moon Bar, 125
Blue Sky Grill, 87
Boaters Choice, 21
Boettcher Concert Hall, 66
Bongo Billy's, 202
Boogie's Diner, 150
Boulder, 2–10
Boulder Creek Path, 7
Boulder Dushanbe Teahouse, 7

Boulder Museum of
    Contemporary Art, 8
Bravo!, 218
Breckenridge Ski Area, 117
Briar Rose, 9
Bridgestone Winter Driving
    School, the, 55
Broadmoor, The, 170
Broadmoor's Golden Bee, The, 172
Broadmoor's Lake Terrace Dining
    Room, The, 173
Broadmoor's Spa and Fitness
    Center, The, 173
Brown Palace Hotel, 73
Brown's Canyon, 179
Brush Creek Ranch, 48
Byers-Evans House, 73
Bubba's Barbecue, 46–47
Buck Snort Saloon, 190
Buckhorn Exchange, 87
Burrito Co., the, 215
Butterfly Pavilion and Insect
    Center, 67–68

C

C Lazy U Ranch, 24–25
Cabin, the, 55
Cache la Poudre River, 39
Cadet Chapel, 174
Camp 4 Coffee, 197
Canyon Rim Trail, 160
Canyon Wind Cellars, 161
Carlson Vineyards, 161
Caroline's Cuisine, 25
Carver's Bakery, 102
Casa de las Chimeneas, 218
Castle Marne, 69
Cave of the Winds, 172

Celestial Cafe, 4–5
Celestial Seasonings, 4
Central City, 27–33
Central City Opera, 30
Challenge Unlimited, 171
Chap's Grill & Chophouse, 123,
    127, 128
Charter, the, 130
Chateau L'Acadienne, 30–31
Chautauqua Dining Hall, 4
Chautauqua Park, 4
Chef's New World Cuisine, 163
Cherry Creek North, 64
Cherry Creek Shopping
    Center, 64
Cherry Cricket, 69
Cheyenne Mountain Zoo, 173
Cheyenne, Wyoming, 43–44
Cheyenne's Old West Museum, 44
Chipeta Sun Lodge & Spa, 205
Churchill Bar, the, 74
Ciao Vino, 41
Cielo, 69
City Market Deli, 187
Claremont Inn Bed and
    Breakfast, 92
Cloud City Coffee House, 138
Club at Crested Butte, the, 196
Club Car, 101
Coal Creek Coffee Company, 47
Colorado Avalanche, 86
Colorado Bicycling Adventures, 15
Colorado Cellars Winery, 161
Colorado History Museum, 73
Colorado National
    Monument, 159
Colorado Rapids, 86
Colorado Riff Raft, 153

Colorado River Headwaters Scenic and Historic Byway, 22
Colorado Rockies, 86
Colorado Ski Museum and Colorado Ski Hall of Fame, 128
Colorado Springs, 166–76
Colorado Springs Fine Arts Center, 170
Colorado State Capitol, 73–74
Colorado State University, 34
Colorado's Ocean Journey, 68
Columbine Café, 135
Columbine Victorian Hotel, 192
Coors Field, 82–83
Copper Mountain Resort, 117
Cordillera (See Lodge & Spa at Cordillera)
Corley Vineyards, 161
Corner Bar, 7
Country Bounty, 179
Coyote Springs, 56
Cozens Ranch House and Museum, 102
Craftsmen in Leather, 13
Crested Butte, 193–99
Crested Butte International Hostel, 199
Cristiana Guest Haus Bed and Breakfast, 198–99
Cross Orchards Historic Farm, 162
Cruise Room, 84
Cry Baby Ranch, 76
Crystal Cafe, 157
Cumberland Pass, 188
Cupboard, the, 36
Cyprus Cafe, 204

D

Daily Bread Cafe and Bakery, 144
Dakota's Bistro, 183
DeBeque Canyon Winery, 161
Delaware Hotel, 139
Del's Triangle 3 Ranch, 58
Denver, 62–70
Denver Art Museum, 65
Denver Botanic Gardens, 67
Denver Broncos, 85–86
Denver ChopHouse and Brewery, 85
Denver Firefighters Museum, 77
Denver Museum of Nature and Science, the, 76
Denver Nuggets, 85
Denver Pavilions, 82
Denver Performing Arts Complex, 66
Denver Public Library, 71, 73
Denver Zoo, 67
Destinations West, 104
Devil's Thumb Guest and Cross-Country Ski Center, 104
Dinosaur Expeditions, 158
Dinosaur Journey, 158
Dirt Camp, 120
Discovery Center Science Museum, 39
Divide Grill, 105
Doc Holliday's grave, 144
Doc Martin's Restaurant, 213
Dolan's, 9
Dolce Vita, 158
Dostal Alley, 32
Dot's Diner, 4
Double Diamond Stables, 38–39
Downtown Denver, 71–79

Dozens, 71
Dragonfly Anglers, 195
Durango, 200–8
Durango & Silverton Narrow
    Gauge, 203

E

E.G.'s Garden Grill, 22
Eagle Vail Cafe, 157
Eagle-Vail Golf Course, 127
Eagle's Nest Adventure Ridge, 125
Edgewater, Keystone Lodge, 120
El Chapultepec, 84
Eldora Mountain Resort, 8
Elkhorn Avenue, 13
Ellyngton's, 75
Embassy Suites, 78
Enos Mills Cabin and Gallery, 16
Enstrom's, 157
Ernest L. Blumenschein Home and
    Museum, 212
Eske's Brew Pub, 211
Espresso Broadmoor, 168
Estes Park, 11–18
Estes Park Aerial Tramway, 16
Estes Park Area Historical
    Museum, 16
Estes Park Brewery, 13
Estes Park Center/YMCA, 17
Estes Park Golf Course, 16–17
Estes Park Mountain Shop, 15
Expeditions, 109

F

F.M. Light & Sons, 52
Fado Irish Pub, 87
Farm Heritage and the Farm at
    Lee Martinez Park, the, 39–40

Farrell's Restaurant, 187
Fechin Institute, 212
Fiesta Mexicana, 183
Fish Creek Falls, 53–54
Fishpaw Trading Company, 44
Fiske Planetarium, 8
Flagstaff House, 5–6
FlatIron Crossing, 68
Fontenot's Cajun Café, 105
Footloose and Fancy Things, 150
Fort Collins, 34–41
Fort Collins Museum, the, 40
Fourth Story Restaurant and
    Bar, 64
Fraser River Trail, 101
Fraser Valley, 98–106
Fraser Valley Tubing Hill, 103
Frenchy's Cafe, 188
Frontier Historical Museum, 145

G

Garden of the Gods, 169
Garfinkel's, 127
Garlic Mike's Italian Cuisine, 186
Garner Galleria Theatre, 66
Gates Planetarium, 76
General Palmer Hotel, 207
Georgetown, 108–14
Georgetown Energy
    Museum, 110
Georgetown Gallery, 109
Georgetown Loop Railroad, 110
Georgetown Mercantile, 107
Gerald R. Ford Amphitheater, 129
Gerald R. Ford Park, 128
Gilpin County Historical
    Museum, 31
GISDHO Shuttle, 160

Glen Eyrie Castle, 169
Glenwood Canyon Brewing
   Company, 143
Glenwood Caverns Adventure
   Park, 144
Glenwood Springs, 140–47
Glenwood Springs Center for the
   Arts, 143
Gold Hill, 7
Golden Bear, the, 125
Golden Eagle Inn, 127
Grand Adventures, 24
Grand County Historical
   Museum, 23
Grand Junction, 155–64
Grand Junction Symphony, 162
Grand Lake, 19–26
Grand Lake Art Gallery, 21
Grand Lake Golf Course, 23
Grand Lake Lodge, 25
Grand Lake Lodge Restaurant, 25
Grand Lobby, 144
Grand Mesa, 162
Grand Pizza, 21
Grand Valley, 155–64
Grande River Vineyards, 161
Great Rocky Mountain
   Outfitters, 48
Guanella Pass Road, 112
Gunnison, 184–92

H

Hacienda Martinez, 212
Hamill House, 109
Happy Cooker, the, 107
Harmel's Ranch Resort, 191
Harwood Museum, 212

Harvey's Wagon Wheel Casino and
   Hotel, 32
Hat Creek Saddlery & Trading
   Post, 44
Hawthorn Suites, 158–59
Haymaker Golf Course, 54–55
Healy House, 137
Hearthstone Inn, 175
Hearthstone Restaurant, 121
Helen G. Bonfils Theatre
   Complex, 66
Heritage Aspen, 151, 152
Hickory House, 94
High Valley Center, 180
Historic Atlas Theatre, 47
Historic Georgetown, Inc., 109
Historic Governor's Mansion, 44
Historic Old Town Square, 36
Historic Taos Inn, 218
Home Ranch, the, 58
Horsetooth Mountain Park, 38
Horsetooth Reservoir, 38
Hot Springs Pool, 142
Hot Springs Pool Deli, 140
Hot Sulphur Springs Resort and
   Spa, 23
Hotel Boulderado, 6
Hotel Colorado, 143
Hotel Denver, 146
Hotel de Paris, 109
Hotel Monaco, 78
Hotel Teatro, 69–70
Hudson Gardens, 68
Hungry Elephant, 67
Hyatt Regency Denver, 87

I

Ice Palace Inn Bed and
    Breakfast, 139
Idle Spur, 196
Il Fornaio, 76
IMAX Theater, 76
Ingrid's Cup and Saucer, 146
Inn at Loretto, 215
Inn at Silver Creek, the, 25
Inn at the Spanish Peaks, 217
Inn of the Anasazi, 218
Into the West Furniture & Art
    Gallery, 53
Invesco Field at Mile High, 85–86
Iron Horse Resort, 105
Isle of Capris, 32
Italian Underground, 146

J

Jay's American Bistro, 41
Jimmy's: An American Restaurant
    and Bar, 153
Joe's Famous Deli & Homemade
    Ice Cream, 131
Jorgensen Park, 186
Josephina's Ristorante, 74
Junz Restaurant, 94
Jurassic Tours, 160

K

Kauffman House, 21
Kawuneeche Visitor Center, 15
Keystone, 117
Keystone Mountain, 120
Keystone Ranch, 119
Keystone Resort, 119
Keystone Stables, 120
Kid's Fishing Pond, 188–89

Kit Carson County Carousel and
    Old Town, 91
Kit Carson Home and
    Museum, 212
Kitchen, the, 105

L

La Tour Restaurant, 125
Lady Falconburgh's, 207
Lake Dillon, 119
Lake Terrace Dining Room, 171
Lambert's of Taos, 218
Larimer Square, 76
Larkspur Restaurant, 131
Latigo Ranch, 25
Laughing Ladies, 183
Le Rendezvous Swiss Bakery, 204
Leadville, 133–39
Leadville Country Inn, the, 137
Leanin' Tree Museum of Western
    Art, 8
Leland House, the, 207
Lexie's Mesa Grill, 44
Limbo Restaurant & Lounge, 9–10
Little Nell, the, 154
Lodge and Spa at Cordillera,
    127, 131
Lodge at Sunspot, 101
Lodge at Vail, 131
Loews Giorgio, 66
Lollypops, 47
Long Lake, 54
Lory State Park, 38–39
Los Altos, 164
Lounge at Saratoga Inn, 44–45
Lower Downtown (LoDo), 80–88
Lucci's, 150
Lucile's, 6–7

Lumber Baron Inn, 78
Lumina North Fine Art and
    Sculpture Gardens, 216

M

MacKenzie's Chop House, 176
Mad Adventures, 101
Manitou Springs, 172
Marigold Cafe and Bakery, 169
Mario's Pizza, 192
Market, the, 85
Maroon Bells, 151
Marys Lake Lodge, 17–18
Mary Lawrence Inn, 187
McCormick's Fish House, 84–85
Meadows Terrain Park, 179
Mel's Restaurant and Bar, 64
Mesa Lakes Resort, 162
Mesa Verde National Park, 205
Mi Casa Restaurant, 121
Mild to Wild Rafting, 205
Millicent Rogers Museum, 212
Mineral Belt Trail, 137
Minturn, 129
Minturn Market, 129
Mochas!, 192
Moffat Market at West Portal
    Station, 105
Molly Brown House Museum, 77
Mom's Kitchen, 45
Monarch Scenic Tram, 179
Monarch Ski & Snowboard
    Area, 179
Monarch Sno-Cat Tours, 179
Moose Cafe, 23
Morrow Point Reservoir, 191
Morton's of Chicago, 83
Mount Crested Butte, 193–99

Mount Princeton Hot Springs, 181
Mount Princeton Riding
    Stables, 180
Mount Shavano Trout Hatchery
    and Rearing Unit, 180
Mountain Spirit Winery, 181
Mountain Spirit Winery &
    Gallery, 182
Mountaintop Lodge, 106
Museum of Indian Arts and
    Culture, 215
Museum of International Folk
    Art, 215
Museum of Western
    Colorado, 158

N

Nagel Warren Mansion Bed and
    Breakfast, 49
National Center for Atmospheric
    Research, 8
National Mining Hall of Fame and
    Museum, 135
National Sports Center for the
    Disabled, 103
National U.S. Marshals
    Museum, 47
New Belgium Brewing
    Company, 37
New Mexico Museum of Fine
    Arts, 215
Nineteenth Street Diner, 146
Noah's Ark, 179

O

O's Steak and Seafood
    Restaurant, 32
Odell Brewing Company, 37

Ohio City, 190
Ohio Pass, 197
Old Town, 92
Operatique, 31–32
Ore House, the, 207
Otero Cyclery, 180
Ouray, 204
Oxford Hotel, the, 84

P

Palace of the Governors, 214
Palettes, 64–65
Palisade, 160
Palisades Restaurant and
    Saloon, 195
Panda City, 110
Paradise Bakery, 152
Paradise Cafe, 197
Park Meadows, 68
Pearl Street Mall, 4
Penrose Room at The
    Broadmoor, 172
Perennial Gardener, the, 36
Phantom Canyon Brewing
    Company, 170
Phoenix Theatre, 66
Pickle Barrel, 203
Pikes Peak, 171
Pikes Peak Cog Railway, 171
Pines Inn Bed and Breakfast,
    the, 106
Pint's Pub, 78
Pioneer Museum, 186
Pitkin, 188
Pitkin Historical Society
    Museum, 188
Pizza on the Plaza, 119
Plum Creek Cellars, 161

Poppycock's, 151
Positano's Pizza, 41
Poudre River Kayaks, 39
Powderhorn Resort, 163
Prairie Rides, 48
Prehistoric Journey, 76
Primate Panorama, 67
Primitivo Wine Bar, 176
ProRodeo Hall of Fame and
    American Cowboy
    Museum, 174

Q

Quality Inn and Suites Boulder
    Creek, 10
Queen Anne Inn, 88
Quincy's Steak & Spirits, 136

R

Rancho de San Juan, 217
Raven Hill Mining
    Company, 110
Redstone Inn, 146–47
REI, 86
Remington's Restaurant, 21
Rendezvous Gallery &
    Framing, 195
Restaurant at Inn at Loretto, 215
Ridgway, 204
Ridgway State Park and
    Reservoir, 204
Rim Rock Drive, 160
Rimrock Adventures, 160
Ritz-Carlton Bachelor Gulch, 130
River Suites at Monarch
    Shadows, 183
Rochester Hotel, the, 202
Rockslide Brewery, 164

Rocky Mountain Adventures, 39
Rocky Mountain Biological
    Laboratory, 198
Rocky Mountain Connection, 13
Rocky Mountain Home
    Collection, 36
Rocky Mountain Institute, 153
Rocky Mountain Meadery/Rocky
    Mountain Cidery, 161
Rocky Mountain National
    Park, 11–18
Romantic Riversong Bed and
    Breakfast Inn, 18

S

Sacred Grounds Coffee House and
    Delicatessen, 146
Salida, 177–83
Salida Golf Club, 179
Salida Hot Springs Pool, 182
Salida Museum, 182
San Geronimo Lodge, 211–12
San Juan County Historical
    Museum, 203
San Juan Mountain Bakery and
    Cafe, 204
San Juan Skyway, 204, 206
Santa Fe, New Mexico, 209–19
Santa Fe Opera, 216
Saratoga Inn, 45
Saratoga, Wyoming, 42–49
Sardy House, 154
Savory Inn & Cooking School of
    Vail, 131–32
Scot's Sporting Goods, 15
Shack Cafe, the, 53
Shed Southwestern Grille and
    Cantina, the, 102

Sheraton Crested Butte
    Resort, 195
Sheraton Steamboat Golf Club, 55
Silver Dollar Saloon, 135–36
Silver Grill Cafe, 34
Silver Plume Antique Shop, 113
Silver Plume General Store, 188
Silver Queen Gondola, 151
Silver Queen Quad Lift, 196
Silver Saddle Restaurant, 46
Silverton, 203
Sitzmark Lodge, 132
Six Flags Elitch Gardens, 86
Sixteenth Street Mall, 82
Ski Cooper, 138
Ski Purgatory at Durango
    Mountain Resort, 206
Ski Tip Lodge, 120, 122
Ski Train, 100
Slogar Bar & Restaurant, 197
Slopeside Grill, 58
Smuggler's Brewpub and
    Grille, 208
Soda Creek Homestead, 122
Sopp and Truscott, 113
Sopris Restaurant and Lounge, 146
Soupçon Restaurant, 195
Spirit Mountain Ranch, 22
Sports Shaq, 119
Sprague Lake, 15
Spruce Lodge Cabins, 162
St. Kathryn Cellars, 161
St. Moritz Lodge &
    Condominiums, 154
St. Regis Aspen, the, 150
Stanley Hotel, the, 13–14
Starbucks, 62
Starry Night Coffee Company, 36

Steamboat Grand Resort Hotel, 53
Steamboat Springs, 50–59
Steamboat Yacht Club, 52
Steaming Bean, 208
Steamworks Brewing
    Company, 202
Storm King Mountain
    Memorials, 143
Strater Hotel, the, 207
Stratton, 89–95
Stratton City Park, 93
Strawberry Park Hot Springs, 56
Strings, 78
Su Casa, 152
Summit County, 115–22
Summit Guides, 118
Summit House, 171
Sundeck Restaurant, 151
Sunlight Mountain Resort, 145
Swan, the, 70
Sweet Basil, 132
Swetsville Zoo, 40

T
T-Lazy-7-Ranch, 154
Tabor Center, 82
Tabor Opera House, 138
Tailgate Tavern, 91
Tall Timber Resort, 207
Tamayo, 65–66
Taos, New Mexico, 209–19
Taos Plaza, 211
Taos Pueblo, 214
Taos Ski Valley, 216
Tattered Cover Book Store, Cherry
    Creek, 64

Tattered Cover Book Store,
    LoDo, 85
Teller House, 29
Temple Hoyne Buell Theatre, 66
Tennessee Pass Cookhouse, 139
Theatre on Broadway, 66
Tiger Run Tours, 120
Timberline Tours, 127
Tincup, 187–88
Tincup Cemetery, 188
Toll Memorial, 16
Tommyknocker Microbrewery &
    Pub, 112
Torian Plum, 58
Trail Ridge Road, 15–16
Tread of Pioneers Museum, 55
Trimble Hot Springs, 206
Trios Enoteca, 84
Tropical Discovery, 67
Trough, the, 190
Tudor Rose Bed & Breakfast, 181
Turntable Restaurant, 132
Tuscany Room, 70
Two Rivers Winery, 161

U
U.S. Air Force Academy, 173
U.S. Mint, 65
U.S. Olympic Complex, 174
Union Station, 74
University Bicycles, 7
University of Colorado, 2
University of Wyoming Art
    Museum, the, 48
Upper Arkansas Valley, the, 177–83

V

Vail, 123–32
Vail Cascade Resort & Spa, 125
Vail Mountain, 127
Vail Nature Center, 128
Vail Village, 125
Van Vechten Lineberry
    Museum, 212
Village at Breckenridge, the, 121
Vista Verde Guest & Ski Touring
    Ranch, 58

W

Walter's Bistro, 176
Wanderlust Adventures, 39
Wapiti Bar & Grill, 18
Wazee Lounge and Supper
    Club, 88
Wedding Canyon, 160
Western Colorado Center for the
    Arts, 157
Westin Hotel, The, 70
Westin Westminster, 32

Wheeler Opera House, 152
Wienerstube Restaurant, 154
Wild Horse Inn, 102
Windswept Farms, 40
Winery, the, 164
Winona's, 55
Winter Park, 98–106
Wizard's Chest, the, 64
Wolf Hotel Restaurant, the, 45
Woodstone Deli, 196
Woodstone Grille, the, 196
Wyndham Peaks Resort and
    Golden Door Spa, 208
Wynkoop Brewing Company, 82
Wyoming Territorial Prison & Old
    West Park, 47

Y

Yampah Spa and Vapor Caves, 144

Z

Zaidy's Deli of Cherry Creek, 67
Zephyr Express Chairlift, 101

About the Author

SHERRY SPITSNAUGLE has lived in Denver since 1980 and has spent years exploring the main attractions of Colorado, as well as those out-of-the-way places known only to locals.

After earning a degree in journalism and mass communications from Kansas State University, Sherry began her career as a reporter and photographer at the *Great Bend Tribune* in western Kansas. She has covered destinations in Colorado and around the world and is published in major newspapers and regional magazines. She is a member of the Society of American Travel Writers, Colorado Authors' League, and the Denver Woman's Press Club.